Edward Jerman

for

Philippa

John and Jonathan

Edward Jerman

1605-1668
The Metamorphosis
of a Master-Craftsman

Helen Collins

The Lutterworth Press

The Lutterworth Press
P.O. Box 60
Cambridge
CB1 2NT

www.lutterworth.com
publishing@lutterworth.com

First Published in 2004

ISBN 0 7188 3038 5

British Library Cataloguing in Publication Data
A catalogue record is available from the British Library

Printed in Malta
by Interprint

Contents

List of Illustrations

Preface

Edward Jerman (1605-1668) was the architect of eight City company halls, the Royal Exchange and St Paul's School following their destruction by the Great Fire of 1666. Jerman came from a dynasty of master-carpenters who lived and worked in the City of London for 150 years and who had, in each generation, widened their horizons from master-carpenter to designer and contractor, and finally to surveyor and architect. His buildings were commissioned by the City Corporation and the City companies, so the circumstances surrounding their design and construction are well documented in City and company record books. Jerman's post-Fire buildings were large in number and high in quality, symbolising the City's mercantile importance, and although none remains today, there are many contemporary images of them.

This book discusses in detail the variety of work available, and indeed undertaken, by Edward Jerman, a metropolitan master-craftsman, and for the first time, presents his complete oeuvre. It relies closely upon City Corporation and City company record books to examine the life and work of the Jerman family, to reveal the complexities of their individual careers, and the influence of the designs and executed works of Inigo Jones, Sir Roger Pratt and Peter Mills upon Edward himself. An assessment of each of Jerman's buildings is made with reference to the City patronage that commissioned them and to both the immediate and subsequent critical assessment of them. Attention is drawn to the fact that the speed of the City's revitalisation, so imperative for the nation's survival, was in large part due to Edward Jerman's phenomenal output of work between 1666 and his death in 1668. The book provides a more thorough appraisal of Jerman's work than has hitherto been attempted.

Acknowledgements

My thanks must, first of all, go to my husband, who persuaded me to undertake my thesis, paid my fees, and learnt to accept a diet somewhat less than cordon bleu. Secondly, I am indebted to my daughter, Philippa, who bullied me to keep going and who was responsible for the final presentation of the thesis. Her continued support on both a practical and emotional level during the preparation of this book has been inestimable. Dr Christine Stevenson convinced me that I had something worthwhile to impart, and supervised my work for three years. My love and gratitude also go to Jim, my beloved West Highland Terrier, who patiently sat beside me through the long hours of writing. To my son, Jonathan, and all my friends who have encouraged me, I give my thanks. Bobbie Taylor introduced me to the world of architectural history; the patience and humour of Ursula Carlyle sustained me through my thesis; and Prue Corp tolerated my mood swings and kept faith. To them, and to all the staff of the Guildhall Library, I give my heartfelt thanks for their cheerfulness and helpfulness in dealing with my countless requests, and especially to Jeremy Smith in the Library's manuscript department. Elizabeth Wiggans has earned my profound admiration for her accurate work on the index of this book.

Finally, I should like to thank the Courts of Assistants of the Mercers' Company, the Drapers' Company, the Fishmongers' Company, the Goldsmiths' Company, the Haberdashers' Company and the Wax Chandlers' Company for their financial support in the production of this book.

Abbreviations and Notes on the Text

CC	Carpenters' Company
CLB	Calendar of the Letter Books of the City of London
CLRO	Corporation of London Record Office
CSPD	Calendar of State Papers Domestic
GC. CB	Goldsmiths' Company Court Book
GLMS	Guildhall Library Manuscript
JOR	Journal of the Common Council
LTS	London Topographical Society
MC. AC	Mercers' Company Acts of Court
MC. GR	Mercers' Company Gresham Repertory
OED	Oxford English Dictionary
REP	Repertory of the Court of Aldermen
R.I.B.A.	Royal Institute of British Architects

I have followed the scholarly convention of dating the early months of the year both by the Julian and Gregorian Calendars, for example 24 March 1663/4. Where I have incorporated quotations from record books, I have used modern spelling and punctuation. The units of measurement and money have not been modernised, and are given respectively in feet and inches, and in pounds, shillings and pence. One noble was the equivalent of 6s 8d, and one mark, 13s 4d. All folio numbers are recto unless indicated, and have been provided where they are available. Dates have been quoted whenever possible.

All illustrations accredited to GMLS are reproduced by courtesy of the Guildhall Library, Corporation of London.

Introduction

The main aim of this book is to confer upon Edward Jerman the recognition he deserves as the designer of a group of the most prestigious secular buildings in the City of London following the Great Fire of 1666. Considered "the City's most able known artist",[1] in 1667 Edward Jerman was invited by a committee composed of the Corporation of the City and the Mercers' Company to make designs for the new Royal Exchange. Forty-four halls of the Livery Companies had been destroyed by the Fire, but so crucial was their renaissance for the business life of the City that forty-one were speedily rebuilt. Of these, Edward Jerman designed eight, while of the thirty-three remaining, only four had designers whose names have been recorded. Among those forty-four, nine halls of the "Great Twelve Companies" were damaged beyond repair. These companies were the wealthiest and most superior, whose members included the most eminent citizens. Four of the replacements were designed by Edward Jerman and one by his brother Roger. Thus Edward Jerman was chosen as architect by many of the rulers of the City, an august body of men of authority and privilege who controlled its affairs both politically and commercially. Together with Sir Christopher Wren, whose City work was mainly confined to ecclesiastical architecture, Jerman was responsible for the most important City buildings of the post-Fire period.

Most books on the subject of the City Livery Companies contain only one chapter on the company hall and its contents, and in many cases the contents rather than the hall building seem to have attracted the attention of authors. This may be partly due to the fact that the problem of terminology is ever present in any discussion of the building industry in Britain up till the late seventeenth century. The word "architect" was not in general use, and as we shall see, some other titles can be misleading. Of the authors who do discuss post-Fire rebuilding, only Priscilla Metcalf, Jean Imray and Ann Saunders have provided a detailed account of Edward Jerman's contribution.[2]

Because Edward Jerman worked, in various capacities, for both the City of London and the City companies, more documentation of his employment and undertakings exists than for comparable craftsmen-designers of that time who were working for other patrons. Indeed, one can go as far as to say that Edward Jerman is unique in this respect, for the City archives abound with details of his commissions, and with images of those commissions that were brought to fruition. Yet, no scholarly study has been undertaken to assess Jerman's contribution to seventeenth-century City architecture.

This book celebrates that contribution. Jerman's major designs – the Royal

Exchange, eight Livery Company halls and St Paul's School – received acclaim from contemporary critics. His town planning for the Goldsmiths' Company was innovative and his pageants exemplified his versatility and ingenuity. His palette was wide and the City of London in the third quarter of the seventeenth century proved fertile ground wherein Jerman's artistic talent could take root and flourish.

CHAPTER 1

Setting the Scene –
Edward Jerman in Context

The Jerman dynasty of seven master-craftsmen, of which Edward belonged to the fourth and last generation, lived and worked in the City of London from 1520 until 1678, a period spanning six reigns. Their working lives are chronicled in the record books of the City companies by whom they were employed, mainly in court minutes and wardens' accounts, as well as in the Repertories of the Corporation of the City of London,[1] Journals of Common Council and various City account books.[2] From these archives one learns that Edward Jerman held appointments with the Corporation of the City from 1633, and before the Fire was Company Surveyor to the Fishmongers and Haberdashers, and Company Carpenter to the Goldsmiths.

He designed pageants to celebrate both the coronation of Charles II and several Lord Mayors' days, documentation of these being found in company records and in pageant pamphlets or programmes of the days' events. In the post-Fire period, Edward Jerman was approached by eight City companies to plan new halls for them, and was chosen "to order and direct the affair of rebuilding the Royal Exchange.[3] He acted as a surveyor to fire-damaged halls and oversaw the building of St Paul's School. Details of these works are sometimes haphazard, sometimes fragmentary, depending upon the assiduousness of the reporting clerk or the condition of the record books.

These record books are factual accounts that, in some cases, give details of meetings of building committees, shedding light on Edward Jerman's negotiations with both the companies and the workforce. Some describe the materials used and the costs incurred, the court minutes usually being supplemented by wardens' accounts in this field. They give a fascinating insight into all aspects of Edward Jerman's working life, allowing us to follow his path from craftsman to designer. Every now and then, it is possible to catch a brief glimpse of the characters, not only of Edward Jerman, but also of those members of the family whose work is recorded, and we find evidence of them being argumentative, dependable, long-suffering or greedy. In the absence of any visual images of these men, such glimpses are helpful in building up a mental picture.

Entries in the records of the Carpenters' Company reveal the approximate dates and ages of the family members, and their relationships with each other, while the Christ's Hospital records indicate where they lived and worked, affording a picture of the background from which Edward Jerman emerged to become such a sought-after designer in the post-Fire period. Had the Fire not occurred, he might, like his father, Anthony, be remembered merely as a City Viewer and Carpenter, a creator of pageants, a speculative builder and a surveyor to three of the Great Twelve Companies. Instead, the Fire afforded him the opportunity to demonstrate the talents that many in the City of 1666 realised he possessed, talents that vindicated the rulers of the City in their choice of him as a surveyor and architect.

Unfortunately, Wren's dictum "si monumentum requires, circumspice" cannot be applied to Edward Jerman, Apothecaries' Hall being the only one of his designs still extant in any recognisable form.[4] However, there remain many images, mainly engravings, of the facades of his company halls, together with the Royal Exchange and St Paul's School. As nearly all of these buildings were completed after Jerman's death in October 1668, finer detailing cannot always be reliably ascribed to him, although, as we shall see, certain "trademarks" recur in many of his buildings, leading one to believe that his designs suffered little adaptation.

Contemporary written descriptions of any of the company halls are meagre. John Strype, in his edition of Stow's *Survey of London*, commended many of them as "spacious" and "noble", but gave little indication of their architectural details.[5] Edward Hatton's writing is more architecturally descriptive. He acknowledged that most of the halls were brick-built (in compliance with the Rebuilding Act of 1667), and mentioned that several incorporated the orders of architecture, praising their elegance.[6] However, most writers laid greater emphasis on the antiquity of the guilds and their coats of arms, rather than their premises, and none of them mentioned a designer.

Edward Jerman, the craftsman-turned architect, and his forebears have also been neglected by subsequent historians, even those documenting the Carpenters' Company itself. Little or nothing relating to the first two generations of the family is to be found in published literature, save an occasional sentence in a company history. E.B. Jupp, in his history of the Carpenters' Company (1847) mentioned the family in a table of Masters and Wardens.[7] B. Alford and T. Baker (1968) omitted any reference to the Jermans,[8] while Jasper Ridley, writing on the Carpenters in 1995, simply acknowledged a cup given to the Company by Edward's father, Anthony Jerman, on his appointment as a Warden in 1628.[9] Anthony has also been deemed worthy of note for his work in connection with the rebuilding of Goldsmiths' Hall in 1635 and the Church of St Michael le Querne in 1638, probably because both projects involved the intervention of Inigo Jones, the King's Surveyor General.[10]

Howard Colvin's *Dictionary*, of course, supplies the fullest biographical details of Edward Jerman, and refers to his post-Fire designs for the halls of the Apothecaries, Barber-Surgeons, Drapers, Fishmongers, Haberdashers, Mercers, Wax Chandlers and Weavers, together with those for the Royal Exchange and St Paul's School.[11] Fuller accounts of Jerman's work for the Mercers are provided by Jean Imray and Ian Doolittle,[12] while his commission at the Exchange is described in Ann Saunders' chapters in the recent publication by the London Topographical Society.[13] Edward Jerman's long association with the Fishmongers' Company has been thoroughly chronicled and appraised by Priscilla Metcalf.[14]

This lack of documentation is perhaps understandable, given the paucity of research that has been conducted into Jerman himself,[15] or indeed into secular, post-Fire rebuilding, which seems to have been considered something of an architectural backwater by many writers. Margaret Whinney considered Edward Jerman's work for the Mercers' Company and the City, namely the Mercers' Hall and the Royal Exchange. She mentioned the "confused Serlio-like form" of the Hall, and the Flemish influence evident in the Exchange, which she compared with the King Charles block at Greenwich, designed by Jerman's contemporary, John Webb.[16] For Whinney, the contrast demonstrated the gulf between the taste and knowledge of the City and the court patrons and artists, a point as we shall see, taken up by Sir John Summerson and Cynthia Wall. Kerry Downes, who described Jerman as a mason rather than a carpenter, believed that the Exchange represented a middle-class taste "noticeably and almost archaically conservative in its time."[17] Summerson dismissed it as "typically mannered and coarse as one would expect from City artificers", and erroneously accredited Jerman with the rebuilding of Merchant Taylors' Hall.[18] Even if one accepts that Jerman's style was coarse and mannered, how much of that style was due to his own artisan background, and how much was dictated by his City patrons is open to question. Certainly, the rulers of the City showed little interest in emulating the cultivated court architecture of the West End, if only because of its cost.

As we shall see, the reconstruction of the City was, of necessity, executed with speed and thrift, but the unsophisticated taste of many City dwellers certainly influenced the design of buildings in that immediate post-Fire period. Summerson, discussing City taste, remarked that it was "a subject of mockery and disdain in the West End. . . . They [City folk] liked cornices and enormous iron-work shop signs, just as they liked starting the day with a draught of sack, over-eating and pinching each others' fat wives. The City contributed nothing to the art of the Stuarts or the Georgians, it was content with the robust second-rate".[19] Wall also makes this distinction between those merchants of the City and the cultivated courtiers of Westminster, with reference to Restoration theatre: "The most obvious reason that Restoration drama deals so little with the City life is the usual one, the Restoration playwright and the Restoration audience were emphatically not of the City, but . . . members of the court, of prominent literary and social circles. . . . The City housed the Puritans, the money-makers, the recalcitrant Commonwealths. What had City life to do with cultivated urban court life?"[20] As with the theatre, so also with architecture, between the court and the City lay a great aesthetic divide.

Most writers on the reconstruction of the post-Fire City have focused on Wren, although Paul Jeffery stressed the important role played by Robert Hooke, and especially Edward Woodroffe in church rebuilding.[21] Wren's own contribution to the rebuilding of the City was confined mainly to ecclesiastical buildings, St Paul's and the City churches, together with a very few public buildings, including the Custom House. Both W.G. Bell and Reddaway gave thorough and detailed descriptions of the Fire and its aftermath, and factual accounts rather than aesthetic judgements of post-Fire buildings.[22]

The writings of Bell and Reddaway have recently been superseded by Stephen Porter's comprehensive book, *The Great Fire of London*.[23] Porter has condensed and amended these seminal studies, incorporating research and publications that have become available in the intervening years. He has especially taken into account the research of A.L. Beier and Peter Earle, who have concentrated on social topography and the culture and society of Restoration London. Beier, in his essay "Engine of Manufacture: The Trades of London",[24] stressed that, in the seventeenth century, the City of London was probably the greatest trading centre in the world, and by the 1660s was also a major manufacturing centre, with the parish of St Giles Cripplegate (where Edward Jerman was buried in 1668), for example, supporting 390 different trades. The abundance of merchants and masters living within the City walls reflected the fact that, for such people, their workplace was commonly also their residence. Understanding this helps one to realise why speed of rebuilding after the Fire was so crucial, to avoid the loss of income caused by the collapse of this all-important manufacture and trade.

Peter Earle, in *The Making of the English Middle Class*, attempted to rationalise Daniel Defoe's seven classes of society (which he had described in 1709) into three: the upper or "West End society" of aristocracy and gentry; the middle, commercial and industrial capitalists and professional men; and the working class, Defoe's "mechanic part of mankind". However, as Earle admits, in the seventeenth century, some independent artisans such as Edward Jerman, with their own workshops and tools, had most of the attributes of the middle class, and had a great chance of improving themselves over the course of a lifetime.[25] Although, at the time, these classes would have been identifiable by their speech, dress, behaviour, bearing and income, the status quo was constantly fluctuating. Society was a continuously ascending hierarchy, and for artisan families of the calibre of the Jermans, each generation was a little better off and a little more genteel than the previous one.

The craftsman's role, his conditions of work, his position in society and within the trade guilds of the seventeenth century have been elucidated by both Donald Woodward and Steve Rappaport. Although Woodward discussed the working conditions of building craftsmen in the towns of northern England,[26] circumstances prevailing in the City were not very dissimilar. Woodward considered contracts and methods of payment with reference to Wren's oft-cited discourse, addressed to the Bishop of Oxford, on ways of working.[27] He demonstrated the wage differentials among building craftsmen arising from different levels of skill and responsibility, and also discussed the provision and transport of building materials. These subjects are particularly pertinent to Edward Jerman's work at Fishmongers' Hall, the Goldsmiths' Hall and the Royal

Exchange. Rappaport discussed the position of the City companies in the sixteenth century, and stressed the powerful part they played in the protection and succour of their members and explained the hierarchy that existed within them.[28] This issue is taken up here in relation to the Jermans' status within the Carpenters' Company. The importance of the companies was indeed waning in the City by the seventeenth century, due to the growth of the suburbs and migration of provincial workmen, but for craftsmen such as the Jermans, still under their jurisdiction, both structural inequalities and patterns of mobility remained pertinent.

The Company Halls

The predecessors of Jerman's company halls cannot be easily classified as a building type because their individual evolution resulted in a very disparate group of structures. The great majority of them had developed, or, like Topsy, just grow'd,[29] in their different ways, from City houses of varying degrees of grandeur, usually bequeathed to the company by a wealthy member. Livery halls (great halls in which the livery met), company offices and parlours were subsequently added to such houses wherever sites permitted, and often by jettying when they did not. By the mid-seventeenth century, therefore, they were a heterogeneous group, as we shall see, united only by their incorporation of a livery hall. By this time, too, the companies' financial resources had been gradually eroded by a fall in membership and by demands not only of the Crown, but also of Parliament during the Commonwealth. The wars with France and the Netherlands were both costly and unpopular, and were trebly burdensome for those companies involved in the building industry. They were obliged to pay taxes towards the wars, they lost craftsmen, sent to Tilbury for defence work, and their trade suffered from a shortage of timber, used for shipping. Any building programmes the companies might have envisaged were therefore curtailed, and very few had the resources to build anew.

By 1666, the companies must have agreed with Claudius when he said, "When sorrows come, they come not single spies, but in battalions."[30] Their finances were depleted, and the plague of 1665 had further reduced their membership and so their revenue. The Fire destroyed not only their halls, but also their plate and memorabilia, and they also found themselves responsible for the homeless dependants of their gutted almshouses. They were indeed walking a financial tightrope. To compound their woes, floods in October 1666 were followed by the most severe winter in living memory, rendering any immediate attempt at reorganisation impossible.

Although, of course, there was no fire insurance, most companies did manage to rebuild, but speed and thrift were their priorities. Very few company minute books or account books mention the actual rebuilding process, only remarking on livery dinners which were held to celebrate the new halls.[31] Account book entries concerning both the expenditure on and the design of these post-Fire halls are similarly scanty, but do indicate that following their initial rebuilding, the new halls continued to evolve, as had their predecessors, as company fortunes grew. Thus they always were, and still are today, a miscellaneous group, not easily categorised. One need look no further than Goldsmiths' Hall and its near neighbour Plaisterers' Hall to appreciate this difference. In the City of London, contained within its walls, space has always been at a premium and the individuality of City building has always reflected this.

The reason why the "Puritans, the money-makers, the recalcitrant Commonwealths" of the City chose Edward Jerman to design not only eight company halls, but also the Exchange, is a good question until one remembers that the professional architect, as we understand the term today, was all but unknown in Restoration England. Educated "amateurs", gentlemen with an interest in architecture, as well as craftsmen – carpenters, bricklayers and masons – filled that position. Thus the King's choices for Commissioners for Rebuilding the City were Christopher Wren, Hugh May and Roger Pratt.[32] Both Pratt and May had country-house building experience, but Wren, at this time, had only university buildings to his name. All three were, of course, Royalists, and not readily acceptable to those "recalcitrant Commonwealths", when it came to designing halls.[33] The City's commissioners were Robert Hooke, a discreet Royalist, a gentleman and scientist, "brilliant, cantankerous, secretive and always in ill-health",[34] Peter Mills, a bricklayer by training, and Edward Jerman, a carpenter. Although the Court of Aldermen had approved Hooke's plan for the new City, preferring it to that of Peter Mills, Hooke had as yet no building to prove his worth. Mills' activity as a surveyor and architect can be traced back as far as 1638, and he is credited with the designs for several country houses; he had worked alongside Jerman for the City Corporation for thirty years when they held posts of City Viewers, City Bricklayer and Carpenter, and City Surveyors. In the post-Fire period, so whole-hearted was Mills' commitment to street surveying that his health deteriorated. This enabled Jerman, whose artistry and craftsmanship were already known to several of the City companies over many years, to gain contracts that might otherwise have been offered to Mills and finally to win that for the Exchange.

Edward Jerman was a well-known City man with local knowledge and a sound reputation. He was manifestly the City's candidate for the rebuilding and it becomes clear why he was chosen by the companies to design their halls. Although he had received no formal training as a designer (Webb being unique at this time in having been instructed in classical architecture as a pupil of Inigo Jones), and most of his inventions must have sprung from observation and discussion, [35] his experience as a master-craftsman, then as a surveyor and speculative builder would have rendered him conversant with mensuration and the drawing of plots and uprights. While the designs of Jerman's post-Fire buildings were determined by the amalgamation of a variety of influences – other company halls, Gresham's

1.1 Cromwell House, near Smithfield. John Crowther watercolour (1880).

Exchange, the mansion houses of City merchants, his association with Inigo Jones and with Mills, Pratt and May, and the printed works of architectural masters which were becoming available – it must not be forgotten that the companies required that their halls be rebuilt along the lines of their predecessors, rather than re-designed in some entirely new form. With no extra land available, and little time or money to spare, the companies were conservative in their ambitions.

Jerman was familiar with many of the halls that had been destroyed by the Fire, especially those he had visited in connection with his pageant work, or knew in his capacity as a company surveyor. They included those of the Fishmongers, Haberdashers, Grocers, Skinners and Clothworkers. While conducting his business in these halls, he became familiar with officials who, as we shall see, considered him a skilful and dependable worker. He was also no stranger to some of the recently erected halls which had escaped the flames, including those of the Carpenters, as a member; the Goldsmiths, on which his father and brother had worked for several years and where he was the Company Carpenter; and the Leathersellers, where his advice had been sought in 1632.

Jerman had been a frequent visitor to Gresham College while creating his pageant props because many of them were both fashioned and assembled there. As he crossed its quadrangle, he must have compared its arcaded walks with those of Gresham's other edifice, the Royal Exchange. When he came to design his Exchange, there were already many images, both engravings and paintings of this nerve centre of the City to which he could refer when he considered his replacement for this much admired building.

Walking through the City during his working week, Jerman would have passed the mansion houses of City merchants, some from Tudor times and before. Such houses included Crosby Place (1466), Thomas Cromwell's Mansion which had become Drapers' Hall, Thanet House (1644), Bacon House, which had been acquired by the Scriveners' Company, and Browne's Place, situated on the Thames next to Askham's Place which was the site of Fishmongers' Hall.[36] Notably in his rebuilding of the Apothecaries', Drapers' and Fishmongers' Halls, Jerman perpetuated the courtyard form of these houses, about which Hatton remarked in 1708,

> Those especially . . . around the Royal Exchange are so numerous and magnificent with courts, offices and all other necessary apartments enclosed to themselves . . . because of the great quantity of ground they are built on, generally situate backwards, and by that means, the City appears . . . not near so stately and beautiful as it really is . . . were these ornaments exposed to public view.[37]

A glimpse at Ogilby and Morgan's City of London map of 1676, together with illustrations of Jerman's buildings here provided, will confirm Hatton's observation.[38] Jerman's Fishmongers' Hall, however, boasted an imposing river front, while the Mercers' façade dominated Cheapside. The pedimented centrepieces of Drapers' Hall and the north front of the Royal Exchange introduced a classical element to Bishopsgate and Threadneedle Street respectively. Edward Jerman thereby bestowed on his new buildings a grandeur which fitted their function as the nucleus from which commerce would again emanate and the future of the City be assured.

Thus Edward Jerman's halls were a disparate group, from that of the mighty Mercers' to the more humble Wax Chandlers'. The lack of reportage of the evolution of the designs and process of building these halls is interesting. In the case of the Mercers, Jerman's surveys of properties owned by them are recorded in great detail, together with his lengthy and intricate negotiations with the argumentative and formidable tenants, but sparse reference is made to hall rebuilding. The possibility of litigation must have loomed large with properties so closely juxtaposed, and with boundaries and ancient lights so frequently contested.[39] The progress of hall rebuilding, as long as it proceeded smoothly, was not a cause of concern to the Courts of Assistants, and even if it were debated, it was not recorded. Discussion of architectural elegance was not the province of those "money makers" of the City. Happily for these courts, in Edward Jerman they engaged not only a first-rate artificer and a tactful negotiator, but also an accomplished architect.

After Jerman's death, his colleagues John Lock, Thomas Cartwright and John Oliver continued his work.[40] Theirs was the last generation of craftsman-organised

1.2 Carpenters' Hall, built 1664. Thomas Shepherd watercolour (1830).

building, for changes were taking place in the building world that had already touched the lives of the post-Fire designers. Speculative building was playing an increasingly large part in urban development, pioneered by Nicholas Barbon, who speculated in both land and houses. Architects such as Edward Jerman designed and often oversaw the materialisation of their schemes, but no longer shaped them in a craft capacity. The direct labour mode of payment was being replaced by one in which work was contracted out to one or more surveyors, men necessarily literate and numerate enough to be able to measure and calculate the size and cost of the proposed work, to organise the provision of materials and to check the finished buildings in accordance with the drafts set down by the designer. And of course, the vernacular style which had predominated in the City was giving way to a more classical one, as Figures 1.1 and 1.2 demonstrate, and brick and stone were, by legislation, replacing wood and infill for external walls. As we shall see in the ensuing chapters, each of these changes directly affected Edward Jerman's working life, the nature of his employment and his remuneration.

Edward Jerman's life can be conveniently divided into three categories that ran more or less consecutively. He was elected to the first of his City posts, that of City Carpenter, in 1632/3 and was subsequently appointed City Viewer and City Surveyor, but by 1657, Jerman had resigned from all these positions to become an independent contractor. From 1656 until 1664, his pageant work for the Lord

Mayors' Shows was well received by the organising City Companies, and through it, he was becoming known to officials of those companies, acting as a surveyor to three of them. The Fire formed the watershed between Jerman the artificer and Jerman the architect, and between 1666 and 1668 his skills as a designer/ surveyor were much sought-after by many Courts of Assistants. It was in this brief period that he designed the Royal Exchange, St Paul's School and eight company halls, but as we shall see, it was his pre-Fire work for those very particular City patrons that ensured these post-Fire commissions.

CHAPTER 2

The Jermans from the Records
of the Carpenters' Company

Although the minute books and account books remain our most illuminating source of information about the history and finances of the City companies, readers should always remember that they must have been compiled with a marked bias towards the perspective of the Courts of Assistants who instigated such records, rather than towards the more lowly artisans who made up the bulk of the membership. However, kinship between these highest and lowest members was perpetuated by charity in time of need, company dinners at times of celebration, and arbitration at times of dispute, even if the voice of the yeomanry was somewhat indistinctly recorded.

Through the court books and wardens' accounts of the Carpenters' Company, a comprehensive picture of four generations of the Jerman family over a period of 130 years can be built up. In all, seven members of the family were active during this time; two died young, but all the rest were called to the livery, three were elected Warden and one became Master. We have, therefore, a short dynasty of highly successful master-craftsmen, carpenters in the City of London between 1550 and 1680. No other name appears with such regularity over so long a period in the Company's records, and it is interesting that, as the family wills confirm, all the sons followed their fathers into the trade. Information about actual work done by those of the first two generations is not very plentiful, but there is some documentation of their lives and activities in entries in the Carpenters' Company archives. However, the names of those of the third and fourth generations appear more regularly, not only in the Carpenters' books, but also in the archives of many of the other City companies, as well as in the Repertories of the Court of Aldermen of the City of London, the Journals of the Common Council and various City account books.

In order to understand this world in which the Jermans spent their working lives, and to discover the background from which Edward Jerman emerged, some knowledge of the history of the Carpenters' Company will be helpful. The Carpenters' Company was fairly typical of one of the lesser trade guilds, and the regulations the Company tried to impose on its members in order to maintain control over them were similar to those of the Masons', Bricklayers' and Joiners' Companies. An incursion into the history of the Company will also serve to introduce members of the Jerman family from 1545 onwards. Inevitably, several members of the family bear the same name, but I hope to lessen confusion by the

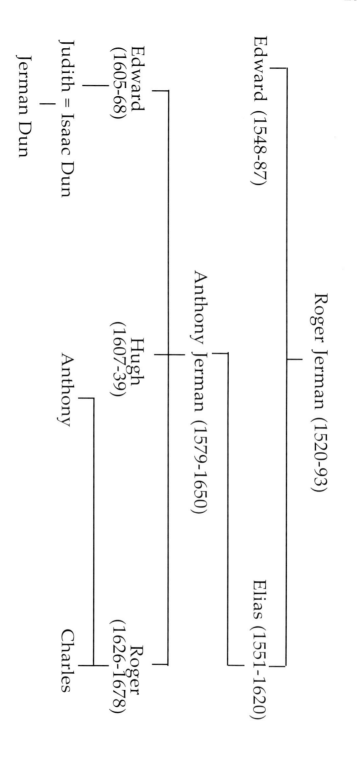

Jerman Family Tree

provision of a simple family tree (Figure 2.1), and by discussing the family members chronologically. The commonest spelling of the name is Jerman, although many variations appear in the records, from Jarmayne to Germin. With such a diversity of spellings employed, care has been taken to check that all the men under discussion are of one and the same family. As many of them refer to each other in the records, or are mentioned as being related, it has been possible to cross-check from several entries. A brief outline of the family members and their relationship to one another will help to reinforce the fact that here were six men, all sons, grandsons and great-grandsons of Roger Jerman, successfully pursuing their craft from the same place in the City of London for over a hundred years.

Roger Jerman was probably born about 1520, this date being calculated from his admittance as a freeman of the Carpenters' Company in 1545,[1] and he died in 1593, his will being dated 22 January 1592/3. In his will, he described himself as a citizen and carpenter of London, in the parish of St. Botolph without Aldersgate, where he wished to be buried, "near the place where my son Edward lieth buried". He left forty shillings "to the poor children of Christ's Hospital so that they do accompany my body to the burial".[2] A sermon was preached at his funeral, implying that he was a man of substance, and indeed he made sizeable bequests to eleven members of his family as well as to servants and friends. One of the witnesses to his will was Ralph Treswell, Painter-Stainer, whose surveys of London are well known, and one of whose earliest works in London was a drawing of the church of St. Michael le Querne in 1585, a church with which Roger's grandson, Anthony, would be associated 50 years later.[3]

Edward Jerman, Roger's elder son, was born about 1548. He was made a freeman of the Company by his father in 1577,[4] and died in 1587, his death being recorded in the Carpenters' records.[5] Elias Jerman, Edward's brother was apprenticed at Christmas 1568, setting his date of birth at 1551. His apprenticeship lasted nine years, and he was made a freeman in 1578.[6] No will of Elias has come to light, possibly because he died in Ireland. However, he must have died before 1620, when the Carpenters' accounts record him as deceased.

There is no record that Edward had any children, while Elias seems to have had only one son, Anthony, who must have been born around 1578-80. Like Edward's, Anthony's name does not appear in the presentment of apprentices in the Carpenters' records,[7] but it is listed among those made freemen in 1600.[8] In the Goldsmiths' records of 1639, Anthony described himself as "of the parish of St. Botolph without Aldersgate, carpenter, aged fifty-nine years or thereabouts",[9] establishing that the family was still living in the same parish, and that Anthony thought he was born "about" 1580. The Christ's Hospital Treasurer's Accounts confirm that the same property (to which reference is made below) was still being leased to the Jerman family. Anthony, whose will is dated 8 February 1649/50,[10] died shortly thereafter. Anthony appointed his two sons, Edward and Roger, as his executors, while "it hath pleased God to take to his mercy one of my sons named Hugh Jerman". Hugh and Edward must have been very close in age, as they were both presented for apprenticeship in 1623, Hugh by his father, and Edward by one Thomas Fawcon, whom we shall meet again. Anthony and Hugh worked together for the Goldsmiths' Company in 1635,[11] but thereafter, there is no mention of Hugh. Both 1636 and 1641 were particularly bad plague years (although nothing compared with 1665), so perhaps Hugh succumbed and died during this period.

As Edward was apprenticed in 1623, he must have been born about 1605. Further confirmation of this date is found in his marriage licence, granted on 10 September 1631, when he was said to be "about twenty-six". Edward continued to rent the family leasehold property from Christ's Hospital until his death in November 1668, and indeed a new lease was drawn up on behalf of the Hospital in 1666.[12] The property clearly escaped the worst ravages of the Fire, and there were consultations regarding the expiry of the lease between Edward and the Hospital during 1667. However, in his will, dated 9 September 1668, Edward described himself as "citizen and carpenter of the parish of St. Giles Cripplegate", a parish lying adjacent to that of St. Botolph Aldersgate, and it was in St. Giles that he was buried on 26 November 1668. The burial register entry reads, "Edward Jerman: City Surveyor: consumption: church".[13] This terse entry implies that, because of his status as a City Surveyor, Edward was allowed burial in the church itself.[14] No sermon was preached during the service, probably due, as J.C. Whitebrook suggested, to Jerman's poverty.[15] Indeed, Edward's widow had to appeal for financial assistance from several of the companies for whom her husband had worked. In his will, Edward's only bequest was a freehold tenement in Whitechapel, which passed to his three grandchildren, the sons of his daughter, who was married to one Isaac Dun. Edward's oldest grandson, appropriately named Jerman, graduated from Cambridge in 1673, and was admitted to the Inner Temple.

Edward's brother, Roger Jerman, Anthony's youngest son, was made a freeman of the Carpenters' Company in 1650, twenty years after his brothers, and so he was probably born around 1626. He had two sons, Anthony and Charles, and took Anthony as an apprentice on 3 October 1676.[16] Charles seems to have been the only son for four generations who did not follow in the carpentry tradition. Anthony became free by patrimony on 4 January 1680/1, two years after the death of his father on 24 October 1678. Roger's will suggests that life as a master-carpenter had paid him extremely well, for he left property, lands and tenements in Kent, and his Cophold estate in East Ham, as well as houses and tenements held by lease from the Earl of Dorset, together with land on which was built the Dorset Garden Theatre, said to have been designed by Wren in 1670.[17] As well as all this property, he made bequests totalling over £1,300 to his relations, and left plate and jewels to his wife. For Roger, work as a master-craftsman was clearly very much more remunerative in post-Fire London than employment as a surveyor or architect like brother Edward.

The Carpenters' Company, history and regulations

The Carpenters' Company, like many other trade guilds, probably originated from some sort of craft organisation or secret fraternity which operated more as a friendly society than as a trade organisation, and had a religious basis and often a patron saint. The members of such fraternities usually established a set of rules, as much for their mutual guidance as for any sort of governance, so that they might further and safeguard their craft, and at the same time, mitigate the suffering of their fellows in time of need. Thus, from the beginning, they were benevolent societies and were formed not only in the metropolis, but in every important city in the country.

From early times, in an attempt to regulate buildings and builders in the capital, certain master-carpenters were elected by the City authorities as overseers. This gave the craft association a degree of control over the City's affairs, but the first positive evidence of any formal organisation of the Craft or Fraternity of Carpenters is found in 1333.[18] In his royal charter of 1319, Edward II had proclaimed that no stranger could be admitted as a citizen of London unless he were supported by six men of the craft he wished to follow. This meant that citizenship and craft membership were tantamount to one and the same thing. The charter may have spurred the Carpenters into formalising their association, for in 1333, the "Brotherhood of Carpenters of London" drafted its Book of Ordinances. These ordinances dealt mainly with the provision of charitable aid to sick or injured members, to orphans and widows. The only ordinance touching on any aspect of trade was that directing any member who had work available "to work his own brother before any other", as long as he were sufficiently skilled to perform the work in question. The rest of the ordinances dealt with the day-to-day running of the fraternity, and formed the basis of regulations still operative when the Jermans were members of the Company. Penalties of a pound of wax had by then been replaced by fines of shillings and pence, but the misdemeanours giving rise to such penalties were very much the same. Quarterages were to be paid. New members could only be admitted to the fraternity by the unanimous vote of all members, and members were to be expelled for bad behaviour. Four wardens were to be chosen annually, and any disputes between members were to be dealt with by the Wardens and the fellowship. The fraternity was, therefore, very much a friendly society, within which the wellbeing of its fellows, and the maintenance of high standards of workmanship and behaviour were paramount.

The Black Death in 1381 brought about a sudden change in the labour supply of the City, and in the finances of the emerging Brotherhood. From 1189, there had been some attempt to regulate artisans' wages and to restrict the number of "forrens", country craftsmen, working in the City. There was now an acute shortage of labour, and those carpenters who survived the pestilence could ask, and did receive, much higher wages. On the other hand, the charitable aid that had to be disbursed to the sick and needy of the fraternity must have been a strain on those wages, however augmented. Perhaps this give-and-take situation, the higher wages and the strengthened bargaining powers of the individual craftsmen, consolidated the bonds between brothers, for the association flourished in the post-plague period.

The very nature of carpenters' work, being, on the whole, small-scale and peripatetic, made any strict organisation very difficult to operate in practice. It was all too easy for employers to use "forrens" who were willing to work for lower wages, and this proved to be a recurrent problem throughout the history of the Carpenters' Company. The fines imposed on members who were in contravention of the rules were never sufficiently punishing to deter malpractice, and in fact, these fines proved a regular source of income in the early days to the City authorities and the crown, and later to the Company itself.

The late fourteenth century saw an upturn in the fortunes of City carpenters. The amount of royal building, with its associated impressment of labour, declined, freeing carpenters, among others, from its binding obligations. There was more house building, and because most houses in the metropolis were timber-framed, there were exceptional opportunities for the more ambitious carpenters to become small-scale contractors. As a result of this upswing in its circumstances, the Company realised it needed a permanent headquarters, and by 1429, it had bought a piece of land and built a Hall.[19] From this period onwards, we have a continuous record of Company affairs. By 1466, the Carpenters were sufficiently well established to apply for and obtain a coat of arms and a company seal, and in 1477, they received their Charter of Incorporation from Edward IV.

In 1455, new ordinances were laid down, forming the basis of the Company's authority. These ordinances were, to all intents and purposes, the ones that pertained throughout the Jermans' membership of the Company, and the records show that all the members of the family brushed up against the regulations in one way or another. They were all bound by the apprenticeship system, either as masters or apprentices. They all rose through the ranks of the Company and were obliged to pay the requisite fees. Several of them were reprimanded and fined for improper behaviour and for unsatisfactory workmanship. In these respects, they were probably typical of most members of the Company, and it was for these reasons that strict regulations were set down, to maintain discipline over such men.

The Company's fifteenth-century regulations, although re-iterating the need for good conduct, laid more emphasis on trade matters, appropriate to the expanding industry that it had become, and were little changed over the following two centuries. The Carpenters were to be controlled by a Master and three Wardens who were elected annually and could appoint eight assistants. They were to hold a weekly court and present an annual statement of accounts, and it is from these two sources that our knowledge of details of Company business arises. If elected to the livery, freemen were obliged to take it up, refusal resulting in a severe admonition and a fine. Admission to the freedom by redemption had to be approved by the Court of Assistants,[20] to prevent insufficiently qualified men from working under the protection of the Company, bringing it to disrepute. Similarly, no apprentice could be approved without proof of ability. No member was to supplant a fellow craftsman, nor to undertake the work of masons, plasterers, joiners or tilers. The different crafts were thus strictly demarcated and contempt of such boundaries could result in a reproach. The Master and Wardens had powers to inspect all timber, to ensure that it complied with standards set down by the City. In addition, the prestigious office of Master Carpenter of the Guildhall and of Bridgehouse, which involved the supervision of all carpenters' work at the two buildings, was to be held by a freeman of the Carpenters' Company. Thus the Company assumed considerable control over much of the building work in London, and the members it elected to such eminent positions must have wielded considerable influence.

The Finances of the Carpenters' Company

In the sixteenth century, the income of the Company was derived from five main sources: quarterage payments, the apprentice system, small fines for disciplinary misdemeanours, fines arising from the Company's attempt to control the craft in London and, finally, property, gifts and bequests. At this time, each freeman was required to pay four pence quarterly at the hall, and from 1550 onwards, the Wardens' Account Books reveal countless such entries. At the same time, liverymen were also obliged to pay subscriptions towards the costs of the Company dinners, including those celebrating Election Day, Lord Mayor's Day and the Company Feast Day.

The apprentice system was a source of considerable income to the Company by way of a series of different fines. On the presentation of an apprentice at the Hall, the presenting master paid a fee or fine of two shillings and two pence, while the payment for turning an apprentice over to another master was twelve pence. Failure to conform to these regulations, or setting an apprentice to work before his term of servitude was completed involved another fine. In certain circumstances, such as the employment of more apprentices than the regulations permitted, the Court of Assistants might waive the rules – against the payment of yet another fine. Although such transgressions undermined the authority of the Company to a certain extent, they were a further source of income. On completion of apprenticeship, admittance to the freedom was secured by a fine of three shillings and four pence, while freedom by patrimony, as mentioned, was open to bargaining between the individual and the Court. By the mid-sixteenth century, the total membership of the Company had reached between 250 and 300, ensuring a steady income by way of the series of fines involved.

In many City companies, especially the Great Twelve, there was a distinction between the yeomen, freemen who exercised the craft, and the livery. In such companies, the livery might be composed of Aldermen or Common Councilmen, successful City fathers who did not necessarily have any working connection with the company.[21] This was not the case with the Carpenters: with them, the distinction lay between the more successful and therefore the more prosperous group, and the rest. The path to seniority and prosperity was seen as available to all, and in the Jermans' time, the livery of the Carpenters' Company was composed of about forty members. Even so, there were degrees of equality. In 1571, a group of liverymen of a less egalitarian complexion decided that their elevated status should not go unrecognised. They determined that four dozen special napkins should be bought for the exclusive use of the livery at Quarter Day and Election Day dinners, the liverymen bearing the cost, not only of the purchase of such table linen, but also of the laundering of the same![22] Details of such an Election Day dinner, a sumptuous-sounding feast, are given in Appendix 1. The Carpenters were particularly enthusiastic about Company dinners, and wives were made welcome at such festivities.

As laid down in the 1455 ordinances, those elected to the livery, or to the office of Warden of the Company, were obliged to take it up; yet again, however, the payment of a fine would enable exemption.

Throughout the sixteenth century, the Carpenters were in contention with such allied trade crafts as the Woodmongers and Joiners, particularly in connection with demarcation disputes.[23] Fines arising from the Company's attempts to control the trade in London, especially regarding the purchase of timber, building licences, the standard of workmanship and the control of "forrens" were a steady source of income. Until the early sixteenth century, timber had been cut and sawn outside London by timbermen and boardmen who then brought it to London and sold it directly to the relevant companies, especially the Joiners and Carpenters.

Gradually, during the sixteenth century, woodmongers and wharf owners along the Thames began to oust the traditional suppliers, the timbermen and boardmen. They bought as much timber as they could, seasoned or unseasoned, and charged customers for carriage and storage. It was easy for "forrens", not under the control of the Carpenters' Company, to obtain supplies from these dealers, dismantling the time-honoured modus vivendi that had existed between the timbermen and carpenters.

The recurrent need to pass new regulations and to issue building licences was the result of a failure to satisfactorily enforce existing rules. As we have seen, the fines imposed were merely regarded as a small taxation, easily passed on to the client. Although they generated some small income for the Company, they never succeeded in deterring malpractice by the determined perpetrators, the record books reveal countless instances of such fines imposed for various misdemeanours.

Although the various fines enumerated above generated a considerable annual income for the Company, the greatest source of income came from gifts and bequests, but especially from property. From early times, Carpenters' Hall had been rented out to companies and fraternities that had no permanent headquarters. Other property on land that the Company had bought, or had had bequeathed to it, was leased with an initial fine and an annual rent. This was such a profitable aspect of the Company's affairs that the Master and Wardens "viewed" all properties annually with great care and vigilance. The fine Hall, its furniture and fittings and its accumulation of silver and plate was evidence that the income generated by property generally exceeded the Company's expenditure.

Expenditure considered necessary for the aggrandisement of the Hall was a constant worry to the Court of Assistants, but its grandeur was thought to make membership of the Company more attractive. The Hall served not only as the administrative centre for Company affairs, but also as a place of relaxation, in its adjoining garden and bowling alley, and as a place of entertainment. The first major alterations to Carpenters' Hall, described simply as a "timber building" were made in the early sixteenth century, with the addition of a new parlour. Renovations followed, and the garden layout was improved with the help of a subscription levied on the members.

Expenditure on festivities, dinners and the like were met by quarterage receipts and special collections from the freemen and liverymen. The Carpenters, being one of the lesser companies, were not involved in heavy expenses for City pageantry such as the Lord Mayor's Shows or royal entries. They could enjoy such occasions without the financial worry incurred by the more prominent players.

The Company's greatest expenditure was, however, on the extension of charitable aid, as laid down in the ordinances. The irregularity of carpenters' work, and the seasonal nature of the industry, together with its vulnerability to the vagaries of the weather, meant that many members were reliant on some kind of alms from the Company during times of unemployment. Carpenters living in London were completely dependent on their craft, unlike their country brothers who had the opportunity to turn their hand to agricultural work during the lean periods. For City carpenters, therefore, admission fines and quarterage fees were but a small insurance premium to pay for the benefits that could then ensue.

The Crown was, for very many years, to be a constant drain on the City companies' finances. Possibly the first application from the Crown for a loan was made by Henry VIII in 1544 to pay for his wars in Scotland. As Herbert stated, "in pursuing the companies' history, it will be seen to what a ruinous extent the precedent was afterwards carried".[24] Further demands on the City companies followed in the 1570s and 1580s. In 1578 and again in 1580, the livery and yeomanry of the Carpenters' Company (including the Jermans) were obliged to contribute towards the charges for soldiers mustering at Mile End Green.[25] As the war with Spain intensified, culminating in the Armada of 1588, we again find the Jermans subscribing towards the charges of the thirty-two soldiers "which did muster before the Queen in Greenwich Park".[26] From this time onwards, the Crown regularly demanded money from the City companies, with ever-increasing avarice, and under the James I and Charles I, the companies were propelled to the verge of bankruptcy when they were obliged to contribute towards the Virginia Plantation and the Irish settlements.

In the early seventeenth century, the Company tightened the rules concerning all aspects of its members' working lives, from control over the apprenticeship system to distinctions between carpentry and allied building crafts, and from the quality of timber used to checks on all work completed. But try as it would, the Company could not keep strict control over the craft. There was always a large number of "forrens" working in the City. Company members felt threatened by these non-citizens,[27] and the ease with which they avoided detection is plain to see. The ubiquitous nature of carpentry encouraged a "here today, gone tomorrow" modus operandi, and faced with such a large area as the City to patrol, the Company's resources proved woefully inadequate. New ordinances were again drawn up in 1655, allowing more apprentices per freeman, but one is left with the feeling that this was merely some attempt to lend an air of legitimacy to a situation which the Company could not hope to control.

Demarcation disputes continued, and the thin line between carting and trading was constantly breached. The Carpenters had always maintained that they represented all aspects of building, although in practice they were mainly involved with structural work. The Joiners, wishing to strengthen their position, had claimed for themselves those branches of woodworking not directly categorised as structural; doors, windows and the like. Matters got so bad that in 1632, the Court of Aldermen had to step in and adjudicate between the two Companies, laying down rules as to who could do what. As a result, the Joiners were granted the finer work, while to the Carpenters was assigned the rougher building and jobbing work.

By the time of the Fire, a wide variety of work had become available to master-carpenters, especially to those with ambition and drive. From the late fourteenth century, some had become small-scale contractors, and those at the top of their craft could be elected City Viewers, City Carpenters and, as we have seen, Master of the Guildhall and of the Bridgehouse. They might also become, as did Anthony Jerman, wholesale suppliers of building materials, or City Company Carpenters or Company Surveyors. Some were invited to submit designs for modest building programmes, while others engaged in small-scale speculation. The Fire was to open up even wider possibilities. Those with flair and enterprise, such as Edward Jerman and John Wildgose (see Chapter 3), grasped the opportunity to become designers and surveyors on an altogether grander scale than heretofore. They were – to all intents and purposes – architects. Other, more financially astute master-carpenters, including Roger Jerman, chose to become large-scale contractors, a very lucrative field of activity. However, such men represented only the tip of the iceberg. Most carpenters continued to practise their craft as had their forebears, sometimes venturing into small-scale design, contracting or speculation.

The Fire of 1666 swept away not only the greater part of the City of London,

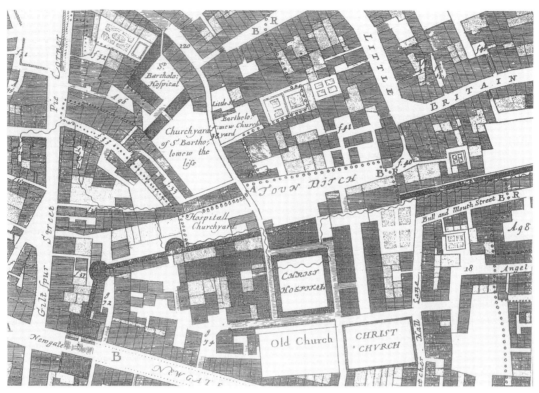

2.2 Section of Ogilby and Morgan's 1676 map showing the Jermans' carpenters' yard (f.40).

but also many of the City's old traditions and institutions. For a short while, demarcation disputes were forgotten as the Fire brought prosperity to all sections of the building industry. The Carpenters' Company petitioned the City authorities to check the credentials of the many "forrens" who flooded the capital in the hope of work, but the City turned a blind eye to any hindrance which might hamper the rebuilding process, while in these unique post-Fire circumstances, some of the more ambitious and enterprising master-craftsmen, especially carpenters, masons and bricklayers, seized the chance to widen their horizons. Edward Jerman was probably the prime example of a craftsman for whom the Fire provided the opportunity and conditions to further his career, to break with the carpentry tradition of his father, grandfather and great-grandfather. How he took advantage of such an opportunity will be revealed in subsequent chapters.

The Jermans as Carpenters

As a freeman of the Company, Roger Jerman, Edward's great-grandfather took five apprentices between 1552 and 1591. He seems to have been a rather contentious man, with several entries in the record books pointing to his argumentative nature. On one occasion, there is evidence of controversy between Roger and two fellow carpenters during which "they abused themselves unto the other misadvisedly in lewd and opprobrious words". They were each fined six shillings and eight pence by the Company.[28] Roger Jerman was also having trouble with bad debts. He was owed money by three people, and was attempting to involve the law in its recovery.[29] Perhaps in refusing to join the livery in 1582, at the age of sixty-two, Roger felt too old to make a useful contribution to Company affairs, but even at that advanced age, he was fined forty shillings for his refusal. In 1591, a year before his death, Roger took on his last apprentice, and in the same year, he was paid by the Company for some carpenter's work done for them in Threadneedle Street.[30]

Edward Jerman, the older of Roger's sons is recorded as having taken only two apprentices, in 1583 and 1584.[31] One of the Company's ordinances must have stipulated that no craftsman should carry out work for a client who was in debt to a fellow carpenter, and for 1585, Edward was involved in an interesting contretemps on this account: "Edward Jerman complaineth against Thomas Fawcon for that he did work at a baker's house where the said Edward Jerman had money owing. It is ordered for that the said Thomas shall well and truly pay unto the said Edward the sum of three shillings and four pence".[32] Commonly, fines exacted for such offences were paid to the Company, and this seems to have been a rare example of settlement being made directly to the injured party. A further point of interest about this case is that the aforesaid Thomas Fawcon (or perhaps his son of the same name), would, thirty-eight years later, take Edward Jerman (this Edward's great-nephew) as an apprentice.

Elias Jerman, Edward's brother, presented at least nine apprentices which suggests that his business was a very thriving one. It is difficult to know whether the Jerman family was particularly litigious, but here again we find another member in contention with fellow carpenters over several issues, including the wrongful transfer of apprentices, unpaid debts, and again the use of opprobrious words.[33] Certainly, record books do not abound with reports of such disputes – perhaps the Jermans were a particularly spirited family.

In 1593, Elias took over the house and yard that his father had been renting from Christ's Hospital since the mid-1570s, and continued to pay the same rent of five pounds per annum. The Register of Evidences of Lands belonging to Christ's Hospital gives us some idea of the neighbourhood of the Jerman property: "Elias Jerman, carpenter, a house and yard opening into Little Britain Street. Christ's Hospital holdeth a green yard or placement adjoining to the aforesaid Jerman house and yard right west, called or known by the name of the Town Ditch, being a place of recreation for children of this house and for the laying of timber".[34] Ogilby and Morgan's 1676 Map of London indicates precisely this carpenter's yard and the children's playground as described, at the east end of the Town Ditch and connected to Little Britain by a long, narrow alley (Figure 2.2).

Elias was an auditor to the Company, and his symbol appears in the account books between 1604 and 1607, sometimes with and sometimes without an

2.3 Signatures and symbols of auditors of the Carpenters' Company, including that of Elias Jerman (1607).

accompanying signature (Figure 2.3). He was elected New Warden in 1605, and was a Warden again in 1606, 1608 and 1610. His election in 1610 was to replace a fellow member who had died: "received at the burial of Mr. Bentley towards a drinking, twenty shillings, and received of Mr. Jerman, the same day elected Warden in his place, twelve shillings towards the same drinking".[35] Elias was clearly a very active and lively member of the Carpenters' Company, standing for and being elected to posts of importance, as well as participating in Company dinners and entertainments. It is amusing to find that he was paid "eleven shillings and eleven pence for sugar by him laid out several times this year",[36] roughly equivalent to £40 today!

2.4 A silver-gilt cup presented to the Carpenters' Company by Anthony Jerman in 1628.

Ironmongers' Hall is the only major building in the City with which Elias' name is linked. Brief entries in the Ironmongers' minutes of 1586-88 record that Elias and Edward were asked to draw a plan for a new hall, and then to "treat, build and set up the new form", while Elias promised to "well workmanly and sufficiently finish all his work".[37]

In 1610, together with another member of the Company, Mr. Cobb, Elias was paid "at his going to Ireland about the building there, five pounds". In 1609, James I had put forward proposals to plant a Protestant colony in Ireland, towards which the City was requested to contribute £60,000. A precept from the Lord Mayor on 1 July 1609 requested the Carpenters, along with the other companies, to appoint four members to a consultative committee.[38] The companies were required to form themselves into groups, each headed by one of the Great Twelve, and to each was allotted a portion of land. Each company sent representatives over to Ulster to view their designated territory, and so it was that Elias Jerman, at the age of sixty, set forth to Ireland about the building, a long, uncomfortable journey on a boat from the Pool of London. It was no small undertaking for a man of his age, but he must have found the place agreeable, for, having returned briefly to England to collect his wife, he spent the rest of his life in Ulster and became one of the nine Aldermen of Coleraine.[39] Elias and Peter Cobb had originally been employed to oversee the carpenters who were working on the new houses in Derry, but how long Elias continued to work in this capacity is uncertain. In 1612, Bishop King, the Bishop of Derry, instructed John Rowley, the agent, receiver and treasurer for the affairs of the City of London's Plantation in Ireland (item 39): "for the two master carpenters that have eighteen shillings a week, we now hold one to be sufficient".[40] Perhaps Elias spent his last years in civic government in Coleraine, for there is no evidence of his resignation from his position as an Alderman there, nor of his return to the City of London.

What a long, fascinating and varied life Elias had led. He was obviously a highly talented and respected master-craftsman, shown by the high offices to which he was appointed, both administrative and financial. He seems to have thoroughly enjoyed the social side of Company life, and was prepared to take up the challenge of such a venture as the Irish Commission at an age when most men would have been ready to relax. Such brief entries as there are in the record books only serve to tease the imagination, but engage it enough to follow any reference which may throw light on such interesting characters.

After he became a freeman of the Carpenters' Company in 1600, Anthony Jerman, Elias' son, presented a steady stream of apprentices, one every three

2.5 Window glass from the Master and Wardens' room at Carpenters' Hall (1664) showing the Arms and Carpentry mark of Anthony Jerman, Master in 1634.

years until 1636. In this time, therefore, twelve young men received their training in his workshop, including his son Hugh. The premises and carpenter's yard must have been quite sizeable to accommodate Anthony and two or three apprentices, possibly one or two labourers and stacks of wood in some state of preparedness. Presumably, his unworked timber was still being stacked round the edge of the Town Ditch. Anthony could have been using his father's house and yard from 1609 onwards, after Elias had settled in Ulster, but in 1614, he leased another house and garden next to Elias' property. Rent continued to be paid on the properties until Anthony's death, when Edward took over both leases. A very detailed survey was made of Anthony's property on 22 January 1639/40, and this is transcribed in Appendix 2. The trapezoid yard was indeed a very good size, approached by a long, narrow alley, useful for security but rather difficult for the negotiation of timber-laden carts. Thus, although no image of the Jerman family has come to light, we do have a detailed description of their living and working environment, and we are able to build up some assessment of their personalities.

Anthony was elected to the livery in 1615, and was a regular subscriber to the Election Day dinners, also subscribing to the "allowance and view", presumably an official inspection of his livery gown. He was a specially appointed auditor eleven times between 1631 and 1647, and was a Warden in 1628, 1630 and 1632, culminating in his election as Master in 1634.[41] When appointed Younger Warden in 1628, Anthony Jerman presented the Company with a silver-gilt cup which is now held in the treasury at Carpenters' Hall (Figure 2.4). The cup stands about twenty inches high, and around the rim is engraved, "The gift of Anthony Jerman, Younger Warden of the Carpenters' Company and Master Carpenter to the Chamber of London and one of the four Viewers of the same City. August 12, 1628." Anthony was clearly proud of his achievements. His presentation to the Company of such a cup (not a common practice, it would seem, from an investigation of the Carpenters' treasury), a tangible reminder to posterity, would ensure that his name would not be forgotten. Indeed, his name is not forgotten because on display in the entrance hall of Carpenters' Hall is a small glass panel that has survived from the east window of the 1664 Hall. It bears the Arms and carpentry mark of Anthony Jerman, master in 1634 (Figure 2.5). His work as a City Viewer and City Carpenter, together with his work for the City companies and his association with Inigo Jones will be discussed later. Anthony died in 1650 and was buried in St. Botolph's Aldersgate alongside his grandfather and Uncle Edward.

Edward Jerman chose to become a freeman by patrimony along with his brother Hugh in 1630,[42] seven years after his presentation as an apprentice. It seems that he took on only one apprentice, in 1633. Perhaps this is indicative of the way his working life would develop, less the master-carpenter and more the designer, surveyor, and indeed architect. There is only one reference to his being a liveryman, but he was nominated for the post of Youngest Warden in 1650.[43] He failed to be elected that year, and was nominated again in 1651, finally securing election on 10 August 1652, only to decline the appointment three days later.

In September 1655, Edward Jerman and Thomas Jordan, both City Viewers, requested permission to resign from their positions. As, by this time, the post of City Viewer was in the gift of the Carpenters',[44] their resignation and the nomination of their successors had to be put to the Court of Assistants. On 11 September 1655, the matter was discussed:

> Our Master intimated unto this Court that Mr. Edward Jerman, a member
> of this Court, and one of the City Viewers, and Thomas Jordan, one other
> of the City Viewers, were minded to surrender their said places . . . and
> that the right of presenting to the said places doth belong to this Company
> as well by the ordinances as by ancient custom, and that the said Mr. Jerman
> and Mr. Jordan were willing to invest the same again in the Company
> upon two able persons as this court should nominate.[45]

From this record, it is clear that Edward Jerman was a member of the Court of Assistants although he had never been a Warden. This was a most unusual situation, as Courts were usually composed of past or present Wardens and Masters of the Company. Perhaps Edward's influential position as a City Viewer secured his exalted status within the Company. From this time on, Edward Jerman seems to have been very much his own man, an independent operator rather than a company official. He appears to have severed all links with the Company, and after 1655, there is no further mention of him in Company records.

There is surprisingly little reference to Roger Jerman in the Carpenters' records for someone who spent his whole working life as a successful master-carpenter. One would expect to find him presenting apprentices on a regular basis, as his father had done, but he appears to have taken only three, one of whom was his son. As he had so much work, and made so much money, he must have had some assistance in his workshop. Much of his remunerative work was carried out after the Fire when restrictions on the employment of "forrens" had been relaxed. Perhaps he took advantage of the situation.

Having been made a freeman in 1650, Roger was elected to the livery in 1656. The entry in the Carpenters' records gives us a delightful insight into the formalities of the procedure: "This day, the twenty persons newly summoned to be of the livery, every of them paid their fines and fees were called into this court, and had their livery gowns and hoods put on them and were admitted, accordingly ranked and placed according to their antiquity and priority of freedom viz. number sixteen, Roger Jerman".[46] He was elected a Warden twenty years later, thus maintaining the family tradition of being called to hold high office in the Company. Roger Jerman died in 1678. Robert Hooke, in his *Diary*, records simply "Thursday October 24, 1678, Jarmin, City Carpenter, died".[47] The two men seem to have enjoyed a close relationship, for there are several references to Roger in Hooke's *Diary*.

References to members of the Jerman family are scattered widely through the Carpenters' Company minutes and account books, through many and diverse City records, through the records of fourteen other City companies, through view books, diaries and pageant pamphlets. However, it has been possible, with a degree of determination, to build up the outline of a picture of this intriguing family. Through the four generations of these talented and successful master-carpenters, we can gain some insight into the work and conduct of such men who played so important a part in the day-to-day life of London in the sixteenth and seventeenth centuries. All the members of the family seem to have led very different lives, and it becomes clear that the label of master-carpenter could be a spring-board into varied fields of activity. Had Peter Mills hailed from such a dynasty of bricklayers, a comparative study with Edward Jerman could have been fascinating, but the dynasty of the Jermans was unique in the world of master-craftsmen of their time. Following the fortunes of the Carpenters' Company alongside those of the Jermans, we can appreciate the attempts of the Company to control the craft in the City of London, and at the same time, we can recognise that the thread binding the three institutions of companies, City authorities and Crown was a very tenuous one.

CHAPTER 3

Edward Jerman: City Worker

> The great majority of London houses were wholly built of wood, and thatched with straw, reeds or stubble, and hence it was that, upon the occasion of the Great Fire which happened in the King's reign, beginning at London Bridge, it destroyed St. Paul's Cathedral, and burnt all the houses as far as St Clement Danes . . . warned by this misfortune, the most opulent among the citizens rebuilt their houses with partition walls of freestone, and covered their roofs with thick tiles.[1]

The reader of this account might suppose that it refers to the Great Fire of 1666. However, the extract describes a fire during the reign of Stephen (1135-1154), and is a starting point for consideration of the control of building in the City of London, and of those who exercised that control. The post that Edward Jerman held as City Surveyor in the 1650s had thirteenth-century roots, but its parameters had gradually evolved through the centuries. The men who held such posts were master-artificers, carpenters and masons, and those who operated the controls were City fathers, Aldermen, and Officers and Wardens of the craft guilds. Thus, there had always been an intermingling between the Corporation of the City and the City companies, a situation which would prove beneficial to Edward Jerman when, after the Fire, he gave up his City work completely, to work for the companies.

The Control of Building in the City of London: the Genesis and Development of Edward Jerman's position of City Viewer

The fire in King Stephen's reign eventually resulted in an Assize of Building in 1189,[2] under the auspices of the first Mayor of London, Henry Fitz-Alwyn. This Assize aimed to protect the City from future devastation by fire, and was probably the first English "building act". It laid down precise details about the structure of houses, their party walls, gutters, aumbries, gables and "necessary chambers", although building materials, which one might think in the circumstances to have been of supreme importance, were little mentioned. Party walls, which would assume an ever greater concern as overcrowding in the City led to the subdivision of buildings and subsequent litigation, were to be three feet thick and fifteen feet high, constructed of freestone. The houses consisted of only a ground and first floor.

Another great fire, at the end of Fitz-Alwyn's mayoralty in 1212, led to a second Assize of Building. This Act was more stringent than the first, and some of its clauses were re-iterated in the building proclamations of Elizabeth I in 1580 and Charles II in 1666. In this second Act, building in stone was strongly encouraged and the removal of internal partitions ordered, to prevent owners using their premises as hostelries, which was occurring in contravention of City regulations and which would become a major problem again in the seventeenth century. No brewing or baking was to take place at night, and Aldermen were to provide themselves with a "proper cord and hook" and to encourage households to place water-filled vessels outside their property.[3] The wages of carpenters, masons, and bricklayers, whose services were much in demand for the construction of so many new buildings, were to be strictly controlled, and "strange workmen", the antecedents of the "forrens" who were later to cause the Carpenters' Company such problems, were to be brought before the Mayor if they declined to abide by the same scale of wages.[4]

Pertinent to Edward Jerman's role as City Viewer (a role which, during his tenure was almost subsumed by that of City Surveyor), is the fact that this Second Assize of Building called for a "view" of all wooden houses in Cheap, the principal market place of the City. The fear of fire was ever-present. The view was to be conducted by the Mayor, Sheriffs and "discreet men of the City". These discreet men were probably Aldermen with little specialist expertise, but by around 1270, sworn masons and carpenters had become involved both in the assessment of buildings and in disputes between neighbours. The Assize of Nuisance, probably pre-dating the thirteenth century, dealt with these disputes and stressed that no-one might complain of a nuisance unless he were a freeholder, and that any property in contention was to be "viewed".

Richard de Wytham was the first Viewer to be mentioned by name. In 1301, he came before the Mayor and Aldermen and swore "to give proper consideration to all men of the City and suburbs of London concerning . . . stone walls between neighbours and touching other things pertaining to his office". At the same time, two carpenters, Robert Osekyn and John de Writele were required to report on the state of the gutters and boundary walls,[5] and in 1303, de Wytham and Osekyn, sworn to the Assize of Nuisance, reported on a ruinous wall, and advised on repairs.[6] Such Viewers were therefore required to fulfil the dual role of assessor and judge. These master-masons and carpenters, sworn to the City, the chosen representatives of their crafts, gradually achieved privileges appropriate to their status. In February 1370/71 two chosen carpenters and masons were "to be discharged of all taxes of tenths, fifteenths and others subsidies to our sovereign lord the King raised and levied in the City" as long as they remained in office.[7] By 1442, the Viewers had achieved further privileges, when they were discharged from serving on juries, inquests and other offices because so much of their time was taken up "by a great work that they have taken speedily for to make at Leadenhall . . . for the profit of this City".[8] In 1454, the formal title of Viewer was applied for the first time to these masons and carpenters who "from time out of memory" had been viewing and adjudicating nuisance in the City. In that year, "Edward Stone and John Wise, carpenters, admitted by the court to the office of Viewers were sworn before the Mayor and Aldermen well and faithfully to superintend certain nocuments [sic] of the City between neighbours, and thereof truly to report before the Mayor and to execute well and faithfully all that appertains to the office in this respect".[9]

By the sixteenth century, Viewers received a striped gown annually from the Chamber of London, provided that they gave their diligence and attendance when called by an Alderman of the City to survey illegal encroachments and other nuisance. It seems that they received no salary, for no records report any such payments, and the striped gown was forthcoming on the condition of their attendance "without anything taking for their labours in that behalf".[10] However, the sworn Viewers were able to charge a fee for every view they conducted which did not include the City as one of the parties involved. Although each man received only a share of five shillings, the fee most commonly mentioned, this share, multiplied several hundred times over a few years, must have added up to a very substantial income. The public aspect of the Viewers' duties continued to be that of reporting nuisance in which the City had an interest, particularly encroachments such as jetties, bay windows or even whole new building on to public streets and lands. The Thames and its waterfronts also came under the watchful eye of these men who thus kept the whole City under their surveillance.

These sixteenth-century Viewers were men who had risen to the top of their chosen careers of masons and carpenters, and were retained as contractors to the City. Many of them had held the position of Warden or even Master in their own City company, as well as that of Carpenter or Mason to other companies. They were required to be "ancient" (at least elderly and experienced), "sad" (merely serious) and "discreet", as well as being honest, able craftsmen. The Carpenters' and Masons' Companies presented candidates for the Viewers' positions when they fell vacant, and most commonly, one of their nominees was elected and sworn until, by the early seventeenth century, the Master and Wardens of the Carpenters' Company were able to appoint Viewer Carpenters directly.

The Viewers' oath, recorded at intervals since the early fourteenth century, continued to reflect the requirement to consider both public and private nuisance, but through the years, the emphasis veered from the private to the public. The fourteenth-century oath had laid stress on impartial adjudication:

> You shall truly learn the right between party and party in all manner and size of nuisance that you are charged in without any favour of any party, and true report make to the Mayor and Aldermen after your wit and cunning . . . sparing neither for made favour, dread nor hate of any person, but well and truly therein behave yourself.[11]

However, by 1580, indiscriminate building in the City was the main cause for concern:

> You shall swear that you shall truly present . . . all such building and
> purprestures as you shall find made upon any part of the common ground
> of the said City . . . you shall search all manner of nuisances, buildings and
> edifyings between party and party . . . and make true report to the Mayor.[12]

Similarly, the oath sworn in 1667 by Robert Hooke and Peter Mills upon their
appointment as Surveyors for the Rebuilding of the City echoed those earlier
oaths taken by the City Viewers:

> You shall swear that you shall well and truly see that the rules and
> scantlings set down in the Act of the present Parliament for building within
> the City of London . . . be well and truly observed. And that in all other
> things, you shall truly and impartially execute the office of Surveyor to
> the best of your skill, knowledge and power.[13]

The rules and scantlings set down in the Rebuilding Act of 1667 were long,
precise and detailed. It would take the Surveyors an enormous amount of time
and energy to ensure that they were "well and truly observed".

The Great Fire effectively destroyed the medieval London of the City Viewers,
the crooked alleys and overcrowded tenements that had come under their
surveillance. The 1667 Act was to ensure that the irregular buildings and
purprestures that they had so painstakingly measured should not, phoenix-like,
rise again. At the same time, the Act sounded the death-knell of the City Viewers
themselves. Since 1655, when Edward Jerman and Peter Mills had been appointed
Surveyors of the City Works, the work of the Viewers had diminished, and although,
in the aftermath of the Fire, there was some division of labour between the Surveyors
and Viewers, it was to the Surveyors that the enormous task of staking the streets
and measuring foundations in preparation for rebuilding fell. Meanwhile, the
Fire Court arbitrated between any contesting parties and policed compliance with
the Act. The office of City Viewer did, in fact, continue until 1737, but by then it
had really become a sinecure, the work being carried out by the Surveyors "as be
used to do of the views of the Common Viewers of this City".[14]

Most of the records pertaining to Edward Jerman's work for the City of London
as City Viewer, City Carpenter, Surveyor of the City Works and Surveyor for
Rebuilding, as well as his private work for the City are found in the Repertories
of the Court of Aldermen, the Journals of Common Council, the City Cash
Accounts, the City Lands Grant Books and the Coal Dues Accounts. These are
held in the Corporation of London Records Office. To understand better the
relationship between the City and the companies at this time, to understand how
Edward Jerman could be wearing three hats – those of designated City worker
(be it Viewer, Carpenter or Surveyor), private speculator-cum-builder and
company craftsman or surveyor – an appreciation of City and company hierarchy,
and their interdependence is helpful. Jerman's work for the companies that
engaged him before the Fire, namely the Fishmongers and Goldsmiths, will be
considered here while his post-Fire work for the many companies that sought
his services will be considered later.

The Hierarchy of the City Corporation and the City Companies: Edward Jerman's Position in each of them

In many respects, the hierarchy of the City Companies in the seventeenth century resembled that of the City Corporation itself, for both were pyramidal structures. At the peak of the company pyramid stood the Master, elected annually by a Court of Assistants. Below the Master were two or three Wardens, also elected annually. The Court of Assistants effected the administrative duties of the company, dealing with financial affairs of charges and expenditure, as well as controlling, in the case of the craft guilds, the apprenticeship system by scrutiny of work discharged. All members of the Court of Assistants were liverymen, most having served as Warden or Master. They were invited to join the Court, usually on the basis of seniority, when a vacancy arose. Liverymen were elected from the ranks of freemen in a rather haphazard way. When company funds were low, more liverymen would be elected, for there was a fine to be paid on election, but a greater fine for refusal. This process therefore boosted a company's coffers in a bad financial year. As a result of this electoral system, some liverymen might have been freemen only a short time at the date of their call, whilst others might be experienced freemen of twenty years or more. Freemen were admitted to the company upon the termination of their apprenticeship, which was commonly seven years. It was also possible, as was the case with Edward and Hugh Jerman, to be made a freeman (at the age of twenty-one) by patrimony, as the legal child of a freeman of the company, or by redemption (by the payment of a fine). At the base of this pyramid stood the apprentices and journeymen, often known as the commonalty. The company had jurisdiction over their day-to-day work.

At the apex of the City's pyramid stood the Lord Mayor, elected annually by the Aldermen. There were twenty-six Aldermen, each representing a City Ward, but unlike a Company Court of Assistants, the Aldermen were elected by the Wards, not by the next layer down in the hierarchy, the Common Council. The Aldermen were rich, powerful men who dealt with the City's day-to-day administration, overseeing the estates and interest of the Corporation, as well as supervising a multitude of public services. These included the enforcement of law and order, the control of trade in the port of London, the management of markets such as Leadenhall and Blackwell Hall, the condition of the streets and sewers, and the provision and maintenance of water supplies. In these duties, the Aldermen were assisted by the Common Councilmen (234 of them by the time of the Fire), returned each year as representatives of the Wards. Since the twelfth century, they had been summoned, appointed and elected to assist the government of the City, being variously defined as *probi homines*, "the best men of the Wards", "the sufficient men of good and wisest discretion" and "the most discreet and worthy citizens". As well as providing practical help with aldermanic duties, they were able to provide the Aldermen with impartial views from the citizens at large, thus permitting a more democratic government than might have otherwise existed.

Below the Court of Aldermen and the Common Council was the "Common Hall", composed in the mid-seventeenth century of about 4,000 liverymen from the more privileged companies, including the Great Twelve. In theory, Common Hall meetings were called to nominate such City officers as the Lord Mayor, the City Chamberlain, one of the two Sheriffs and four Members of Parliament who represented the City. In practice, its voice could be heard in outbursts against the national government, or indeed the City's own leaders. Below the Common Hall were the citizens, members of the Corporation by virtue of their freedom. In the seventeenth century, the City freedom was a practical necessity for most people who wished to work within the City of London or its liberties – that part just outside the walls, but under the jurisdiction of the City. Non-freemen could be prosecuted and fined by the Corporation, which not only derived valuable income from freedom fees, but wished to limit the numbers of the electorate, which was confined to freemen. To be free of the City, one had first to be a freeman of one of the City companies, or to be born the son of a City freeman, in the same way that a young man might become free of his father's company by patrimony. No-one but a freeman could keep a shop or exercise a trade in the City, neither claim exemption from taxes at markets or in the port of London. When Edward Jerman described himself in his will, as a "citizen and carpenter of London", he meant that he was a freeman of both the City and the Carpenters' Company. Valerie Pearl has estimated that in the mid-seventeenth century, three-quarters of adult males in the City belonged to City companies, and were therefore freemen of the City.[15]

Thus the City and the companies were mutually dependent, being held together by a combination of self-interest and mutual respect. To progress up the rungs of one ladder, it was necessary to be on one's way up the other. Time and time again, the archives tell of the same men simultaneously performing civic and company duties. Such men were, in the main, holders of high office in the Great Twelve Companies, for they were the rich City merchants. However, as we have seen in Chapter 2, the Master and Wardens of a craft company such as the Carpenters were elected from their own ranks: they were working craftsmen, not City merchants.

Edward Jerman's work for the Corporation of the City

Edward Jerman's first appearance in the record books of the City of London is found in the Repertory of the Court of Aldermen when, on 15 October 1632, Anthony Jerman presented a petition to the Court requesting that Edward should be admitted as a City Carpenter. Although most buildings in the City did not rival those under the surveillance of the Office of Works in grandeur or importance, the markets, gates and prisons needed constant adaptations and repairs. This work was carried out by specially appointed master artificers, that is, masons, carpenters and bricklayers who worked alongside the City Viewers. Anthony Jerman's request was granted: "This day upon the humble petition of Anthony Jerman, the City's Carpenter, this Court doth admit Edward Jerman his son (who hath been brought up under his father in the trade of carpenter fourteen years and upwards and is well known to have good experience and sufficiency in that art) to join with his said father in the execution of his said place".[16] Thus, at the age of twenty-seven, Edward Jerman was already considered a fine, experienced craftsman by the City authorities. Although these records do not make it totally clear, it seems that the City employed only one carpenter, mason and bricklayer at any given time. Perhaps, therefore, Edward's appointment to work alongside his father was unusual, and for this reason, it was necessary to seek the Lord Mayor's approval. This was granted the following year. Anthony and Edward were to work together until Anthony's death, when Edward would assume total responsibility as City Carpenter. Tenure of the post was dependent upon good workmanship as well as good behaviour, and the men were to be paid a fee, unspecified in the records.

Twelve years later, in March 1644/5, Anthony Jerman (already a past Master of the Carpenters' Company), was required in his capacity as a City Viewer to report on property adjoining Bethlm Hospital. Together with the three other City Viewers, Anthony made an extremely detailed survey of this property, clearly set out in full in the Repertory of the Court of Aldermen.[17] Anthony had been a Viewer since 1627 and the other Viewers named were all holders of high office within their companies. They were Thomas Jordan, a Carpenter Viewer; Thomas Birkett, another carpenter, who had had a distinguished career as a Warden of the Carpenters' Company in 1635 and 1637, and Master in 1639 and 1649; and Peter Mills, the bricklayer. Peter Mills was a few years older than Edward Jerman, having been born in 1598. He was apprenticed to a tiler and bricklayer in London in 1613 at the unusually early age of fifteen, presumably becoming a freeman of the Bricklayers' Company around 1621-1622. At the age of forty-five, in March 1643, he was appointed City Bricklayer.[18] Peter Mills also had an interest in design, for in 1638, he had made a plan of the church of St. Michael le Querne, and around 1640, he was probably the designer of houses in Great Queen Street. By the 1650s, he was employed more and more as a surveyor and architect.[19] He may have accepted the post of City Bricklayer to ensure that his name would be in the forefront of the minds of City patrons when building projects were in the offing. On the other hand, he seems to have been an extremely public-spirited man, who as we shall see, devoted much of his time to the City, surveying devastated building sites in the aftermath of the Fire.

Edward Jerman was elected a City Viewer in July 1650 on the death of his father, joining Peter Mills in the office. A clear insight into the nature of the Viewers' work in the mid-seventeenth century is found in a Christ's Hospital View Book entry for August 1651. The four sworn Viewers, including Peter Mills and Edward Jerman, were required to view, consider and report on some building work planned by an Alderman who had "pulled down certain houses of his situated in Fenchurch Street, and intends as himself declared to erect the same two houses two storeys higher than the old houses were, which will, as is conceived, much darken and obscure the ancient lights of three several tenements near thereunto adjoining, belonging to the said hospital".[20] These seventeenth-century Viewers were confronting the same type of problems that had engaged their forebears since the thirteenth century and had been considered at the Assize of Nuisance.

Around 1650, the Committee of Common Council realised that the Corporation's building programme in the City, comprising rebuilding, adaptations to existing buildings and repairs, had exceeded the terms of reference of the Viewers and the City craftsmen. They concluded that a total reorganisation of manpower and materials was needed, and decided to make a detailed examination of all workmens' bills. As a result of this investigation into a more satisfactory use of resources, the Committee concluded that two Surveyors should be appointed to report on any necessary construction work and to keep a check on all building materials stored in the City. These Surveyors were to draw up contracts with the workmen regarding labour and materials, while the Chamberlain would be responsible for the payment of wages. On 22 June 1655, Edward Jerman and Peter Mills were duly appointed Surveyors of the City Works. Thus Jerman, now aged fifty, and Mills, aged fifty-seven, were the two men singled out above all other City craftsmen by this Committee which, we must remember, would have been composed of the most influential men of the City Corporation and the companies. As Surveyors, Mills and Jerman received an annual salary of sixty pounds. Officially, it was recorded that they were considered "fit persons to survey the City work to be done, they being willing to relinquish the benefit of doing the same works and all other salaries and fees and liveries". The terms seem to imply that the two men were henceforth debarred from any private practice, although Jerman contrived to undertake City company work. In the City Cash Account Book the two are described as Surveyors General, and the Chamberlain deducted four pounds and eight shillings from each of their first year's salary for "fees, liveries and other things". Perhaps their livery still resembled the striped gown presented to their sixteenth-century predecessors.

The record books from this time reveal an interesting alternative route to the attainment of the City freedom. The Corporation commonly granted its officers a certain number of freedoms to dispose of in lieu of salary, the officers then presenting that number of people to be made free of the City "by redemption". The Repertories of the Court of Aldermen record that in 1654, for their work in the meal markets recently erected in the City, Mills and Jerman were owed

> fifty four pounds besides what allowance shall be fit to be made to them for their oversight and pains taken in the said work, for discharge thereof and for sparing the costs to the Chamber, it is ordered . . . that Mr. Mills and Mr. Jerman shall have the benefit of making four persons free of the City by redemption, the same being first presented to and allowed of by this Court,

and paying to Mr. Chamberlain to the City's use the sum of forty-eight shillings and sixpence in full of the said disbursement and all other demands touching this business.[21]

Clearly, the Court had to approve the officers' choices and each applicant was subjected to some kind of interview before being accepted. The applicants were also obliged to show the colour of their money at this point. The grant of this "privilege" to City officers was a very profitable exercise for the City Corporation, for not only did it avoid paying the officers' salaries, it also received a good fee from the applicants. One wonders quite what the officers got out of the deal – perhaps there was a certain obligation towards their sponsors by those who had acquired their freedom in this way, or even a discreet exchange of money. Mills and Jerman wasted little time in implementing the privilege, and by 25 September 1655, they had presented the second of their four candidates, one Thomas Imps, to be admitted a freeman by redemption in the Carpenters' Company.

The City records fail to furnish us with much detail regarding the work done by Mills and Jerman as City Surveyors. Scattered through the record books are such sketchy entries as "1655 . . . Edward Jerman was required to cause a bar to be fixed across the dock at Bridewell for the safekeeping of lighters". Perhaps the paucity of evidence stems from the fact that the several City offices that Mills and Jerman held were salaried. Had they been paid for each piece of work completed, more detailed accounts of work done and payment made would have been recorded. It must also be remembered that, under the Commonwealth, there were no great City building projects, so perhaps the greater part of the Surveyors' and Viewers' time was spent dealing with repairs to existing fabric rather than building anew.

By September 1655, Edward Jerman had, as we shall see, branched out into property development in the City, and he, together with Thomas Jordan, who had held the post of City Viewer for eleven years, resigned their positions. They were replaced by Richard Frith, who had been a Warden of the Carpenters' Company in 1650, and was again holding office in 1655. He was to become Master in 1657. The other appointee, John Wildgose, was a similarly eminent carpenter who, having been Warden of the Company in 1652, would be elected to that post again in 1656 and 1658, finally becoming Master in 1660. In 1664, he was to design an addition to Carpenters' Hall, and after the Fire, was to go on to design new Halls for the Coopers' and Salters' Companies. The status attached to the office of City Viewer, and the competition faced in the attainment of that office can be judged by the calibre of these men who were appointed, for they all held the highest positions in their own craft organisations.

Two years later, in October 1657, Jerman resigned from his post of City Carpenter, and the position was taken up by one Benjamin Warden, who held it for less than five years before resigning in favour of Roger Jerman on 24 July 1662. At Christmas 1657, Edward Jerman resigned from the third and last of his City appointments, that of Surveyor. He must have thought that there was more profit to be made in private practice, including work as an independent contractor in the City, and by this time, Jerman's reputation as a fine craftsman and his experience in dealing with the City elite must have left him in no doubt that he would receive plenty of commissions. He had already been appointed to eminent positions in two of the Great Twelve Companies, the Goldsmiths' and Fishmongers', as Company Carpenter and Company Surveyor respectively.

Edward had succeeded his father, Anthony, as Carpenter to the Goldsmiths' Company in 1650:

> At this Court as read the petition of Mr. Edward Jerman and Mr. Roger Jerman, two of the sons of Anthony Jerman late Carpenter of this Company, and also Robert Warden carpenter, they being suitors for the Company's place. And it appears, upon reading of the said Jerman's petition, that the younger of the two desired the place and that the other would be assistant to him upon all occasions. It was by this court taken into consideration that the younger was not so fitting for the place as others might be, and thereupon, Edward Jerman the older brother was called in and told if he would stand for the place himself, the Court would further consider thereof . . . he gave the Court his thanks and did become suitor for the same . . . it was resolved by the ballot box sixteen to three that the said place should be given to Edward Jerman.[22]

How clearly this extract conjures up an image of the three men anxiously waiting in an ante-room while the Court deliberated, called Edward back in, and then announced their decision. In 1650, Roger would have been only twenty-four, and a freeman for just one year. Perhaps Edward encouraged Roger to apply for the position, thinking that it might be his younger brother's chance to get his foot on a ladder up which his career would advance; he could guide his brother in his first appointment by working alongside him, as his father had done for him in 1632. It would seem that Edward was a generous and sympathetic man, qualities remarked upon by Tatham in his pageant pamphlets of the 1650s and 1660s,[23] and after Edward's death, by the Courts of many of the City companies by whom he had been employed. Edward's association with the Goldsmiths continued until his death in 1668, and so highly was he regarded by them that the Company extended financial help to Rose, his widow.[24]

Edward Jerman was appointed Surveyor to the Fishmongers' Company in 1654. Back in 1639, aged 34, he had measured "the mason's work, the plasterer's joiner's, carpenter's and painter's work at Fishmongers' Hall". His father, then a City Carpenter and the Goldsmiths' Company Carpenter, had been called in as an outside expert to inspect some work recently completed on the roof of the great hall, and Anthony must have been instrumental in Edward being chosen for this job. As we shall find in Chapter 5, it was the start of an association that was to last twenty-eight years.[25] It was about the time of his appointment to the Fishmongers' Company that Edward's interest in buying and selling timber developed, for the Fishmongers owned extensive woodlands at Bray (Berkshire), close by their almshouse, the Jesus Hospital. The management of these woodlands was Jerman's responsibility, and there are several records of his timber transactions in the City around this period.

At this point, we must side-step from Jerman's work for the City Corporation and consider his venture into real estate in the City, together with that of Peter Mills. Although Mills resigned as a City Viewer in September 1657, he continued to work as a City Surveyor until the office was abolished in November 1668. Having (probably) designed the houses in Great Queen Street around 1640, Mills went on to design Thorpe Hall (Cambridgeshire) in 1653, and possibly several other large houses in East Anglia in the later 1650s. Although Mills professed to being a Parliamentarian, and was a member of the Committee for the City of London Militia, commissions seem to have been more important to him than politics,[26] and he was able to forget any Parliamentary sympathies he had nurtured when he was invited to design the triumphal arches to celebrate Charles II's coronation in 1661, as well as the water pageant *Aqua Triumphalis*, to welcome Charles and his Queen to Whitehall in 1662.

Peter Mills' first foray into the City property market was in 1629 when he bought two dilapidated tenements, probably half-timbered structures, which he demolished, rebuilt in brick (gradually becoming the favoured material) and then sold on at a considerable profit. In December 1654, the Committee of City Lands granted him "a piece of void ground near Moor Ditch . . . from north to south 60ft. and from east to west 152 ft. for sixty-one years at the yearly rent of forty shillings, and a fine of £160 . . . upon condition that he well and substantially build upon the front of the said ground three double houses three storeys high, besides cellars and garrets according to the form, manner and conditions agreed upon by this committee".[27] This was a more adventurous project than the previous one, quite a sizeable piece of property development, but to be constructed within strict guidelines laid down by the City. However, Mills did not develop the land, but surrendered the lease fifteen months later in favour of Edward Jerman. Jerman, having built the houses as specified by the City, two years later relinquished "all claims and interest of this grant unto the Lord Mayor and Commonality of London".[28]

At the same time that he acquired this land from Mills, Jerman took the lease of another two pieces of ground. Presumably he built the requisite number of houses on both plots in the form required, for he was paid £1,100 by the City "for new building several tenements on the postern, his relinquishing his rights therein to the ground there". Jerman was clearly buying the land, building houses thereon, then selling the houses and land to the City authorities.[29] The type of houses "three storeys high besides cellars and garrets" which Jerman was building would have been those described as the "second" category under the Rebuilding Act which laid down guidelines after the Fire. Such houses were built on streets and lanes of note, resulting in an homogeneity of appearance, furthered by a uniformity of roof lines.

The concluding section of this chapter considers the legislative measures that were put into force following the Fire and the role played by the Surveyors in the reconstruction of the City. The Fire was to prove a turning point in the career of Edward Jerman, for he was chosen by no fewer than nine of the City companies to either re-design or repair their halls, as well as to provide plans for the Royal Exchange and St Paul's School. However, of immediate concern in this discussion of his work for the City is Jerman's role, albeit brief, as a Commissioner for Rebuilding in that immediate post-Fire period. The nature of this role would be spelt out by Charles II's Proclamation of 13 September 1666, by resolutions of the Corporation of the City and by the Act for the Rebuilding of the City. Parliament's immediate priorities in the first days of the Fire were to avoid civil disorder, to provide some kind of shelter for those who had lost homes, and to get business operating again. These it managed with surprising ease. The next priority was a plan for a new City which would reduce traffic congestion, eradicate much of the overcrowding which had exacerbated the risk of fire, relocate food markets in more convenient situations, and open up a riverside quay. Grandiose plans by Wren, Hooke, Evelyn, Mills, Valentine Knight and Richard Newcourt all set to address these problems with wide boulevards and grand piazzas, but by mid-September, after much deliberation by the King, Parliament and the City, it was concluded that speed of rebuilding was all-important if London were to retain its pre-eminent position as a trading centre.

On all sides, there was a sense of urgency. A large proportion of the City's income came from property which had been consumed by the flames, whose occupants had dispersed and were unlikely to return to the metropolis unless they were permitted to rebuild their homes quickly and to start to pick up the threads of their lives. The King needed the customs and excise duty he collected from the City's trade, and the City feared losing its ascendancy as a centre of business over the suburbs and the provinces. The practical and financial difficulties in adopting one of the ambitious plans were apparent – there was simply no time to effect them – and more modest plans took their place. Even the modified plans became more modified as building progressed.

On 13 September 1666, Charles II issued a Proclamation "to prohibit the rebuilding of houses after the Great Fire of London without conforming to the general regulations therein premised".[30] He stressed that "mature deliberation must be given to rebuilding", that streets would be widened and building would be in brick and stone; that the waterfront would be opened up to provide "a fair quay" and smoky, disagreeable trades would be relocated. Finally, the King proclaimed:

> We do hereby direct that the Lord Mayor and Court of Aldermen do with all possible expedition cause an exact survey to be taken of the whole ruins . . . to the end that it may appear to whom all the houses and ground did in truth belong, what term the several occupiers were possessed of . . . so that provision may be made, that though every man must not be suffered

to erect what buildings and where he please, he shall not in any degree be debarred from receiving the reasonable benefit of what ought to accrue to him, that no particular person's right and interest should be sacrificed to the public benefit or convenience without recompense.

He anticipated that, by the time the survey had been taken, "a plot or model would have been made for the whole building through those ruined places". This question of a survey must have been much under discussion as the inhabitants of the City walked among the ruins. On 10 September, Henry Oldenburg, in correspondence with another Fellow of the Royal Society, Robert Boyle, remarked, "I was yesterday in many meetings with the principal citizens whose houses were laid in ashes who, instead of complaining, discussed almost of nothing but a survey of London and a design for rebuilding".[31]

Nine days after the Proclamation, The *London Gazette* reported that the Lord Mayor and Aldermen "desired all corporations, companies and persons . . . that the last occupiers do within fourteen days bring into the Beadle's booth set up in the respective wards . . . a perfect survey of the ground whereon his house, shop or warehouse stood and his term therein, to the end that the whole may be there recorded".[32] This attempt to collect data from all interested parties was a failure. Most people were too busy trying to piece together the fragments of their lives to stand in queues outside Beadles' booths.

An important meeting of the Common Council was held a fortnight later, when "the great business of rebuilding the City" was debated. It was reported that the King

> was pleased to appoint Dr. Wren, Mr. May and Mr. Pratt to join with such surveyors and artificers as should be appointed by the City to take an exact and speedy survey of all the streets, lanes, alleys, houses and places destroyed by the late dismal fire, that every particular interest may be ascertained and provided for and the better judgement made of the whole affair. This Court doth therefore order that Mr. Hooke, Mr. Mills and Mr. Jerman do join . . . in taking the said survey . . . which shall be taken in every ward.[33]

These six men, entitled Commissioners for Rebuilding, were ideally suited to such a wide-ranging assignment. Wren was a professor of astronomy and an amateur architect; May, a royal officer with architectural experience; Pratt, a practising architect; and Hooke, the curator of experiments at the Royal Society and professor of geometry at Gresham College. The other two men chosen by the Committee, Jerman and Mills, had vital local knowledge of the City, its problems and its modus operandi. The recommendations of these men, together with the ideas contributed by Charles II and the City, would become the basis of the first Rebuilding Act on 8 February 1666/7. Speed, simplicity, economy and improvement were crucial, and these men contributed significantly to the achievement of such goals.

The following week, the Committee instigated a second survey, dealing more specifically with foundations, to be conducted by Hooke and May on behalf of all the Surveyors. They were to be paid eighteen pence by the proprietor of each foundation surveyed. It was hoped that, by giving adequate notice of an impending survey, the attendance of all interested parties could be assured, minimising disputes between neighbours, and between landlords and tenants. In fact, many people refused to set about clearing rubbish, and the authorities finally undertook the task themselves. No records of any measurements made at this time exist, and probably, few were made until the spring. Hooke, Mills and Jerman were formally appointed City Surveyors on 31 October 1666 when they were desired to "meet and consult with Mr. May, Dr. Wren and Mr. Pratt . . . concerning the manner, form and height of buildings in this City, the scantlings of timber, removing of conduits and churches and the alteration of streets".[34]

Although it detailed recommendations set out in the royal Proclamation, together with exact specifications of houses to be erected, the Rebuilding Act of 8 February 1666/7 left decisions concerning widths of streets to the King and the City. Until such decisions were taken, no streets could be staked and therefore no building could proceed. Pepys reported Thomas Hollier, a surgeon, as saying "he would be a builder again, but knows not what restrictions there will be, so it is unsafe to begin".[35] However by the end of February 1666/7, the Court of Common Council had drawn up a comprehensive list of streets and their designated widths, together with thoroughfares which were to be promoted to "lanes of note". At the same time, the Court ordered that consideration should be given to Mills' and Jerman's payment "for their pains for the times past, and of what salaries shall be allowed them for the time to come". On 5 March 1666/7, Mills and Jerman were ordered to provide stakes for setting out the streets and lanes "in order to rebuilding". Costs involved were to be borne by the Chamber, who would subsequently be repaid by the builders.

In effect, the City's choice of Commissioners for Rebuilding were being re-appointed as City Surveyors: "Mr. Peter Mills, Mr. Edward Jerman, Mr. Robert Hooke and Mr. John Oliver are chosen to be Surveyors and Supervisors of the houses to be built in this City . . . and the said Surveyors [shall] forthwith proceed to the staking out of the streets as is ordered in the pursuance of the Act".[36] Hooke and Mills were sworn in the next day, taking the Surveyors' oath quoted above. John Oliver, at this time, declined the post, and Edward Jerman absented himself. He was already so involved with work for the City companies, measuring and designing halls and surveying devastated sites, that staking streets prior to rebuilding may have seemed an unfeasable proposition or an unattractive one.

On 29 April 1667, an Act of Common Council finally provided the definitive list of streets and alleys to be widened. Even so, builders were not free to begin work immediately, for the Act contained directions:

> for the defraying charges of measuring, staking out . . . sweeping the street
> and grounds, each builder before he lay his foundations, or such survey
> be taken, do repair to the Chamberlain of London and there enter his name

with the place where his building is to be set out and pay to the Chamberlain the fine of six shillings and eight pence for every foundation to be rebuilt for him, for which Mr. Chamberlain shall give him acquittance, upon receipt of such acquittance, the Surveyor proceed to set out such person's foundations . . . and it is ordered that Mr. Edward Jerman shall be allowed fifty pounds for the time past.[37]

Thereafter, Mills and Hooke were to receive annual salaries of £150. A vellum-covered book in the Corporation of London Records Office entitled "Day Book for Receipts of Money for Staking out the Foundations within the Ruins of the City of London" contains records of all the foundations surveyed by Hooke, Mills and Oliver between 13 May 1667 and 5 February 1668/9, demonstrating that between these dates, about 3,500 sites had been surveyed.[38] The book is a remarkable piece of evidence of the enormity of the task that was accomplished. At the back of the book are columns of payments made to the Surveyors, including only two to Edward Jerman on 10 October and 15 October 1667.

Only when the Surveyor's views were contested was a case referred to the Fire Court. The aim of this Court was to settle disputes between landlords and tenants, to hasten rebuilding with all speed on the basis that everyone concerned should bear a proportionable share of the loss. Petitions were brought to the judges, whose decisions were almost incontestable. They took no fees, and worked for six years dealing with over 1500 cases. The Fire Court completely won over the confidence of the citizens who could, and often did, conduct their own petitions. All contending parties pleaded their case to the judges, and when necessary, the judge enlisted expert advice from one of the Surveyors. At this point, Edward Jerman or (much more frequently) one of the other Surveyors was called in.

Although Edward Jerman's name only appears twice in the Receipts Book, the payment to him of fifty pounds must imply that he did a considerable amount of work for the Corporation of the City in those months following the Fire. Perhaps records of his work were lost, or perhaps his work went unrecorded. Similarly, only four references to him appear in the reports of the Fire Court. The first report, on 1 May 1666/7, concerned the respective responsibilities of a landlord and tenant in rebuilding a house and shop destroyed in the Fire;[39] the second, on 9 July 1667, dealt with a disagreement between two parties over a "front" house and a "back" house and the yard between them.[40] The third case, on 22 December 1667, involving Hooke, Jerman and Oliver was to determine the rights of tenants in a property in which the rooms lay intermixed, and the fourth and last case was viewed by Jerman one week before his death, on 21 October 1668.

There is one recorded instance of Jerman viewing a property together with Peter Mills, a case which was not referred to the Fire Court, but was settled between the Surveyors and the interested parties. On 6 October, 1667, Mills and Jerman viewed Squire Austen's property near Foster Lane:

and did set out the same, and did then with some of the Goldsmiths' Company view the old stone wall separating the said Austen's mansion house and the churchyard . . . and upon our view do find in our judgement that the said wall doth belong to Mr. Austen so far in depth east and west as the said Austen's old building did stand, as may appear by many ancient stone windows that stood in the same, and by the returned wall at the end of the old building extending northward from the stone and is branded into the old stone wall and wrought with the same materials.[41]

Each of the Surveyors covered a particular area of the City: Hooke, the eastern part; Oliver, the centre; and Mills, the western section. Few of their foundation certificates have survived, as these were the property of the payees. However, Mills' and Oliver's surveys were transcribed (though not Hooke's), and these indicate that the Surveyors also inspected the superstructures erected on their approved foundations, ensuring compliance with regulations laid down in the Order of Common Council of 29 April 1667. The Surveyors were instructed, among other things, to encourage all builders "for ornaments sake" to use rubbed brick on all decorations and projections on the fronts of their buildings, where the surfaces of bricks were to be "neatly wrought". Breast-summers and roofs were to be set a uniform level, breaking only where ordered by the Surveyors. By 1670, 6,000 foundations had been set out and paid for. During 1667 and 1668, the Fire Court had arbitrated in 800 cases. What enthusiasm and stamina Peter Mills must have had, to spend his days, at the age of seventy, scrambling in and out of gutted buildings, measuring them and composing surveys, dealing with distraught and frightened people.

Although Edward Jerman's post-Fire work for the City was minimal compared with that of Peter Mills, to warrant the remuneration he received he must have done more than these recorded surveys suggest. To achieve a complete appraisal of Jerman's work for the City of London, more precise evidence of that work would have been illuminating. However, he had given the City many years of service before the Fire, holding three principal posts. Looking back over his years of work for the City, one realises just how many times Jerman must have appeared before the Court of Aldermen, and how often his name must have been mentioned and his proficiency discussed in their private meetings. When it is remembered that these same men were also holding positions of importance in their Livery companies, it becomes clear why so many of those companies sought Jerman's expertise and experience when it came to rebuilding their halls. Although Jerman resigned from the last of his City posts in 1657, he had in the previous year become the designer of the annual Lord Mayor's Show. He continued to devise most of the shows until 1665, when the Plague and then the Fire caused an interruption in the festivities. It is to his pageant work that we must now turn, to conclude this account of Edward Jerman's pre-Fire work.

CHAPTER 4
Edward Jerman as Pageant Maker

A solemn oath-taking ceremony before the sovereign, a watch to maintain law and order, folk customs celebrating the turning of the year and its seasons, royal entries honouring the monarch, the observance of saints' days and other recognised dates in the Christian calendar – from these evolved the Lord Mayor's Show. It took inspiration from some of these festivities and replaced others until it became the principal, and finally the City's only regular annual pageant, a magnificent, colourful display portraying both mythological and historical scenes. By the second quarter of the seventeenth century, it attracted some of the finest artists and dramatists of the day and, as David Bergeron states, "it came to rival in magnificence and opulence the entertainments presented to the sovereign".[1] However, it was interrupted, like so many other entertainments between 1640 and 1655, under Cromwellian austerities, and again between 1665 and 1671, as a consequence of the Plague and then the Fire.

From the late sixteenth century, and throughout the seventeenth century, the Lord Mayor's Show was commonly described as a "pageant" or "triumph". The *Oxford English Dictionary* provides two definitions of the word "pageant": a public entertainment consisting of a procession of people in elaborate colourful costumes, and, historically, a scene erected on a fixed stage or moving vehicle as a public show. Whenever possible, "show", and sometimes "triumph" will denote the former meaning, and "scene" for the latter. When "pageant" is used, the discernment of the reader should elicit the implied definition.

Edward Jerman became the principal artificer for the Lord Mayors' Shows between 1656 and 1664. He worked alongside the poet, John Tatham, and the scenes that Jerman contrived demonstrate another aspect of the virtuosity of this widely talented man. In order to understand his inventions, and the form the Shows took, some knowledge of their history, and the nature of the pageantry is essential.

As described in Chapter Three, in the seventeenth century the City of London was ruled by an oligarchic elite drawn from the ranks of the City companies. This had developed by the late fifteenth century, when the right to participate in civic elections was limited to only those freemen who were members of the livery, instead, as formerly, to all freemen. At the same time, entry to the livery was restricted to certain freemen who, amongst other criteria, would and financially could fulfil various ceremonial obligations, resulting in an estrangement between merchants and artisans. In the sixteenth century, this elitism was carried even further, when the twelve so-called "great" companies formed themselves into a distinct and formal group from whose numbers the new mayor would, in the future, be elected. About the same time, the title of Lord Mayor began to replace that of mayor, and the appointment carried with it the automatic conferral of a knighthood on retirement from the office.[2] Concurrent with this gradual exclusivity in the role of mayor was the increasing magnificence of the inauguration, from the early "ridings" to the oath-taking trip by barge to Westminster, to the full panoply of the seventeenth-century Shows. By following the development of mayoral inaugurations over the years, it becomes apparent why Edward Jerman's scenes took the form they did. They were both an expression of the glory of the office of Lord Mayor and a demonstration of the tradition and longevity of the Show itself.

In this chapter, a similar pageant, the City's Guildhall entertainment in June 1660 will also be discussed. This was one of several that were staged in honour of Charles II around the time of his coronation, and was again a collaboration between Jerman and Tatham. On this occasion, Roger Jerman was appointed master-carpenter.

The History and Development of the Lord Mayors' Show

The first seeds of the Lord Mayors' Shows were sown sometime around the dawn of the thirteenth century when Henry Fitz-Alwyn, a draper, was required to ride from the City to Westminster to seek the King's approval for his appointment as the first Mayor of London.[3] John Stow tells us that about fifty years later, Henry II commanded watches to be kept in all cities for the maintenance of peace and quiet. These Midsummer watches, whose origins were buried deep in folk custom, developed into marches with street entertainments.[4] The most ancient pageants were portable images, such as the giants mentioned by Stow, and were carried or drawn in procession. Other, more bulky scenes were of necessity static, often erected around the crosses and conduits of the City streets. They resembled the tableaux of the early Mystery Plays which were performed on scaffolds in the open street.

Royal entries had, since medieval times, been costly processions with elaborate and accomplished dramatic scenes enacted at certain points along the designated route as the monarch passed by. The themes of these richly allegorical vignettes were taken from history and myth, and they were both didactic and complementary to the sovereign. City dwellers were thus diverted by street spectacles of varying grandeur and execution, both royal and civic. All these shows were extremely popular events, and drew great crowds of noisy and excited onlookers. They all contributed to the composition of the Lord Mayors' Shows such as those staged in seventeenth century when Edward Jerman's inventions beguiled the spectators.

Towards all these spectacles, the craft guilds were obliged to subscribe considerable sums of money which increased as the events became more

4.1 John Norman, Mayor 1453-4, in aldermanic robes.

ambitious. In 1401, the Grocers' Company paid but forty shillings for six minstrels to accompany the Mayor in his "riding" to Westminster, and four pence for the use of a horse for the beadle – clearly a workmanlike rather than a festive event. By 1436, however, the same Company had augmented its expenditure to £100 for clothing for the Mayor, who was accompanied by twenty liverymen, minstrels and a horseman. The seedlings of the mayoral progress were beginning to flower.

By the third decade of the fifteenth century, a new development in mayoral inauguration was evident. The Mayor progressed from the City to Westminster for the oath-taking by barge – the riding had been replaced by floating. Sir John Norman, Master of the Drapers' Company and Mayor in 1453 (Figure 4.1) made the journey in style in his own barge, attended by "graceful ladies and sweet-singing youths". This transition from a land-based progress to one incorporating London's river was clearly considered a very significant development, for it was referred to nearly two centuries later by the pageant-poets Anthony Munday (in 1614) and Thomas Middleton (in 1623).[5] After 1453, the processions became more and more elaborate, increasing in splendour and ceremony, but were still without accompanying scenes. These remained the prerogative of royal entries and the midsummer show.

A century later, a royal entry and a City company show were combined in the Coronation celebration for Anne Boleyn in 1533. Edward Hall vividly sets the scene in his *Chronicle* of 1548:

> The King's Highness addressed his letters to the Mayor and Commonality of the City, willing them to make preparation as well to fetch her Grace from Greenwich to the Tower by water, as to see the City ordered and garnished with pageants. When she should be conveyed from the Tower to Westminster, commandment was given to the Haberdashers that they should prepare a barge. . .likewise as they used to do when the Mayor is presented to Westminster. Also the other crafts were commanded to prepare barges and garnish them with seemly banners as they had in their halls, and all things necessary for such a noble triumph.[6]

Thus the companies were required by Henry VIII to stage a display for his Queen which surpassed in magnificence and extravagance the annual mayoral Show.

It was about this time that the title Lord Mayor started to replace that of Mayor or Chief Magistrate of London, and more elaborate Lord Mayors' Shows supplanted the simpler mayoral inaugurations. The first of these Lord Mayors' Shows to include a pageant was that of Sir John Allen, a Mercer, in 1535. Complaints were subsequently levelled against the Mercers, accusing them of putting up the cost of office-holding to unacceptable heights with their spectacular display. Similar complaints about extravagance, this time concerning the shrievalty, led Henry VIII to suspend the Midsummer show of 1539, and although several attempts were made to revive it, it continued to decline as the Lord Mayors' Shows prospered. As Michael Berlin states, "The Lord Mayors' Shows lacked the magico-religious element [of the midsummer shows] and dwelt instead on the celebration of the office of the Lord Mayor as the apotheosis of the civic oligarchy".[7]

Henry Machyn, citizen and Merchant Taylor, describes one of the early Lord Mayors' Shows, that of 1553. The Show took place on 29 October, the morrow of St Simon and St Jude's Day (the celebration took place on this day throughout the period under discussion). Machyn relates:

> The Lord Mayor went towards Westminster, attended by the crafts [City companies] of London in their best livery with trumpets blowing, a goodly foist trimmed with banners and guns, waiting of my Lord Mayor's barge unto Westminster, and so to the Exchequer and so homewards, and in Paul's churchyard, every craft were set in array. First were two tall men bearing two great streamers of the Merchant Taylors' arms, then came two great wild men armed with great clubs, all in green with squibs burning, and after came the bachelors all in a livery with scarlet hoods, then came the pageant of St John the Baptist, the king's trumpeters, the crafts, my Lord Mayor's officers and then my Lord Mayor with two good henchmen and all the aldermen and sheriffs.[8]

This fascinating account seems to describe a pivotal moment in the evolution of the Lord Mayors' Show. Looking back, we can see in it the convergence of the essential elements of the three great street spectacles, the Midsummer watch, the royal entry and the mayoral progress. We note the moving pageant of St John the Baptist, but also the giants and wild men from the early folk shows. The pomp, ceremonial dress, musicians and bedecked barges are all particularised. Looking forward a hundred years, not only are all the elements described by Machyn still present in John Tatham's accounts of the Lord Mayors' Shows that he and Edward Jerman devised, but we realise that the procession still follows the same route, and the positions taken up by the City dignitaries within that procession are unchanged. Thus, over the years, the pageants became more ambitious, more elaborate and ornamental, but their basic form remained essentially the same.

Twenty years later, the order of ceremony of the 1575 Show, when Sir James Hawkes, a Clothworker, was installed as Lord Mayor, was described by William Smythe, a spectator:

> The Lord Mayor and Aldermen went by water to Westminster in a most triumph-like manner, and on the return journey, landed at Paul's Wharf, the

4.2. Pageant of 1616: The Fishing Busse.

liveries of every company preceding the Mayor. The streets were cleared by the men dressed like devils and wildmen with squibs, and also by beadles and whifflers in velvet coats and chains of gold. When the streets were clear, came the pageant of Triumph, richly decked with figures, and writing referring to the Lord Mayor and to Justice. Finally, one thousand people repaired to dine at the Guildhall.[9]

Here then, the Lord Mayor's Show had achieved most of its essential characteristics, but as yet, the pageantry was limited, and none of it took place on the barges. George Peele's 1591 Show was the first in which, as well as the land pageant, a speech was delivered on the water by a sea-nymph. It was addressed to the Lord Mayor on his voyage to Westminster, and marks the beginning of the Water Show. The land pageants themselves were generally peripatetic once the speeches had been delivered. They were picked up by porters and carried in front of the Lord Mayor until he reached the next scene.

Until this time, we are dependent on spectators' accounts of the Shows, together with some scanty evidence in the archives of the participating City companies. However, from 1585, pageant-poets, paid to contrive the spectacles and to write speeches, also produced accounts of the days' proceedings in pamphlet form. In 1585, Peele devised the Show for Sir Wolstone Dixie, a Skinner, and Peele's pamphlet, entitled *The Device of the Pageant*, is the first in a long line of such booklets. At first, these contained only the speeches addressed to the Lord Mayor, but later, the accompanying spectacle was also described. Such description as was added tended, in the early years, to be restricted to the aspect of the Show that the poets themselves had helped to create. Stress was laid, therefore, on the spoken, rather than any visual aspect of the show. The pageant-pamphlets were produced annually, and by the early seventeenth century about 400 were printed each year. The printers' names appear on the titles of these publications, indicating that they were for sale to the general public.[10]

From the time of Peele's participation onwards, dramatists renowned for their writing for the legitimate theatre also wrote the Shows. Thus, Ben Jonson, Middleton, Thomas Heywood and Munday, to name but some, were all prominent in the production of these entertainments. The artificers and artists who created the physical part of the Show received little or no mention at this time; nor is there any record of antagonism between poet and artist comparable with that between Ben Jonson and Inigo Jones concerning the relative importance of the "body" (the physical image) and the "soul" (the spoken word) in the early part of the seventeenth century.[11] For Thomas Dekker, author of several pageants, the poet and artificer should work together, "both of them emulously contending (but not striving) with the proprest and brightest colours of wit and art to set out the beauty of that great triumphant day". He emphasised that the artificer should make the words of the poet become flesh.[12] In fact, as we shall see, both the Heywood-Christmas partnership of the 1630s and the Tatham-Jerman alliance of the 1650s and 1660s seem to have been most harmonious, for each more or less spanned a decade.

Perhaps, in the milieu of the City, with their scenes presented to an audience comprised of a cross-section of society from merchants to artisans, from Aldermen to scavengers, the aspirations of both poets and artists involved were not as high as those of Jonson and Jones, and certainly, their abilities were more pedestrian.[13] Pepys complained about the noise of such occasions when he wrote of the coronation day, in 1661, "so great a noise that I could make out but little of the music, and indeed it was lost to everybody".[14] Ned Ward, the journalist, gives a vivid description of the rabble and resulting hullabaloo associated with the Lord Mayors' Shows. Of the crowds watching the 1699 Show, he writes, "I saw such a crowd before my eyes that I could scarce forbear thinking the very stones of the street, by the harmony of their drums and trumpets, were metamorphosed into men, women and children . . . the pageants were advanced within our view, upon which such a tide of mob overflowed the place that every man strove hard for his freedom. . . . I was so closely imprisoned between the bums and bellies of the multitude that I was almost squeezed as flat as a napkin in a press".[15] It is, therefore, not surprising that the spectacle, the visual part of the Show, assumed the greater importance, until, in the eighteenth century, the speeches were abandoned entirely. Kenneth Richards suggests that the decline in the verbal content of the Shows can largely be put down to "Tatham's poetic limitations as a pageant-maker". Richards considers Tatham "an indifferent versifier",

4.3 The Fishmongers' Pageant of 1616: the fourth pageant, The Lemon Tree.

and states that he published two plays, "unacted and arguably unactable".[16]   L.J. Morrissey agrees that after the Restoration, "there was no strong poet to complement the architect".   He emphasises Tatham's declining importance. "Only Jerman was consulted, the poet Tatham was not even mentioned" in the Haberdashers' Show of 1664.[17]

Perhaps the problem of competing with the background noise discouraged poets of the regular theatre, such as Dryden and Shadwell, from adapting their skills to these popular civic Shows. The Jonson-Jones court masques of the early part of the century had been enacted in front of an invited, sophisticated, intelligent, attentive audience, conversant with emblematic references, myth, allegory and historical allusions. The street entertainments, accessible to anyone and everyone were very different. Their subject matter comprised many of the elements found in the masques, as well as company and mayoral allusions, as stated. The speeches must have been almost inaudible, and for most of the spectators, able to catch nothing but a small glimpse of the performance, there could have been little understanding of it in its totality.[18]

The Emergence of the Artificer

A fine, and indeed a rare illustration of a Lord Mayor's Pageant is displayed at Fishmongers' Hall. Anthony Munday's 1616 Show, commissioned for the inauguration of Sir John Leman, is depicted on a long vellum scroll, showing the various scenes or pageants that were employed with the players in situ, together with accompanying horsemen and attendants. This useful piece of evidence helps to establish the complexity of these inventions, and their size relative to the human form; they were truly massive, borne on pageant-wagons whose wheels were concealed by dependent curtains (Figures 4.2 to 4.5). Presumably, they were composed of wood and papier mâché, with silk trimmings, and their variety is as remarkable as their form is ingenious.

The Fishmongers' records give no indication of the artificer with whom Munday collaborated on the 1616 Show, and in fact the first artificer ever named in a pageant-pamphlet for his part in the Lord Mayors' Shows was John Grinkin, who worked alongside Jonson, Munday and Middleton in the first two decades of the seventeenth century.[19] However, it was with Gerard Christmas and his two sons, John and Matthias, that the role of the artificer really achieved prominence. Their work for mayoral pageants spanned the period 1618-1639. It was a unique collaboration, and no other father-sons team served in this way for civic entertainment. They were constantly singled out for praise by Middleton, Dekker, and Heywood, although Middleton's pamphlet references to the artificer seem to have been more conventional than genuinely appreciative. To take an example of Middleton's prodigious acclaim for Christmas, we may return to the 1623 pageant, *The Triumphs of Integrity* (in which he referred to the inauguration of Sir John Norman in 1453). His pamphlet concludes, "For all the proper adornment of art and workmanship in so short a time, so gracefully setting forth the body of so magnificent a triumph, the praise comes as just due to the exquisite deservings of Master Gerard Christmas".[20] Moreover, Middleton concluded his 1621 pamphlet, "Christmas, a man excellent in his art and faithful in his performances", and that of 1622, "Christmas, a man not only excellent in his art, but faithful in his undertakings". This appears praise indeed until we discover that the same words appear in the final paragraphs of most of Middleton's pamphlets, and are directed, not only at Christmas, but also at Grinkin: "The whole work and body of the triumph, with all the proper beauties of the workmanship, most artfully and faithfully performed by John Grinkin".[21] We shall find that Tatham, presumably using Middleton as his model, employed almost identical words in acclaiming Edward Jerman.

The association between Heywood and the Christmas family seems to have been particularly harmonious and productive, and Heywood's eulogies at the conclusion of his pamphlets describe specific components of their artistry, unlike Middleton's bland statements of praise. David Bergeron suggests that Heywood's praise was probably instrumental in Christmas' assumption of a higher status and greater authority in negotiations with the companies. Certainly, in 1632, it was Christmas, not Heywood, who was mentioned in the records of the Haberdashers' Company in connection with their pageant.[22] Gerard Christmas died in 1634, but his sons took his place and the association with Heywood flourished, with John and Matthias, rather than Heywood, assuming responsibility for the Shows. It seems, therefore, that Heywood, in his praise for Christmas, might have been the author of his own demise. The year 1639 marked the end of the Lord Mayors' Shows until 1655, but by 1639, as we have seen, the artificer

4.4 The Fishmongers' Pageant of 1616: the third pageant, The King of the Moors.

had achieved a role of new importance due to the artistic talent and agreeable personalities of the Christmas family. Their mantle was, in 1656, to fall on to the shoulders of another man with artistic talent and an agreeable personality. That man was Edward Jerman.

Edward Jerman's involvement in mayoral Shows was to last almost a decade, a decade that included the Restoration of Charles II and was, therefore, rich in both royal and mayoral celebrations. However, having reached the Interregnum, and a sixteen-year hiatus in mayoral and, of course, royal pageantry, it is perhaps time to consider the purpose behind such Shows, who paid for them, and the route they commonly followed. As Robert Withington remarks, there were flashes of brilliant ceremony, even during the period of the Civil War, including a certain amount of splendour, although no pageants, at the inauguration of the Lord Mayor in 1643.[23]

The primary intention behind the Lord Mayors' Show was to honour the new incumbent and his company. This was effected by speeches directed to him by personifications of the virtues he was said to possess, by likening him to his illustrious forebears and to renowned characters from history, Roman allusions being most popular. Colour symbolism played an important part, enabling the crowd to distinguish the different players in the pageant. The Lord Mayor's Company was praised both for its foreign trade, which brought prosperity to the City, and for its charitable work in helping the destitute and aiding educational establishments. The longevity of the institution was stressed and together with this, the glory and antiquity of the City of London itself. The Show could be said, therefore, to be a panegyric on the City and its ancient rituals. It was designed to be a day of entertainment for the citizens of London, rich and poor alike, an ostentatious show of wealth by the great and the good of the City. It was the excuse for a noisy and colourful celebration, with music and fireworks, giants and wild men, a spectacle with something for everybody. It had, by 1639, in the drama of its presentation, surpassed even those shows which honoured the sovereign.

The expense of the Lord Mayors' Shows always fell on the City company whose Master was elected Lord Mayor for the year. If the Lord Mayor elect were not a member of one of the Great Twelve Companies, it was necessary for him to be accepted into one of them before his installation. This maintained the supremacy of the select group, but meant that the financial burden of the Show always fell on one of the Twelve.[24] The costs were met by fines levied on the yeomanry, the bachelors, and the livery of the organising company. To meet these costs, a company would elevate a group of its members from one category to the next, exacting fines accordingly. Should members wish to be excused from partaking in the celebrations, fines again had to be paid. The costs of Charles II's royal entries and progresses were, however, spread over all the companies and the amount payable by each varied enormously, in proportion to a corn rate levied upon them. The greatest strain therefore again fell on the Great Twelve.[25]

The route taken by the Lord Mayor's procession varied very little from year to year, and more or less followed that described by Machyn and Smythe. From the company hall, the new Lord Mayor and senior company members progressed to the Guildhall where they were joined by the retiring Lord Mayor. Progressing to Paul's Wharf, they travelled by barge to Westminster where the oath of loyalty was taken. Returning to the City, the procession was entertained by a floating pageant, and on landing, was met by the lesser company members, whence it proceeded via St. Paul's to the Guildhall. The pageants or scenes were positioned at locations which varied little from year to year, with St. Paul's, Foster Lane and Gutter Lane featuring regularly, and each pageant, having been enacted, joined the back of the procession.

The Lord Mayors' Shows re-commenced in 1655 with Edmund Gayton's pageant, *Charity Triumphant, or the Virgin Shew,* for the Mercers' Company. In his introduction, Gayton is overtly critical of the regime which prohibited such "anniversary Shows and harmless and merry recreations". His pamphlet was not descriptive, but was in the form of a letter addressed to the Lord Mayor, with an accompanying poem. The only pageant exhibited was the Mercers' Virgin, and Withington states that there seem to have been no speeches. In fact, it must have been a rather subdued event, not helped, as Gayton avers, by the bad weather:

> The sight was rare but envious clouds,
> The glorious day in showers beshrowds;
> And winds in malice or in love
> To sport or court he highly strove.[26]

Edward Jerman: Pageant Maker

The Lord Mayors' Shows for which Edward Jerman was the artificer are recorded in the minute books and account books of the organising City companies, in the Repertories of the Court of Aldermen, as well as in pageant booklets, many of which are held at the Guildhall Library. By 1656, the year of his first pageant, Edward Jerman was already known by the officials of several of the more influential City companies. He was Company Surveyor to the Fishmongers and Company Carpenter to the Goldsmiths. Back in 1633, he had been consulted about the enlargement of the great parlour at Leathersellers' Hall, and in 1655, he had advised the Skinners about a bargehouse they were building together with the Goldsmiths. In 1651, he had been introduced to heraldry by Mr. Allen, the herald painter at Goldsmiths' Hall, when he had helped to create and erect coats of arms of benefactors. In the capacity of City Carpenter, a City Viewer and Surveyor, he was also known to those in the upper echelons of the City hierarchy who were, of course, also officials of the City companies. It is easy to understand why these men chose Jerman as the artificer for their pageants, for they were familiar with his talents. Less easy to understand are Jerman's motives in accepting such commissions. Perhaps it was ambition. He would inevitably be working exclusively with the Great Twelve Companies, and might have hoped for further prestigious surveyorships. Perhaps it was artistic diversion. The enjoyment derived from the creation of such pageants might have appealed to him – a month's respite each autumn from his day-to-day routine.

Jerman devised pageants for four City companies, the Skinners (1656 and 1657), the Clothworkers (1658 and 1662), the Grocers (1659 and 1661) and the Haberdashers (1664). By this time, the form and route of the Shows had become more or less standardised, and Jerman's remit would have been very much the same from year to year, while being particularised by the organising company. A description of one of Edward Jerman's more innovative pageants, the Grocers' Show of 1661, will serve to demonstrate his imagination, artistry and organisational skills in this field. This will be followed by a discussion of more general topics such as the format of the pageant-pamphlets, finances, the creation and storage of props, the preparation of the route, and the spectators.

The October 1661 Show was a magnificent pageant on both land and water for the installation of Sir John Frederick of the Grocers' Company. By this time, Edward Jerman had assumed the role that Gerard Christmas had attained in the

1630s, that of overseer of the preparations as well as designer. Tatham's description of the pageant details the chronology of the day's events, and the composition of the procession. It commences:

> The Lord Mayor's, Grocers' and several companies' barges hasten to Westminster, and near the Temple, his Lordship is accosted by a vessel near the head of which is Galataea drawn in a sea-chariot by two dolphins. In the rear are placed two sea-lions riding on the surface of the water, and on their back, two tritons.[27]

Subsequently, the Lord Mayor and his entourage returned by barge to the City. Near St Paul's School they were entertained by a pageant representing the Temple of Janus. Tatham, in his pamphlet, was at pains to point out all the allusions made in this scene. Janus' globe-like crown, part celestial and part terrestrial, alluded to the revolution of the year. Father Time's sceptre signified his kingly office, and the ploughshare (in his other hand), his knowledge of tillage, while it was he, rather than Janus, who had two faces, a reference to his wisdom. At the angles of the scene sat four persons in colours relating to the King, with branches of palm and laurel wreaths. As the year was 1661, these were presumably emblematic of martyrdom and imperial triumph.

Following a speech by Janus, the whole scene was conveyed to Lawrence Lane "until it did flank the ship and sea-lions formerly on the water and then the whole body did move on". Between Foster Lane and Gutter Lane stood a pageant representing the fountain of Acis, and here, Galataea re-appeared to deliver a speech. The water pageant and the two land pageants then moved on, "and passed by a fourth scene, being a droll of Indians who are labouring". The fifth scene represented an island with a camel and a crocodile, and personifications of Justice and Mercy who addressed the Lord Mayor. While the official party lunched at the Guildhall, the pageants were conveyed to Blackwell Hall.

Then started the afternoon's business. "At about three o'clock, the several scenes return to their former order and are conveyed up the Old Jewry into Cheapside". The Company members re-assembled, passed St. Paul's, and at Bow Church encountered a scene of "drolling Americans (as before), pruning, gathering and planting several sorts of grocery, throwing their fruit about to show the abundance of profit and labour". The whole ensemble then progressed to Foster Lane for the final pageant which represented trade between Europe and America.

This Grocers' Show was typical, if slightly grander than Jerman's other Shows, and it serves to demonstrate several aspects of Jerman's involvement with these entertainments. Such a show was a feat of enormous invention and organisation, with so many and varied scenes to be devised, and so many participants to marshall. The disconnection of scenes and their re-connection in time for the Lord Mayor's arrival at particular points along the route could have been no easy task in narrow streets, thronged with excited onlookers. The pageant-wagons, borne by porters, had to be negotiated through the small lanes and alleys of pre-Fire London, through streets with sharp bends, to arrive at company halls approached by narrow gateways. Some of these wagons were fourteen feet long and eight feet broad, and on occasions, two were coupled together to form a larger stage. Not only did these cumbersome wagons transport the live performers, they also bore the elaborate props, which were not always constructed to scale.[28] This assembly and re-assembly was Jerman's responsibility, as were the negotiations with the organising company, the hire and pay of the actors, the staging of the entire performance and of course the design and fashioning of the props. His role could be compared with that of a theatrical producer, director and choreographer rolled into one. Since 1546 the election of the Lord Mayor had taken place on Michaelmas Day, 29 September, and the Show was always held on the morrow of St. Simon and St. Jude's Day, 29 October. Jerman therefore had only one month to devise and rehearse his pageants, and it is understandable that there are several references to preparations having to be made "in so short a time". However, there are no records of meetings between Jerman and Tatham.

Information is also scanty concerning the extent to which the scenes were suggested or even dictated by the company involved. The only insight into any such negotiations lies in the Grocers' minutes of 1659 and 1661, when it is clear that there were several urgent meetings between Jerman and the Company. Other companies must have faced similar problems, although they were not recorded. The cost of the 1659 Show clearly exceeded the Grocers' estimates, for on 13 October, Jerman was required to tell the Court about "his design and forwardness in the business", and he was directed "to respite what may be with conveniency forborne about the same". Four days later, Jerman reported:

> The charge of the whole business, if finished, will amount to nearly £400, and what is already done will cost at least £150 if a present stop should be included. And that there be diverse public already contracted with for actors and others parts, who will expect and require their pay as if the Show had been wholly carried through.

He went on to say that the time was short, the weather was bad for painting work, and he wanted some money "towards his disbursements".[29] The Show went ahead, and Pepys noted, "I saw the Lord Mayor pass in his water triumph to Westminster, being the first solemnity of this nature after twenty years". Following this Show, the water pageant again became an annual feature.

By the time of their next Show, two years later, the Grocers seem to have realised that, to avoid possible pitfalls and a recurrence of their previous financial embarrassment, they should set up a committee to oversee the organisation of the Show, instead of leaving the arrangements to their Court of Assistants. Negotiations were already under way by 2 October, when the Court ordered that "the designing and management thereof be referred to the Committee, to advise and direct the manner of the said solemnity, and the number and quality of the pageants be entrusted to the care and management of the Committee, and Mr. Jerman to be advised with about the design of the pageantry".[30] The Committee and Jerman were still in negotiation on 22 October, one week before the Show.

Tatham wrote the texts of all the Lord Mayors' Shows between 1657 and 1664. His pageant-pamphlets are small booklets, measuring about 18 cm by 15 cm, and they contain between 14 and 23 pages. Several of the booklets were printed by one Thomas Mabb "at the sign of the Ship". All Tatham's Shows were entitled *London's Triumphs* except the 1660 celebration which called *The Royal Oake*, in deference to Charles II in the year of his Restoration. The texts of these pamphlets follow more or less the same pattern. An address to the Lord Mayor and his company is usually elaborated by a panegyric to the City, its glorious past and the longevity of the mayoral office. This is followed by a detailed description of the day's events and the several pageants, as described above, together with the composition of the accompanying procession and a transcript of the speeches. Finally, the conveyance of the scenes to the safety of the company hall is stressed and the pamphlets end with a eulogy addressed to the artificer. As we have seen, Tatham seems to have modelled the form of his tribute on those delivered by Middleton, first to Grinkin and then to Christmas. In 1657, for example, he concluded, "The several fabrics and structures of the whole day's triumph were performed by the industry of Mr. Jerman, a man not only excellent in his art, but faithful in his undertakings". Tatham, who was no great versifier, needed and relied on Jerman's vision to provide a cogent "body" to his rather unconvincing "soul", viz:

> For aught we do know there's ne'er a lad here
> But may be the Lord Mayor or something as near
> And his Mayoress may take from this innocent rout
> And give her a hood, instead of a clout.[31]

Let us now turn to the remuneration Edward Jerman received from the companies, starting with the 1656 Skinners' Show. For this, Jerman was granted one payment of £5. The following year, when another Skinner was inaugurated, Jerman received £8 "for services done by him for the Company". However, in 1658, we are given a more comprehensive account of the remuneration of the men involved in the staging of the Clothworkers' Show. Eighteen trumpeters were paid £20, while the man who made the streamers and banners received £10-9s-4½d for "silk fringe". Edward Jerman was paid £100 for his part of the bill, and a further £54-9s "towards the charge of the Shows", followed by £10 "for his pains taken therein, of the gratuity of this house". This implies that Jerman paid for his materials and his workmen from these sums, and received £10 for himself. No accounts are available for the Grocers' 1659 Show, and Jerman was not involved with the Merchant Taylors', in 1660. For the Grocers' 1661 Show, Jerman and Mr. Tasker (the keeper of the City Storeyard) were paid £350 "towards the payment of several people for charges of the pageants provided by this Company on the Lord Mayor's Day", but no mention is made of Jerman's individual payment.

In 1662, the Clothworkers paid Edward Jerman £20, "out of the money remaining in his hands for his pains and care taken in the ordering and composing

4.5 The Fishmongers' Pageant of 1616: The Great Pageant.

of the pageants", and he received £30 from the Haberdashers "for his care, pains and oversight" about the 1664 Show. For this Haberdashers' Show, Tatham's remuneration was only £12, and, while Jerman is named in the accounts, Tatham is merely "the poet" (see endnote 17). As no records of earlier payments to Tatham exist, one can only surmise that, as Jerman's payment rose from £5 in 1656 to £30 in 1664, he was responsible for more and more of the production while Tatham's role was correspondingly diminished, in the same way that Christmas' sun had eclipsed Heywood's in the 1630s.

The inventions that Edward Jerman designed and fashioned for his Shows were even more varied than those of the Fishmongers' 1616 Pageant. They ranged from islands with vegetation to sea monsters and wild animals; from "buildings" to "cars", chariots and boats; and from costumes donned by personifications to the devices and emblems they carried. Although, to all intents and purposes, the pageants were ephemeral, some were re-used and some were retained for years as decorations in the great halls of the commissioning companies. Few of Jerman's pageants were architectural, and we have little evidence of the form of any that could be loosely described as such: he fashioned a Temple of Janus and Fountain of Acis in 1661, "a piece of fortification like the Tower of London" and "a representation of St Paul's Church" in 1662, and "a circular building in 1664". Jerman was never required to build anything as "architectural" as the triumphal arches that

Peter Mills devised for the Coronation progress of 1661; his inventions were more fantastic and mythological, and in this context he was an artist with a truly wide palette.

The organising companies provided premises for the making of these pageants, and because of their size, Leadenhall and the under-gallery of Gresham College were commonly used as workshops.[32] The artefacts were clearly very expensive to construct, and, having been transported to the Company Hall at the conclusion of the day's festivities, many were re-used and there is some evidence that the companies borrowed from each other. The third pageant of the Fishmongers' 1616 Show (Figure 4.3), described on the scroll as "The king of the Moors, gallantly mounted on a golden leopard, he hurling gold and silver every way about him", had probably been borrowed from the Skinners' Company. Their Show of 1558, for Sir Wolstone Dixie's Mayoralty, depicted him as "rid on a luzern [lynx] apparelled like a Moor". Similarly, smaller props were exchanged, and Jerman re-used two sea-horses that he had fashioned for the Skinners' 1656 Show in their 1657 Show. When he came to design the City's celebration for Charles II at the Guildhall, the Clothworkers allowed him to borrow two griffins and two lambs as long as he "give a note under his hand for the re-delivery of them again for the use of this Company".

As mentioned above, many pageants were retained as ornaments at the halls, and we shall see in Chapter 5 that structural damage to the roof of the Fishmongers' great hall was probably caused by the suspension of one of the larger artefacts from a Show of years before. Above three of the pageants illustrated on their scroll (described earlier), alongside a brief description, is written, "This remaineth at Fishmongers' Hall for an ornament" (Figures 4.3 to 4.5). Tatham's 1662 pamphlet emphasises that the pageants (scenes) were conveyed to Grocers' Hall "by the care of the master artificers and the City Marshall", and at the conclusion of the 1658 Show, he states that the scenes were taken to Clothworkers' Hall for safe-keeping. The fact that these artefacts survived a long time as ornaments is possibly borne out by an entry in the Leathersellers' minutes. In 1634, a decision was taken by the Court "concerning the hanging of a ship in our common hall, alleging it would be a great ornament to the same in regard of the height of the ceiling; this court agree that he [a warden] should hang it up at such time as he should please".[33] One can imagine that, if this ship were going to enhance such a high ceiling, it must have taken up a lot of floor space. It is clear from the accounts quoted that the Shows were a great, and sometimes worrisome, expense for the companies, but it is reassuring to find that the artefacts were not utterly ephemeral, that many became surprisingly permanent. It should, of course, be remembered that, in this period, props in the commercial theatre (those, which in the 1650s were still playing) were as yet minimal. Painted, sliding panels provided appropriate scenic effects and "machines" or "devices" enabled ascents and descents, but the stage itself was almost bare except for the actors. Jerman's spectacular props must therefore have been all the more exciting.[34]

Finally let us consider the one royal celebration in which Edward Jerman participated, the City's welcome to the returning King at the Guildhall on 5 July 1660. There were two other civic celebrations for Charles II, his Coronation progress on 22 and 23 April 1661, and London's welcome to his bride, Catherine of Braganza, on 23 August 1662. In these, Jerman was ousted from his position of artificer by Peter Mills, and although Tatham was appointed poet for the 1660 and 1662 festivities, to John Ogilby was entrusted the major event, the Coronation progress.

The Guildhall entertainment that Jerman and Tatham devised was to be a celebration not only for the newly-restored King, but also for his brothers, the Dukes of York and Gloucester. It was reminiscent of many of the Lord Mayors' Shows on which the artist and poet had collaborated, the route taken being, of necessity, very much the same.[35] However, the composition of the procession was different from that of the mayoral Shows. It comprised members of the royal family and of both Houses of Parliament, the Privy Council, judges and other dignitaries. Members of the City companies rarely processed on royal occasions, but had privileged positions along the route. On this occasion, because it was very specifically the City's welcome to the King, an exception was made, and certain company members rode in the procession: "note that the Grocers, Skinners, Merchant Taylors and Clothworkers, each of them fifty-two select gentlemen to ride, the rest of the companies but twenty-four".[36] It is interesting to note that these were the four companies that had staged mayoral Shows since their re-introduction proper in 1656 (the 1665 Mercers' Show had been a small-scale event). Perhaps the discrepancy in the numbers of processing members simply reflects the fact that these companies already had sufficient costumes from the previous Shows. The three royal celebrations of 1660-62 were a huge expense for the companies that they could ill afford, prudence was essential wherever possible.

Tatham's pamphlet account of the Guildhall entertainment, entitled *London's Glory*, reproduces the speeches delivered by various personifications, and explains the composition of the procession, but gives very little indication of Jerman's inventions. The Show laid great stress on the City and its companies, and Tatham's choice of the personifications of Time, Truth, Fame and Industry seems more appropriate to the City than to a King recently returned from exile. However, the balance seems to have been redressed the following year, when Ogilby chose Rebellion, Confusion, Loyalty, Concord and Temperance to address the King from Mills' arches during the coronation progress.

Details of Jerman's remuneration for this Guildhall entertainment are more abundant than for the mayoral Shows, and from them, we can deduce that Edward Jerman directed the entire "physical" aspect of the day's events, from devising the scenes, to procuring the necessary materials, to hiring and paying the workmen. In a tall, thin ledger, entitled "Guildhall Entertainment",[37] is a section headed "The Accounts of £3,000 ordered by Common Committee to be lent by all the companies of London proportionally according to a corn rate upon the City's bond to be repaid with interest . . . which sum is to defray the charge of His Majesty's Entertainment at the Guildhall where he dines on 5 July 1660". The demanding tone of such precepts caused considerable disquiet amongst company members,[38] and how much of the money was ever recouped is uncertain. Between July and December 1660, the accounts record four payments to Edward Jerman, amounting to a total of £859-10s. These various payments are described as "preparing the Guildhall in a readiness". In 1661, there are three further payments to Jerman totalling £245-18s-2d to disburse to painters, the plumber and the carver, and including "in full his own sum".

There are also two intriguing entries in the ledger. The first, on 20 December 1660, reads "To Roger Jerman, for his extraordinary attendance upon the preparation for His Majesty's Entertainment, £6", and the second, "Paid unto Roger Jerman, Carpenter at the request of his brother, Mr Edward Jerman, £55". While the other craftsmen had their remuneration disbursed by Edward Jerman, Roger was the exception. We shall discover in later chapters that Roger was very much the businessman, but this discrepancy in the manner of payments seems inexplicable. Roger's role at the Guildhall entertainment was relatively small, but he played a much more vital part in the 1661 Coronation celebrations when he was paid in excess of £600. Here, his work comprised the construction of stages, particularly those in the vicinity of the Royal Exchange and at Cheapside, the provision of posts and rails (to which we shall return) and "the repairing of the late pageants and the houses damnified by the fall of the pageant in Fleet Street". There is no record of his part in the construction of the pageants – only their repair. Among these records held at the Corporation of London Record Office is a warrant signed by Roger for the money he received from the Chamberlain of London for his part in the coronation celebrations. Although Roger would have been obliged to pay for materials and workmen out of his £600, it is clear that his remuneration far exceeded that which his brother ever received as a designer.

Brief reference has been made to Roger Jerman's provision of posts and rails, so perhaps a final overall view of the setting of Edward Jerman's mayoral Shows is appropriate. Some indication of the noise and bustle has already been given, but no mention has been made of the preparation of the streets and crowd control. Tatham, setting the scene for his Guildhall entertainment, remarks that "the streets are railed on both sides" and Pepys, attending the Coronation, noted that he passed "round the Abbey to Westminster Hall all the way within rails". As with royal celebrations, so with the Lord Mayors' Shows. It was customary to separate the participants in the Show from the crowds which, as the day progressed, became more and more lively. This was accomplished by the erection of posts and rails along the entire route. The streets were also gravelled to prevent the horses' hooves from slipping, and to facilitate the porters' carriage of unwieldy items. Shop placards and inn signs were commonly broken or damaged during these festivities, so wherever possible, they were taken down or tied out of harm's way, and in 1657, Edward Jerman was required "to tie up such signs in any of the streets for the clearer passage of the pageants on the Lord Mayor's Day". Brightly coloured carpets, tapestries and tablecloths were hung out of the upper windows of houses lining the route to add to the gaiety of the scene, and, as Ned Ward tells us "for the cleanly leaning-out of the ladies, with whom they were chiefly filled".[39] Immediately ahead of the procession ran "wild men" and "green men", reminiscent of those of the Midsummer shows. With the help of beadles, they pushed the crowds back behind the rails, letting off squibs when necessary, to alarm the stragglers into obedience.

This then was the setting in front of which Edward Jerman's pageants were enacted. His inventiveness, his artistry and his organisational skills were displayed, not only to the crowds in a holiday mood, but also to those men of the City and the companies on whom his career would depend. His participation in the Shows can only have enhanced his reputation amongst such people, for within a very short time, his services would be much in demand by many of them.

CHAPTER 5

Edward Jerman's Work for the Fishmongers' Company

The sequence in which Edward Jerman's work for the City companies is described must, of necessity, be an arbitrary one, since he was involved with so many projects between 1666 and his death in 1668. However, his work for the Fishmongers deserves to take priority on several counts. They had been the first to engage him as their Surveyor, in 1654, and were the first to approach him, post-Fire, to design their new Hall. Their affairs are extensively recorded and all aspects of Jerman's work for them are meticulously chronicled. Within their books is contained a vivid image of a City company in that chaotic period following the Fire, of working practice in the building industry in Jerman's time, of the shortage of timber for building and of the problems confronting the Fishmongers and the people whose lives touched theirs. Their minutes are not only a superb piece of historico-social reportage, they also reveal Jerman's metamorphosis from artificer to architect.[1]

As explained in Chapter 3, a commission by the Fishmongers' Company in 1639 to survey repairs effected on the hammerbeam roof of their great hall may have marked the young Jerman's entrée into the world of the City companies.[2] The pageant props that had been fashioned for Munday's Lord Mayor's Show of 1616 were retained by the Fishmongers to ornament their hall, props that included triumphal "cars", trees, sea monsters, wild animals and dolphins.[3] Herbert has suggested that the deterioration of the hall's roof could have resulted from the strain imposed on it by the suspension of these heavy artefacts from the beams.[4] In such surroundings, Company dinners, such as those attended by Inigo Jones in the 1630s, must have been wonderfully colourful events,[5] even though the creatures of the deep were discreetly wreaking structural damage. Was the young Jerman enchanted by these fantastic inventions when he saw them in 1639? Perhaps he made sketches, or even shaped miniature versions of them, enabling him to accept with enthusiasm and alacrity the position of artificer for the Skinners' pageant in 1656, followed by those of the Grocers, Clothworkers, and Haberdashers.[6] It would be fifteen years before he was appointed Surveyor to the Fishmongers' Company, years in which his time was fully occupied with work for the Corporation of the City as Carpenter and Viewer, and years in which he was becoming well known to the Aldermen and Common Councilmen who also, of course, held positions of power in the City companies.

While Edward Jerman was employed by the City as a Viewer-Surveyor and

Carpenter, he received an annual salary from the Chamberlain. However, his remuneration as Company Surveyor to the Fishmongers exemplifies several of the methods of payment available in the building industry in the seventeenth century, along with the various working methods which were practised at this time, when the role of the craftsman was predominant. Perhaps this is the point at which to discuss seventeenth-century building practice, influenced as it was by the nature of the work, the size of the workforce and the patron.[7]

Until the late sixteenth century, there were only two principal methods of payment for men involved in building, by time or by quantity. In other words, day or task work. Most commonly, labourers and the less important craftsmen were paid for a task done, a fixed price having been agreed upon. The completed work was inspected, measured and confirmed as satisfactory by a surveyor before payment was made. On some occasions, a master-craftsman might enter into a specific contract with the patron regarding a particular piece of work which required the employment of additional workmen. In this case, the artificer concerned, assuming the role of a sub-contractor, would negotiate payment with the extra workers.

Wren's often-cited letter to the Bishop of Oxford in 1681 is a succinct, if rather over-simplified, account of the different methods of contracting which prevailed in Edward Jerman's lifetime.[8] Wren described three ways of working: by the day (i.e. by time), by the measure (i.e. by quantity) and by the great. He did not advocate day work, considering that it encouraged laziness on the part of the workforce. He was doubtful about work done by the great. In this system, the patron purchased the entirety of a piece of work from a particular tradesman, including both labour and materials. The tradesman took over responsibility for the whole work, and with it the carpentry, masonry, bricklaying or any other craft involved. Before price books came into common use, estimates of such costs and charges that might be incurred during any lengthy building operation were clearly very difficult, and Wren feared that either the patron or "the undertaker" would inevitably be financially damaged by such a contract. He favoured working by the measure, when the patron purchased the materials and paid workmen according to the amount of work actually completed, a schedule of prices having been pre-determined, "measuring the work at two or three measurements as it rises. But you must have an understanding, trusty measurer".[9]

The direct labour method of working, synonymous with Wren's first category, that of payment by the day, was most convenient when the labour force was comparatively small. The patron supplied not only the materials necessary for the proposed construction, but also arranged their transport to the site. The workmen, therefore, were merely required to attend on a daily basis and execute their tasks according to orders from their superiors, for which they would be paid a pre-arranged wage. Pratt was in favour of this method, but had some reservations: "if employed by the day, they will make but small haste to finish the building".[10]

Both Wren and Pratt considered that contracting for building work by the great had serious disadvantages. Pratt feared that builders, having given their patrons estimates of costs employing the best materials and the best craftsmen, "would be ready at all turns to obtrude the worst, which are very much cheaper, where they have the choice to do it, especially in this, our London".[11] Pratt was writing with the experience of Clarendon House still fresh in his mind. He stressed that the main difficulty lay in making the bargain, and Wren agreed with him on this point, stating "they shuffle and slight the work to suit themselves". Balthazar Gerbier, too, was in accordance with their views, warning that "when builders put their design to master workmen by the great, or have it wrought by the day, either the workmen will overreach themselves, or the builder will be over-reached".[12]

The favoured method of contracting for building work was, according to Wren, Pratt and Gerbier, by the measure, when payment was made to individual craftsmen on the basis of a pre-determined price for each piece of work completed. This method took into account both the varying complexities of different types of work and their varying inconveniences, for example height and position. This type of contract was also sensitive to the skill of the craftsmen carrying out the work. A trusty measurer was essential to achieve satisfactory pricing, but both Wren and Pratt were fearful that most measurers were too closely associated with the workmen to be reliable. This was, of course, where a craftsman/surveyor of Jerman's character and calibre proved to be such an asset.

The clear dividing lines between Wren's three ways of working seem to have become somewhat blurred when a large building operation such as St Paul's or the Exchange was undertaken. McKellar writes that "a form of contracting by the great" was employed at St. Paul's when separate contracts were made with different trades, spreading the risk.[13] At the Exchange, when hundreds of employees, from labourers to the surveyor, were engaged over several years, the majority of the master-craftsmen were paid on a monthly or even an annual basis, while the labourers were paid weekly by their overseer George Widmerpool.[14] There is evidence, as we shall see, that some craftsmen, including Roger Jerman, were not reticent about asking for "bonuses" intermingled with their regular salaries. Members of the Royal Works, a permanent organisation, received regular remuneration, commonly spending their entire working life within the institution, although many accepted external commissions to boost their regular income. Thus, in the many and varied building programmes executed in the latter part of the seventeenth century, different methods of contracting existed side by side, and from the Fishmongers' accounts, and those of the other companies under discussion, this variety in methods of contracting seems to have been the norm for hall building.

During his eighteen-year association with the Fishmongers, Jerman carried out many and varied tasks for them, but none involved his chosen career, that of a master-carpenter, nor was he responsible for the fabric of the Hall itself. Any work on the Hall was handled by a Warden, backed up by a specially convened building committee that appointed appropriate craftsmen when required. Instead, Jerman's work comprised the viewing and surveying of Company property for which, at the start of his career he was paid on a daily or half-daily basis.[15]

The surviving minute books of the Fishmongers' Company open with a court meeting on 26 June 1592 in a room overlooking the river, the court parlour of their pre-Fire Hall. The Hall formed part of the Company's holdings in Thames Street, close by London Bridge. The meeting was presided over by the Master, one John Porter, who was the Company's tenant of two ancient wharves which had been combined ten years earlier, and were known as Porter's Quay. John Stow, in 1598, explained the reason for this terminology: "in this street on the Thames-side are diverse large landing stages called quays for cranage up of wares and merchandise and also for shipping of wares from thence to be transported. These quays commonly bear the names of their owners, and are therefore changeable".[16] This quay must have remained in the tenancy of the Porter family for many years, for the first mention of Edward Jerman as Surveyor to the Company refers to it. On 24 April 1654, the Court, no doubt sitting in the parlour that Mr. Porter and his colleagues had used, and in fact, as near as can be judged, on the site of the present court room, appointed Edward Jerman Company Surveyor and required him to survey some new building near Porter's Quay.[17]

This minute book entry exemplifies one aspect of mid-seventeenth-century working practice. We learn that both the tenant of the new building and the workmen were to have copies of the work schedule, the tenant's copy being "annexed" to his lease, avoiding any legal battles thereafter. It also discloses that Jerman's position as a Surveyor was not a salaried one. He was to be paid "according to his time and pains", in keeping with a resolution passed by the Fishmongers' Court in 1643: "when any work is done for this Company, the workmen shall come themselves and begin the work, and direct their servants what to do, and oversee them twice or thrice a day at least, to see them perform their work as they ought to do".[18] One must, of course, remember that the seventeenth-century "workman" was a skilled or expert craftsman, his "servant" being analogous with today's workman.

In August 1654, as the new Company Surveyor, Edward Jerman was required to be present at a Court meeting concerning some building work a neighbour wished to execute on a piece of ground he rented from the Fishmongers, next to their garden in Lime Street. This garden, a few minutes walk from the Hall, contained a parlour, not of such grandeur as those found in contemporary Roman *giardini*, but nevertheless, a private place surrounded by foliage where the Fishmongers could relax on summer days. It served as an extension to their Hall, away from the congestion of that noisy, dirty area of the City, and it would later be the site of a very significant meeting. Jerman advised the Company to ensure that the new building should follow the lines of its predecessor, and be sufficiently supported. It should not detract from their garden or adjacent buildings.[19]

At some time between 1654 and 1663 (no indication is provided by the Fishmongers' accounts), Edward Jerman ceased to be paid on a daily basis, but was given fairly substantial sums of money on a more or less annual basis "for his care, advice and pains in this company's business from the time now passed till this time".[20] The "pains" referred to his execution of views and surveys, and the advice, to his expertise as an assessor of timber. Perhaps it was forward thinking on their part, or perhaps it was serendipity that the man the Fishmongers appointed in 1654 as their Surveyor was a carpenter by training, rather than a mason, or, like Peter Mills, a bricklayer. The years that Edward Jerman had spent with his father in his carpenter's yard, followed by his apprenticeship and then his work as a City Carpenter, must have rendered him an expert on the management, use and value of many types of timber. This expertise was to prove invaluable to the Fishmongers in the rebuilding of their Hall, and in the superintendence of their woodlands.

As explained in Chapter 2, the Carpenters' Company was, from the outset, as much a friendly society as a trade organisation, the obligations of charity and benevolence being written into its earliest statutes. So it was, too, with the Fishmongers, and in 1623, a benefactor, William Goddard, had bequeathed to the Company land at Bray in Berkshire, for the building of an almshouse, the Jesus Hospital. This land supported extensive woodlands, planted with a variety of hardwood trees including oaks, much sought-after for house building. By 1662 when, as we shall see, Edward Jerman made his first journey to Bray, there was an acute shortage of English timber, especially oak. The problem had first arisen during the reign of Elizabeth I, when huge amounts of oak were needed for building and repairing ships required for the Spanish wars. The shortage was further exacerbated by James I, who rented the royal woods for the exploitation of their timber, and by Charles I, who sold off woodlands as his financial necessity increased. The official forest policy of the Interregnum proved as destructive as that of the first Stuarts, and the groves of royalist sympathisers suffered severely at the hands of the Parliamentary government. Furthermore, opposing forces in the Civil War had wantonly destroyed any objects, including trees, which lay in the path of their advance.

The Fishmongers therefore found themselves the guardians of a diminishing commodity and a huge asset. Jerman's knowledge of the different varieties of wood and of tree maintenance to produce the best timbers was of inestimable value to them, for as Robert Albion states, "the judging of timber was a fine art. There was much truth in Evelyn's dictum, 'A tree is a Merchant Adventurer, you shall never know what he is worth until he is dead'".[21] The "psychological moment" when an oak yields a greater profit than at any other time is somewhere between 80 and 120 years. It takes an expert to realise that moment, and the Fishmongers decided to rely on Jerman's expertise to know the worth of their "Merchant Adventurers". Instead of buying from timber merchants as they had always done, they began utilising their woodlands for their own advantage, and as a source of income.

To Jerman, this policy was to mean countless journeys westward along the Thames, tramping through muddy ground, marking those trees ready for felling, counting the numbers of oaks, elms and pollards, and checking on the growth of tillers (saplings). On many such visits, the Fishmongers, neither wanting to dispatch two men when one would do, nor desirous to engage a local man, required Jerman, when he had dealt with the trees, to disburse the pensions to the old folks in the almshouse, have a quick look to see if any repairs were necessary to the building, and even to act as arbitrator of the inmates' bickering. Such were the varied duties of a Company Surveyor.

It seems that the Company had been rather neglectful of the "old almsfolks", for in 1661, it was noted that no Court had been held at Bray since 1654. The ensuing entry can be viewed in a somewhat humorous light: "it is ordered that Mr. Wardens and so many of the Assistants of this Company as will and can conveniently sit in two coaches, and as many more of the Assistants as have horses of their own shall please to ride thereon thither, do accompany Mr. Wardens to Bray to visit the Jesus Hospital there".[22] One can imagine so many men squashed into the two coaches – was not a third available? – and those ambitious Assistants, eager for promotion, gritting their teeth and setting off on horseback, no mean journey from London Bridge to beyond Reading. However, the excursion proved worthwhile, for the Company realised the wealth in timber which lay at its doorstep, and within eight months of this visit, Jerman was sent down to Bray to value the trees.

Edward Jerman's journeys to Bray started in April 1662. He was ordered to categorise the various types of timber trees, to survey them for their maturity for felling and selling. He was required to estimate their value and to investigate a possible market for them. He was, however, obliged to have any decisions sanctioned by a higher authority, a member of the Court or a Warden.

Dealing in timber was to become a greater and greater source of income for the Company, and Jerman was probably going down to Bray on a monthly basis. The account books confirm that considerable timber trading was occurring in this period. In October 1663, a goldsmith paid the Company £285 for timber felled on the Company's land at Bray, while Jerman sold, on behalf of the Company, elms, bark – presumably to a tanner – hoops to a cooper and timber that had been felled, cut and peeled. For one consignment of timber, he was also paid for the land carriage to a nearby destination. Perhaps demarcation disputes between the different wood trades, the woodmongers, wharfingers and carters were less common in the country areas than in London, and when a timber merchant "desired to buy the Company's timber", no middle-man was involved, and "Mr. Jerman had order to cut, square fell and sell the same timber either in the field or at the wharf".[23] In November 1663, Jerman was required to obtain a licence for the felling of timber and underwood. No previous mention had been made of licences, but the national shortage of timber had become so acute, and the Navy Board so alarmed that, soon after the Restoration, Charles II introduced a forest policy. This involved the large-scale planting of oaks, encouraged by Evelyn's "Sylva, a Discourse on Forest Trees and the Propagation of Timber in His Majesty's Dominions", delivered to the Royal Society in 1662. Perhaps this forest policy also involved the requirement of a licence for felling timber.

Meanwhile, in April 1663, the Fishmongers were turning their attention to the environs of their Hall, and Jerman was asked to make a detailed survey of a dye-house in Thames Street which lay next to it. A glimpse into the dyers' world is afforded in Jerman's description of huge circular coppers, vats, leaden cisterns with pumps and pipes, and brass stopcocks. The whole area was paved with Purbeck stone to bear the weight of all this equipment.[24] Jerman's interest in and knowledge of the form and layout of this dye-house was to prove beneficial to the Company after the Fire. Also under scrutiny was the road in front of the Hall gate. Jerman was requested to draw up a plan to eliminate carts and carriages from the immediate vicinity, restricting the thoroughfare to pedestrians and horses. Traffic congestion from coaches and carts was becoming more and more of a problem, a problem which the 1667 Act did much to overcome.

The following years are a blank in the minute books of the Fishmongers' Company, and we can only surmise that, for Jerman, life went on very much as before, with visits to Bray interspersed with viewing and reporting on Company property.

The next time we meet Edward Jerman in the records, he is in that "late garden of the Company in Lime Street",[25] which the Company had decided to sell, due to the mounting costs, in the late 1650s. Here he sat, with the Wardens and Assistants, on 13 September 1666, to discuss the ruins of the Hall. The Company officials were aware that they were the trustees of property that involved hundreds of people from tenants to almsfolk, such was their network of dependants. The rents from Company houses paid not only for the running costs of their alsmhouses, but also for pensions for the inmates, as well as out-pensioners. Like other landlords, in the next few months the Company would have to re-negotiate leases with its tenants, and re-adjust fines and annual rents to encourage tenants to rebuild. However, the first decisions taken that day were the same as those being taken all over the City about what was unsafe and must be pulled down, and what was safe and must be secured. Jerman was dispatched to the Hall, and with the Company Bricklayer, decided what was to be done. The Court immediately realised that the woodlands at Bray put the Fishmongers in a better position than most companies, and ordered that no timber felled at Bray and not yet sold should be sold until further order, and no timber should be felled without further order. Even London's new, brick-faced buildings would be constructed on wooden frames, so the timber shortage would become even more acute. The Company arranged to rent space in Bethlem Hospital, both for the holding of meetings, and for the storage of documents, two trunks having been specially purchased for the latter's safekeeping. They decided to sell several items of Company plate to realise money for rebuilding but retained, presumably for sentimental reasons, "one scallop salt with dolphins", still on view at the Hall today.

On 27 September, Jerman was again sent to Bray to review the woodlands and to range all the timber recently felled and yet unsold so that it could be brought to the Company's late Hall to be preserved for the use of the Company. On his return, he was to measure and stake out the bounds of the lands belonging to the Company, and to assist the tenants wherever necessary. Several more journeys to Bray followed, including one in December when Jerman managed to strike a deal with the bargeman to transport elms and oaks at reduced rates. Work in London kept him busy too. He had to intervene in a building dispute concerning one of the Company's tenants in Aldersgate Street, whose rebuilding was proceeding in contravention of the legislation, and was also causing a "nuisance" (an offence). Jerman and the Company Bricklayer were sent along, and found the tenant violating several laws: he had not followed the necessary preliminary procedures; he was building on new foundations; he was infringing the ancient lights rule and was causing a nuisance with his waste-pipe. The law stated that such buildings should be pulled down.

Although, at that initial meeting on 13 September 1666, the Court resolved that the rebuilding of their Tudor great hall and parlour blocks should proceed as soon as possible, it soon became clear that no building would start that year. So much timber was being sent downstream from Bray that its storage was becoming an embarrassment to the Company, and by the following April, Jerman was warning that the timber felled and awaiting transport was becoming sap-rotten. The prohibition on selling timber was temporarily lifted, and in June, it was decided that the ground on which the dye-house stood, on the east side of the Company's Hall, might be a very useful place to lay the Company's timber. The Company tried to persuade the tenant to surrender his lease and, following Jerman's report that there were about 200 loads of timber to be transported, the Court ordered that "he cause a freight thereof, as much as water will bear, to be brought to London and laid upon the ground of the said dye-house if the tenant will give way". The next and final recorded sentence of this meeting on 6 June reads, "And Mr. Jerman was desired to consider of a model for rebuilding the Company's Hall".[26]

Perhaps the Company had always assumed that, as their Surveyor, Edward Jerman would design their new Hall. Certainly, his reputation was extremely high, the Joint Committee of the City and Mercers having already described him as "the most able known artist [beside Peter Mills] that the City now hath".[27] Even so, one might have hoped that the Court would have convened an extraordinary meeting to tender their request, rather than slipping it in as a postscript to their discussions. They met again the next day, requiring Jerman to "make a plott of the ground wherein this Company's Hall did stand and of all the ground of this Company between the Old Swan and the Waterhouse for the better disposing and leasing thereof". The Company was clearly thinking of expansion, and an exact survey was essential with so many tenants and subtenants to persuade and compensate. By July, the tenant of the dye-house must have been persuaded to surrender his lease, for Jerman was ordered to have the ground cleared for "laying the Company's timber thereon, and that the materials of brick and stone may be preserved for the use thereof".[28]

Meanwhile, the staking of the streets in preparation for their widening was progressing slowly, starting with the high or main streets where piles had been driven into the ground. The problems of the lesser streets and alleys would take very much longer to resolve. In July, Jerman was ordered "to take an account of such of the Company's ground as is anywhere staked out to be taken from the Company to enlarge the streets, and measure the same". The Company was evidently anxious to claim any compensation due to it, for such money could be put towards its building programme. In their quest for funds, the Fishmongers decided to "expose to sale the land in Ireland . . . to be sold for raising moneys for building their Hall and other affairs of this Company".

By August 1667, there seemed to be hope of some progress on the Hall building when Jerman attended a meeting with the Court at Bethlem, taking with him "a map or plott of the ground whereon the Company's Hall and divers other tenants belonging to the Company on the east side thereof did lately stand". The Court and tenants were to meet at the ground "to consider of the said map, and to treat with the said tenants about rebuilding their houses or surrendering their leases".[29] However, little headway was made, either with the street valuation or with the tenants, and in December, Jerman was again implored to value the Company land which had been confiscated for street widening. Tenants in some of the Company's houses in Thames Street were proving intractable. Mr. Foster, an obstinate man, who was a past Master of the Grocers' Company and whose family leased a house which had lain intermixed with other rooms of adjoining houses for nearly two hundred years, resolutely refused to rebuild more rationally, rejecting the Company's offer of ground "to build upon upright". Here was an example of an impasse being settled by the Fire Court, this time in the Company's favour. Mr. Foster accepted his compensation, and went off to live elsewhere. Many City dwellers were similarly reluctant to embrace change; they were accustomed to the medieval haphazard, high-density occupancy and they were worried about the financial implications of rebuilding in upright, self-contained units. This was the prejudice against which the Surveyors strove to create a more orderly, safer City.

For Jerman, December 1667 seems to have been spent viewing tenants' ground, staking it out and explaining to the tenants "what quantity of ground the Company can and is willing to lease to them", and by the end of the year, the demolition of those parts of the Hall which were unsafe had been effected, and the rubbish sifted. The site was cleared, ready for building to restart in the better weather of the spring. Normally, little building took place in the winter months, and in spite of the urgency, the winter of 1667-68 was no different. Instead, Jerman was sent down to Bray again, ostensibly to review the timber situation, but in fact, he was acting as a general dogsbody: "The Wardens to give Mr. Jerman £22 to pay the poor at Bray their pensions, and to hear whether the rents at Bray are unpaid, how much thereof and from whom. And to make sale of all this Company's timber felled at Bray".[30]

Finally on 10 March 1667/8, Edward Jerman produced the plan the Fishmongers' Company must have been so eagerly awaiting for the last nine months. Not only was the new Hall to be bigger than the old one, on a much larger site, it would bear no external resemblance to its predecessor. The Court viewed the draft that day, noting the position of the "parlour and rooms to be built". They decided to meet at the ground where the new building would be staked out, and advice from the Assistants concerning the management of the construction was welcomed. They were, of course, anxious to have some idea of the costs involved, and as there was inevitably going to be a paucity of both building materials and craftsmen, the earlier a start could be made, the better chance the Company would have of engaging good craftsmen and acquiring materials. Accordingly, Jerman was ordered "to make arrangement with the bricklayer and carpenter for their workmanship in building so much as the Company shall appoint to be built at Fishmongers' Hall, the Company finding materials and scaffolding, also to agree with the lime-man to deliver lime at Fishmongers' Hall from month to month at the easiest charge he can".[31] Word must have got around that building was imminent because a plasterer asked to be considered when the occasion arose. With a shortage of craftsmen, it is interesting that a plasterer should approach the Company, and not vice versa. However, as plasterers' work would not commence until the major part of the structural work had been completed, perhaps this man was hoping, by applying early, to be appointed to a position which, because of the size and importance of the building, would keep him in employment for a considerable time on a prestigious commission.

By the end of July, construction was really under way. The Wardens visited the site "to see how the workmen go on with the building there, to quicken them therein and to acquaint the Prime Warden with any neglect or obstruction". The building committee resolved to meet weekly, and Jerman promised to attend each meeting to report on progress. As well as 200,000 bricks, scaffolding components and lime were ordered, and at this meeting, the decision was taken to enlarge the great hall to 33ft by 66ft. The bricklayer and carpenter, who were to be paid on account, promised to have the roof completed by the following October. The Court ordered that "the wharf at Fishmongers' Hall be appropriated only to the Company's use, and nothing to be thereon framed but what is or shall be for the use of the Company".

Still, during this critical period of overseeing the beginning of rebuilding, Jerman was travelling to Bray to pay the almsfolk, to arrange for repairs to the hospital to be carried out, and to organise the transport of timber. However, the illness which would bring about his death in a few months time may have already been causing him to feel unwell, and he implied to the Court that he was tiring of these visits. In May 1668, the Court suggested that Jerman should find "some gent or other able man near thereunto to take it as an honour to pay the poor their pensions and see them live in an orderly manner". Unlikely as it seems, the Company did prevail upon a Mercer from Maidenhead to fulfil this time-consuming task, engaging him, coincidentally, on the day Edward Jerman was buried in St Giles Cripplegate on 26 November 1668. Jerman's visits to Bray continued through July 1668, when he was asked to "consider what stone at Fishmongers' Hall will be necessary for amending and repairing the said hospital . . . and to cause the same to be sent thither". Presumably, this stone had been fire-damaged, and although unsuitable for the new Hall, was adequate for patching up the hospital.

Edward Jerman's last recorded visit to Bray took place on 8 October 1668. On that day, the Court granted him £50 "at present, in respect of his pains and service to this Company's affairs, and about the building at Fishmongers' Hall". Three weeks later, the Company requested Jerman to supervise a thorough review of its timber stocks, how much had been felled and sent to London, how much had been sold and to whom. Perhaps the Company had reason to query the timber dealings that Thomas Lock, the carpenter, was conducting, for they wanted to know "how much timber which hath been left to his charge hath been employed at Fishmongers' Hall for this Company's use, or in any other place for any other person or persons", and to give his report to Jerman.[32] As we shall see in the following chapter, Lock's honesty seems to have been brought into question on more than one occasion.

The final mention of Edward Jerman in the Fishmongers' archives is an entry in the Prime Warden's Accounts recording that, in 1672, his widow Rose was paid £50 for the services of her late husband for the company. Those visits to Bray must have been very wearing for a man whose health was fast deteriorating, and who had so many important commitments in the City also demanding his attention. Little wonder then that he died of consumption aged sixty-eight, as Priscilla Metcalf so appositely observed "consumed by over-work".[33]

Thus Jerman died before the Fishmongers' Hall that he had envisaged became a reality, and his death at such an early stage in its construction inevitably renders its attribution solely to him less than watertight. However, although, as we shall see, his draft was slightly modified, the distribution of the rooms as built was little altered from that which Jerman devised, with the exception of the court parlour. Moreover, the river elevation demonstrates similarities with the facades of several other company halls he designed, and with several other buildings which were familiar to him, and had been designed by men well known to him.

To understand Jerman's layout for Fishmongers' Hall, some knowledge of the old buildings that it was to replace is necessary, for the accommodation required

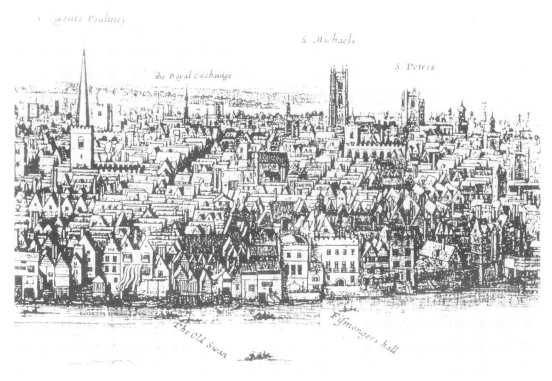

5.1 Wenceslas Hollar: detail of engraving (1647) showing Fishmongers' Hall.

by the Company remained very much the same.

The two branches of the fish trade, the Salt-Fishmongers, who dealt with wet fish, and the Stock-Fishmongers, dealing in dried fish, finally resolved the differences which had bedevilled any attempt at union between them and in 1536, decided to share a common Hall. Its easternmost block was a solidly built, embattled stone structure of three storeys. It resembled a Venetian merchant's house, having access from the water as well as from the street behind.[34] Hollar's drawing of 1639 reveals a precise image of the Hall (Figure 5.1) copied in a woodcut of 1825 (Figure 5.2). This shows a four-bay structure with entry at ground level from a wharf via a central, arched doorway. The four tall, square-headed windows of the piano nobile were adorned with separate balconies to stress the importance of this storey, with its high-ceilinged rooms. The second-floor windows were small and square, and a string course demarcated that storey from the embattled roofline.

In the same way as its Venetian counterpart, the ground floor was used as a storage area because of its easy access to and from the water, the Thames literally lapping at its doorstep. Above, on the first floor lay the great parlour where the 1592 meeting took place and where, in 1654, Edward Jerman was appointed Company Surveyor. Above the great parlour was the great chamber, a more private room, used as a drawing room when wives of the liverymen came to dinner. The rooms behind those

5.2 Fishmongers' Hall before the Great Fire: woodcut (1825).

fronting the riverside were used by the clerk for Company matters, and for family accommodation. Behind, and at right-angles to the riverside, lying north-south, was the Elizabethan great hall. This was a steep roofed building of brick and timber, rising above the battlements of the river block, with bay windows overlooking an open court. Here was the great hammer-beam roof inspected by Jerman in 1639, and here were displayed those pageant props. The first intimation of structural weakness in the Hall had come in the summer of 1624 when the Court recorded that it "sinketh and is weak". It took another fifteen years before repairs were made, and before Edward Jerman's introduction to the Company.

The plan which Jerman finally presented to the Court on 10 March 1667/8, nine months after the initial request, was not exactly the plan of the Hall as it would be built, although the basic layout remained the same. Jerman's plan, preserved and in fine condition in the Print Room of the Guildhall Library, measures 27 ins by 15½ ins and is drawn on vellum (Figure 5.3). Although the plan is unsigned, it might well be the only one left in London that can be definitely ascribed to Edward Jerman.[35] It is drawn in black ink, and coloured washes have been added to differentiate the rooms. Although a scale is set out at the bottom of the page, there are some inaccuracies in dimensions, probably due to the fact that the presence of rubble made measuring difficult. South, and therefore the river, is positioned at the top of the sheet, where two wings labelled "court room" on the east, and "tenement to the Thames" on the west project from the main body of the building. The tenement would probably have been rented out as a source of income. Between, and extending beyond the projecting wings is an area entitled "garden to the quay", in defiance of the King's 1667 proclamation regarding a riverside quay extending from the Tower to the Temple. The proclamation was not made law until 1670, and although Jerman would have

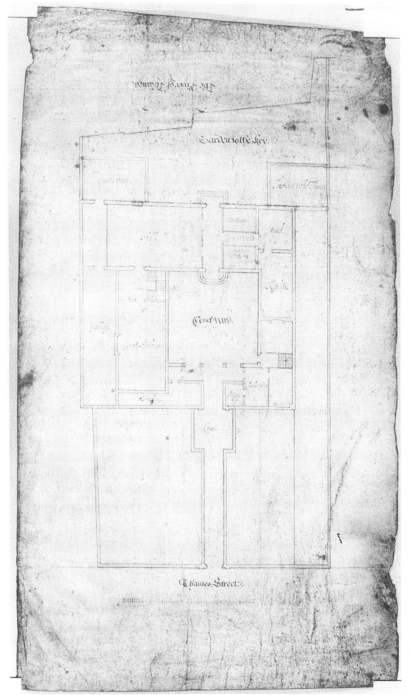

5.3 Jerman's plan of Fishmongers' Hall, March 1668: black ink and wash on vellum.

been well aware of this clause in the Act, he and the Company must have hoped that, because the Fishmongers had always protected their river frontage, extenuating circumstances might be found to enable them to retain their special relationship with the Thames.

Six tenements separated the Hall buildings from Thames Street on the northern aspect. A narrow passage between them gave access to an outer court and thence through a triple-arched portico, called by Hatton a piazza. The portico had columns and arches of the Ionic order, to the courtyard.[36] The construction of this part of the plan was more or less unchanged. It was similar to the arcaded walks that Jerman was designing for the Royal Exchange at this time. At the southern end of the courtyard, three curved steps led up to the screens passage with the hall itself on the east and the domestic quarters,

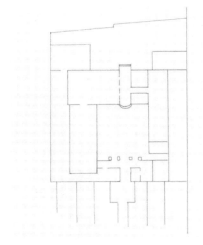

5.4 Diagrammatic representation of ground plans of Goldsmiths' Hall (left) and Fishmongers' Hall (below left).

including a buttery and pantry, on the west. At the southernmost end of the screens passage, a doorway led to the garden and the river. The great hall therefore lay east-west, parallel to the river and street, with the great parlour at right angles to it. To the east of the great parlour, a gallery extended the whole length of the site from the court room to the tenements.

This layout bears a noticeable resemblance to that of Nicholas Stone's Goldsmiths' Hall, 1634-6 (Figure 5.4). Edward Jerman would have been conversant with this plan because his father had been Goldsmiths' Carpenter during the Hall rebuilding, and Edward himself had held the post since Anthony's death in 1650. The orientation of the great halls differed, the Fishmongers being east-west while the Goldsmiths' lay almost north-south. However, the progression from entrance to hall was identical. In both, the courtyard was entered through a triple-arched portico. At the opposite end of the court, a few steps led up to the screens passage giving access to the hall on the left hand side. The great parlour lay at right angles to the hall, forming the left boundary of the court. In both, the domestic quarters lay on the opposite side of the court.

Several alterations were made to Jerman's plan before the clearing of the site got underway and building began. In the original plan, the clerk's office was situated between the southern end of the tenements and the arched portico. In this position, it was as far as it could be from the court room, resulting in great inconvenience. Instead, the court room was moved to the north range alongside the portico, negating the idea of wings projecting to the river. As we have seen, it was decided to increase the great hall's size from 30ft by 60ft to 33ft by 66ft in July 1668, retaining, therefore, the proportions of the pre-Fire Hall.

The riverside block was to be the show-piece section. Here was the front that the Fishmongers wished to present to the City, and because of its proximity to the river, to the wider world. It exhibited forms and motifs apparent in the buildings of Jones, Mills, Pratt and Stone, but Jerman combined them in such a way as to make them his own, and this Jermanian style will be seen to recur in the facades of other company halls he designed.

5.5 River front of Fishmongers' Hall: Sutton Nicholls' engraving (1750).

The dimensions of the riverside block were dictated by the kitchen and parlour ranges that bordered the courtyard behind. As can be seen from Figure 5.5, the river elevation was composed of nine bays, with a projecting pedimented central section, emphasised by alternate stone quoins which echoed those of the angles of the façade, and contrasted with the brick of the rest of the building. Nicholls' engraving shows that the square-headed windows are evenly spaced, and surmounted by alternating segmental and triangular pediments in a way then fashionable in London following their introduction by Jones at the Banqueting House (1619-1622). The Ionic columns of the central doorway support a full entablature topped by an open segmental pediment containing an escutcheon. A modillion cornice underlines the hipped roof, whose dormers repeat the alternating pediments of the main fenestration. The two storeys, of equal height, are set upon a raised basement. The classical doorway was approached directly from the Thames Quay via a pair of lateral steps which alluded to Michelangelo's masterpiece fronting the Palazzo dei Senatori in Rome. Michelangelo had introduced sculptures of river gods in the triangular niches below the steps, but Jerman had no need for such a device with the river itself so close by. Through the incorporation of this powerful motif, Jerman was stressing both the importance of this great Company, the

5.6 Foster Lane façade of Goldsmiths' Hall: engraving (1691).

Fishmongers, and its special relationship with the river.

The organisation and detailing of this riverside elevation therefore resembled many mid-seventeenth-century grand houses, including Thorpe Hall and Coleshill (see Figures 5.10 and 5.11), as well as Goldsmiths' Hall, so familiar to Edward Jerman (Figure 5.6). However, behind this façade, all was not quite what it seemed, there being two "misrepresentations". The riverside block's two rows of pedimented windows belied the single-storeyed great hall behind, and the hall, which dominated the whole plan, was not placed in the centre of the block. Instead, it was set on the eastern side, occupying five out of the nine bays, including the entrance, and extending back through three bays on the eastern aspect. This eastern elevation displayed some idiosyncrasies that contradicted the contemporary aspirations of the river front, for the court room and parlour range were surmounted by multiple gables, harking back to former times. The medieval and the modern were therefore juxtaposed where the great hall and the parlour met (Figure 5.7 and 5.8).

The ground for the river block was not totally cleared of rubbish, nor prepared for building in Jerman's lifetime. It is possible, therefore, that Jerman's elevation could have been modified after his death. Those who may have adapted and refined Jerman's design include Thomas Lock, probably advised by Robert Hooke, and the

5.7 Diagrammatic representation of the eastern aspect of Fishmongers' Hall from a drawing by Richard Suter (1826).

sculptor Edward Pierce. However, the basic form of Fishmongers' Hall remained Jerman's.

At first, following Jerman's death, the Building Committee of the Fishmongers' Company maintained a watchful eye on the construction but, following Thomas Lock's appointment in Jerman's place at Apothecaries' Hall, he assumed a similar position with the Fishmongers, and for a year, was referred to as the Surveyor. In the spring of 1669, Lock surveyed, and made a draft of the building.[37] Neither this drawing, nor indeed any other of Lock's drawings has survived, so there is no way of knowing how closely this drawing did (or did not) resemble Jerman's design. However, as Lock had little practical experience of house design, except that which he had picked up as a carpenter on three of Pratt's houses, Horseheath, Kingston Lacy and Clarendon, much modification seems unlikely.[38]

Edward Pierce, the sculptor, may have been responsible for certain refinements to the stonework of Jerman's façade. He had worked as a mason under Pratt at Horseheath in 1665, and after the Fire, he had masonry and carving contracts with several City churches. The escutcheon in the pediment at Fishmongers' Hall resembled the large shield he had carved at Horseheath, and the exactitude of the carving or the window dressings bears his professional stamp. Thus Jerman's craftsmen-colleagues may have added finishing touches to his design. For that design, Jerman clearly drew on his familiarity with the buildings of four men with whom he had enjoyed a degree of acquaintance, Inigo Jones, Peter Mills, Roger Pratt and Nicholas Stone.

Jerman had ample opportunity to come across and be influenced by Jones in his early life, both on his own account and through his father's association with Jones. From 1633, Edward Jerman was working alongside his father as City Carpenter. Until Jones left London in 1642 to join Charles I, he was, as Surveyor of the King's Works, responsible for the control of new building in London, spending much time in the City overseeing the repairs to St. Paul's Cathedral. When Anthony Jerman submitted a plan for the new Goldsmiths' Hall in 1634, he may well

5.8 South and eastern aspects of Jerman's Fishmongers' Hall: Edward Cooke watercolour (1826).

have discussed his ideas with his son Edward. Although it was Stone's design that was accepted, as Company Carpenter, Anthony Jerman was closely associated with the building, and would have been aware of the part played by Jones in the design of this important edifice.[39] In 1637, Anthony Jerman (and so, possibly Edward) and Inigo Jones were involved with the rebuilding and the associated controversy regarding the Cheapside church of St. Michael le Querne. Anthony was requested by the Vestry to make a wooden model of the church, but the Privy Council intervened in the negotiations. They, wishing to improve and beautify this important area of the City, demanded the demolition of adjacent buildings, the enlargement of the church, and a further model of the church, this time from Peter Mills. Against the Vestry's wishes, Inigo Jones was brought in by the Privy Council and building began "according to the plot and directions made by His Majesty's Surveyor".[40] Recollection of the acrimony surrounding this whole affair, and the high-handedness of the Privy Council may have accounted for Edward Jerman's initial reluctance (as we shall see in Chapter 6) to accept the position of designer/surveyor of the Royal Exchange in 1667. The City's dealings with the Crown had been less than cordial for many years.

Thus Edward Jerman had many opportunities to meet and speak with the Surveyor, and to observe at close hand his various building activities in London, and particularly his suggestions for Stone's Goldsmiths' Hall. The architectural world of the City must have been a small one in the second third of the seventeenth century, and it is most likely that the major players in it were well acquainted with each other, and consulted

5.9 Inigo Jones' unexecuted astylar design for the Prince's Lodgings, Newmarket (1618).

together and exchanged ideas. For this reason (among others) Inigo Jones' influence spread beyond the City of London, and it is probable that when Peter Mills, Jerman's City colleague, was commissioned to design Thorpe Hall (Cambridgeshire) for Oliver St. John, he consulted Jones, for the façade of Thorpe Hall bears a resemblance to Jones' unexecuted astylar design for the Prince's Lodging at Newmarket of 1618 (Figure 5.9). Although the building contract for Thorpe Hall is dated 1654, planning was probably well under way before Jones' death in 1652. The possibility of Jones' assistance at Thorpe Hall is likely when one remembers Jones' involvement at Pratt's Coleshill in 1651. Pratt, the royalist gentleman-architect, who had left England in 1643 to avoid the Civil War and to "give myself some convenient education", had, in his notebooks, advised prospective builders to engage a resourceful designer, preferably one conversant with such masters as Palladio, Scamozzi and Serlio. Perhaps Pratt himself sought Jones' assistance in this capacity, and again, the front elevation of Coleshill is descended from Jones' Newmarket design.[41]

We therefore have three buildings by which Jerman might have been inspired when he considered his river front at Fishmongers' Hall, all three of which had Jonesian connections, and were related to Jones' Newmarket design. Jerman would have been familiar with Thorpe Hall, for he must have been interested to see it, built as it was by such a close working colleague. His association with Pratt appears only to have begun in 1666, but again, he may at that time have seen Pratt's drawings and probably the house itself, so close to the Jesus Hospital at Bray. Jones' compact astylar

5.10 Main front of Thorpe Hall, designed by Peter Mills.

5.11 Main front of Coleshill, designed by Sir Roger Pratt.

prototype can be considered the germ of the idea which developed into Goldsmiths' Hall, Thorpe Hall and Coleshill, and via them into Jerman's Fishmongers' Hall.

Jones' Newmarket elevation displays an astylar form which had become popular by the mid 1600s. The centre of the seven bay elevation is stressed by a projecting, pedimented section whose angle quoins echo those on the corners of the building. Although there is considerable vertical stress, passing from the semi-basement windows, through those of the tall piano nobile to the attic, thence to the tall dormers, there is also substantial horizontal emphasis. This is demonstrated by the stone base line, string courses at the top and bottom of the piano nobile window balconies, another string course connecting the top of these windows and a stressed frieze and cornice. The windows of the semi-basement and attic are low and wide, providing a horizontal feel, counteracted by the tall piano nobile windows and unusually tall dormers (topped by alternating pediments) and by the way our eye is led from the central doorway via a Serlian motif surmounted by a plaque at piano nobile level, to an escutcheon in the pediment and finally to a free standing figure on the apex. Both Thorpe Hall (Figure 5.10) and Coleshill (Figure 5.11) display features in common with this Newmarket design. Both exhibit the same tripartite division of the façade, manifest in different ways. At Thorpe Hall, this tripartite division is indicated by the treatment of the seven evenly-spaced windows, being A-B-A-C-A-B-A, where A are flat lintels, B are triangular pediments and C is a segmental pediment. This formula can be read in two ways, either as A-B-A: C: A-B-A, or as A-B: A-C-A: B-A. The latter interpretation seems the more likely, and the position of the dormers seems to confirm the separation of the two pairs of end bays from the three in the centre. At Coleshill, the tripartite nature of the nine-bay façade is stressed by the three central windows being set much wider than the outer windows. All the windows are square-headed with lintels supported by voussoirs in the upper storey, while below, only the central doorway carries a large segmental pediment.

Both houses display a stronger horizontal emphasis than Newmarket, incorporating accentuated lintels to achieve this, throughout at Coleshill, and in the piano nobile at Thorpe Hall. Low, hipped roofs, string courses and marked cornices complete the horizontal feel, the only verticality being found in the tall chimney-pots. Uneven quoins stress the angles of both houses, as at Newmarket, and there is greater emphasis on the doorways. Each incorporates the orders in the form of columns, each is approached by a flight of central steps, and each is surmounted by elaborate pediments.

The elevation of Goldsmiths' Hall (Figure 5.6) also incorporates Jonesian features, but as John Newman states, Nicholas Stone must have referred to Serlio (Book 7, chapters 55-61) to overcome the problems of a notoriously awkward site, "and it was here that he found the basic motif for his Foster Lane elevation".[42] As at Newmarket, we find the central section of this eleven-bay façade emphasised by projection, by angle quoins, by a more prominent cornice and by an elaborate entrance, but here, the incorporation of a Serlian motif is found in a recessed wings, rather than in a central position. The sheer length of the elevation, with its low hipped roof, string course and prominent cornice gives a horizontal feel, but the fenestration leads the eye vertically.

The river front of Fishmongers' Hall can be seen as an amalgam of three elevations, on to which Jerman has established his own stamp. Although he has maintained a balance between verticals and horizontals, the elevation has less horizontal emphasis than Thorpe Hall and Coleshill, probably because there is less projection of the hipped roof with its stressed modillion cornice, and the angle of Jerman's roof is steeper. Jerman has emphasised the central section in the same way as Jones at Newmarket, and the large segmental pediment over the Fishmongers' doorway, together with the flat-lintelled windows on each side, can be compared with the Newmarket Serliana. This elaborate doorway is a feature common to all Jerman's company halls, most of them incorporating the orders. Another Jermanian feature, used extensively in his facades, is found in the aprons which unite the upper and lower windows, adding to the verticality of the elevation. The lateral steps are unique to Jerman's design; although dictated by the width of the Thames Quay, are a flash of genius.

Fishmongers' Hall was well received by historians of the City, especially Strype. In his version of Stow's survey (1720), he described it as "a curious large building, with a handsome paved passage, paved with freestone. Which leadeth into a large, square court, also paved, surrounded by a hall, the courtroom and other apartments. The front of this Hall towards the Thames is very graceful, giving a pleasant prospect".[43]

Edward Jerman's post of Surveyor to the Fishmongers' Company involved him in a range of activities that testify to his metamorphosis from artificer to architect. He resigned his post of City Carpenter in 1657. Although he had been Company Carpenter to the Goldsmiths since 1650, in the pre-Fire years much of his time was spent viewing and surveying Company property. Only after the Fire, when repairs to the Hall were necessary, did Jerman utilise his expertise in carpentry on behalf of the Goldsmiths'.

CHAPTER 6

Father and Sons at Goldsmiths' Hall

Anthony Jerman and his three sons, Hugh, Edward and Roger, as well as Edward's son-in-law Isaac Dun, had an association with the Goldsmiths' Company spanning thirty-five years, from 1634 until 1669. Anthony served the Goldsmiths in the capacity of Company Carpenter (assisted by his son Hugh) during the rebuilding of the Hall from 1634-36. In the Court books, Anthony is referred to as the Company's "Chief Carpenter" and also as "Workman Viewer", although most commonly, he is "Mr Jerman the Carpenter". Along with the Company Bricklayer, Mr Burridge, Anthony Jerman was, besides his carpentry duties, required to view and measure tenements, shops and gardens on land belonging to the Company. By choosing Jerman to fulfil these tasks the Goldsmiths were making use of his experience as a City Viewer, a post he had held since 1627.

Edward took over the post of Company Carpenter after his father's death in 1650, and his work, too, stretched well beyond that of a carpenter, into the realms of a viewer and surveyor. Throughout the 1650s and up till the Fire, Edward was continually required to take views and measure property owned by the Company as it developed the area around the Hall and Aldersgate Street. After the Fire, he was engaged to make drafts of the damaged Hall and adjacent property. At this time, he also advised the Company about timber supplies, and it seems likely that some of his visits to Windsor and Bray were on combined Goldsmiths' and Fishmongers' business. A strong bond of friendship had grown up between the two Companies, and perhaps these timber transactions were a manifestation of that affinity. Edward continued to work for the Company "with care and fidelity" until his death in 1668, and thereafter, the Goldsmiths favoured his widow with £20 in respect of his faithful service.

Roger Jerman worked for the Company purely in the capacity of a carpenter from 1653, being referred to as "the carpenter" rather than "Company Carpenter", a title reserved for Edward. Interestingly, Roger, not Edward, was responsible for the decoration of the Company barge that escorted the King and Queen from Hampton Court to Whitehall in 1662, although Edward also played a part in these celebrations. Isaac Dun, as a young man in his twenties, seems to have assisted Edward, his father-in-law, in some of his viewing and measuring around 1655, but there is no mention of him as a carpenter in his own right, and he does not seem to have held any official position within the Company.

The training that craftsmen such as Edward Jerman received during their seven-year apprenticeship, together with experience in their early working life, rendered them knowledgeable in a broad spectrum of building matters. The City companies exploited these talents by assigning two such men tasks beyond the bounds of their chosen metier, and for this reason, the term "surveyor" as used in the record books can be misleading. It may cover, as in the case of Edward Jerman, commissions as diverse as reporting on work done by other craftsmen to viewing and measuring company property, urban development and finally to designing and overseeing the construction of a company hall.

As Fishmongers' Hall was appropriately situated alongside the Thames, so Goldsmiths' Hall stands near Cheapside, in that part of the City where working goldsmiths pursued their craft and plied their trade. There is evidence that a guild of Goldsmiths existed in 1180, but in those early days, meetings took place and administration of the ordinances were conducted in taverns, inns or members' houses. Like other guilds, the Goldsmiths realised the advantages of having a meeting-place they could call their own, a hall which would serve as a centre for the social, religious and business aspects of Company life, encouraging firmer bonds between members. So it was that, in 1339, nineteen goldsmiths, acting for the Company, bought a property at the northern end of Foster Lane, just off Cheapside, the site on which the hall stands today, and it is the proud boast of the Goldsmiths that no other City company can claim a longer or earlier tenure. In the first charter, granted to the Company by Edward III in 1327, it was stated that all members of the trade should "sit in their shops in the High Street of Cheap" to ensure that any gold or silver sold in the City should be done so publicly, avoiding illegal dealing. The quality of building in and around this important thoroughfare was to be the cause of constant concern to both the Crown and the Company, and over the ensuing 350 years, steps were regularly taken to maintain its beauty and to limit it to goldsmiths and allied trades. Stow tells us that Goldsmiths' Row, built by Thomas Wood, a goldsmith and Sheriff in 1491, represented "the most beautiful frame of fair houses and shops within the wall of London".[1] It contained ten houses and fourteen shops uniformly built, four storeys high, and "beautified towards the street with the Goldsmiths' arms." The German lawyer, Paul Hentzner, writing in 1598, claimed that Goldsmiths' Row surpassed all other streets "in this handsome and clean" City.[2] However, by 1619, other "meaner" trades had begun to infiltrate some of the shops, and Wardens of the Company were requested to ensure that this should be discouraged. In 1622, James I intervened, declaring his dislike of mean trades in the Row, and demanding that only goldsmiths should inhabit the houses and the shops, for the "continuance of the beauty and ornament" of the City's chief street.[3]

Goldsmiths' Hall, although not situated on one of the City's wider streets was, nevertheless, in a prestigious position close by St Paul's and Cheapside. It was bounded on its west, north and east sides by Foster Lane, Maiden Lane (now Gresham Street) and Gutter Lane respectively, while Company-owned tenements lay on the south side of the Hall abutting Carey Lane which ran parallel to Cheapside. Thus the Hall lay in that part of the City whose beauty had been so fiercely guarded by, amongst others, James I and the Privy Council, and in 1634 an Order of Council was issued. This declared:

> Whereas in the Goldsmiths' Row, in Cheapside and Lombard Street, divers shops are held by persons of other trades, whereby that uniform show which was an ornament to those places and a lustre to the City is now greatly blemished . . . His Majesty, taking notice, is much offended. It is ordered that the Company of Goldsmiths shall take order . . . all the shops in Goldsmiths' Row shall be supplied with goldsmiths and that the Master and Wardens shall give notice to all goldsmiths who keep shops elsewhere to procure themselves shops in Cheapside or Lombard Street.[4]

By the end of the fifteenth century, the Goldsmiths' Company had acquired properties ranging from the houses and shops of well-to-do goldsmiths around Cheapside to the small workrooms of practising smiths, and from taverns and brewhouses to one of the sheriff's prisons. Most of these buildings were, of course, timber framed and in constant need of inspection and repair. The Company had, in 1478, appointed a clerk of works to supervise the building craftsmen engaged on Company property, and to check on the safe-keeping of materials, but in 1496, they found it necessary to appoint an official carpenter, acting as a surveyor, in overall charge of repairs and rebuilding. Thus, the post to which Anthony Jerman was appointed in 1634 had its origins 140 years earlier, and although Anthony, unlike the first incumbent, worked more as a carpenter than as a surveyor – especially during the Hall rebuilding – Edward Jerman, when he became Company Carpenter, again fulfilled the wider role of a surveyor until 1666.

In March 1633/4, a committee of liverymen of the Goldsmiths' Company, realising that much-needed repairs were overdue in their great hall together with some adjoining rooms, met with workmen to view the defects and give their views on repairs and amendments.[5] The buildings on the site that those nineteen goldsmiths had bought, back in 1339, had soon been demolished to make way for the construction of a Hall, resembling an average-sized merchant's house and similar to many others in the neighbourhood of Cheapside. Apart from the great hall, the house had contained a kitchen, pantry and buttery as well as two additional rooms. Constant, partial rebuilding had been carried out and various additions had been made over the next hundred years until, by 1454, the accounts reveal that Goldsmiths' Hall contained a parlour, great hall, chapel, chamber, granary and cellars arranged around a central court or garden. In other words, it was just like the mansion of any citizen of note, with the addition of an armoury, an assay house and a clerk's house. Stow, in 1598, was not much impressed by it. He described it as "a proper house but not large, and therefore to say that Bartholomew Read, Goldsmith, Mayor in the year 1502, kept such a feast in this hall as some have fabled, is far incredible and altogether unpossible [sic] considering the smallness of the hall and the number of the guests which as they say were more than a hundred persons of great estate".[6]

This Hall served the needs of the Goldsmiths well, but by the 1630s, it was beginning to fall into disrepair. Soon after restoration work started in 1634, the Company became aware that the great kitchen and clerk's house would have to be demolished, and once this had been effected, they realised that the extra space thus provided gave them the chance to "enlarge the great hall in the length thereof". With remarkable speed, John Hawes, a past Prime Warden of the Company, presented a plan for an enlarged hall, probably in contravention of building regulations, the last from 1607, concerning building on new foundations.[7] The workmen, "having considered it among themselves", agreed to set the new foundations and proceed with the building. However, it soon became apparent that the entire Hall was in such a decayed state that the whole structure would have to be dismantled and rebuilt.

Inigo Jones was, at this time, making frequent visits to the City, engaged as he was with the remodelling of St Paul's Cathedral. Jones had been appointed honorary architect for the restoration of St. Paul's on 4 February 1633, and work continued until September 1642. On one of his visits, "on some occasion passing by", he met with the workmen of the Goldsmiths' Company to discuss the rebuilding of the Hall. He must have been shown Hawes' plans, and it seems that he found them inadequate for a building which was required to express the wealth, prestige and longevity of the Company. He advised the Court to invite the submission of two or three new plans, and also suggested the demolition, not only of the Hall, but also the tenements, thus considerably increasing the extent of their building site. He encouraged the Company to seek permission from the Commission for Rebuilding, so as not to "offend against the rules of His Highness' Parliament", and, by implication, seems to have recommended that they look beyond Mr. Hawes for a designer.[8]

Of the four plans that were subsequently submitted, one was that of Anthony Jerman, at that time City Carpenter and a City Viewer, who probably hoped to gain the contract for the carpentry work should his design be chosen. Mr. Hawes put forward a plan, presumably a new, enlarged one for the larger site, and two plans were submitted by Burridge and Osborne, the bricklayers. A pleasing note creeps into the Court book here. The plans were all to be left with the Warden, who would show them to Inigo Jones for his approval but, "be it remembered that Mr. Hawes took his plott home with him to mend in some things". Perhaps Mr. Hawes had glimpsed one of the other plans and realised that he could amend his design to his advantage. Meanwhile, the Court realised that there was a "necessity to alter the whole frame of the old building into a more decent and commodious form by some enlargement upon their own ground". However, some members of the Court had second thoughts about contravening the building regulations because they requested that the City Commissioners should view the site, together with Inigo Jones, when he should next come to the City, "as soon as convenience would permit".[9]

At the end of October, Mr. Hawes' hopes must have been raised for, at a Court which sat on 21 October 1634, his was one of the two plans that the Court chose to consider, the other being one of Burridge and Osborne's. At this meeting, the Court also decided to ask Nicholas Stone, the sculptor and mason, to attend the next Court. Not only did Stone attend the next Court, but he took along with him his own plans for a new Hall. This threw the meeting into confusion and, "after much debating thereof, nothing was resolved on", except that Stone was requested to draw some more plans "with what speed he could". At the same meeting, the Court decided that a surveyor for the work must be appointed, "an understanding and skilful man, well experienced in building", and it was concluded that Stone was to be their man, a choice probably encouraged by Inigo Jones.[10] Nicholas Stone was, at that time, at the peak of a very successful career. He had been appointed Master Mason to the Crown in 1632, he was a close working colleague of Inigo Jones following his work as Master Mason at the Banqueting House in 1619-1622, and he was presently completing his year as Master of the Masons' Company.

When the Court met again on 3 December 1634, Stone presented his plan, which was "rectified in some things". By a narrow margin, the Court voted to refer the plan for further consideration so that the workmen whom they appointed, Anthony and Hugh Jerman, carpenters, and Burridge and Osborne, bricklayers, might have a chance to scrutinize it and put down in writing "what exception shall be taken to the plott". This implies that the workmen were given some opportunity to air their views on the design. Two days later, the Court debated the plans and it was agreed that "Mr Stone shall be the Surveyor for the Company's building and direct the workmen therein. And for the better accomodation thereof, Mr. Hooke was entreated to be aiding and assisting him". Robert Hooke had been Prime Warden of the Goldsmiths the previous year. John Parker, one of the Wardens, was required to "take notice of the workmen and labourers of their times of work and absence, and to pay them accordingly". His role must have been that of a clerk of works. Furthermore, Mr. Hooke was desired to "oversee and examine the accounts of the said John Parker . . . and all or any of the Assistants will survey or overlook the work". Perhaps Nicholas Stone was somewhat aggrieved, not only by the appointment of two assistants, but also by the possibility of "all or any of the Assistants" overlooking the work for, a week later, he requested that "in the direction of the workmen in their proceedings, no man may intermeddle but himself [Stone]".[11]

Stone's commission at the Goldsmiths was, therefore, very similar to Edward Jerman's at the Fishmongers, except that Jerman was not saddled with a potentially interfering Court of Assistants. Stone was appointed as a designer/surveyor inasmuch as he both drew up the plans and oversaw the work, and here again we come up against the thorny problem of terminology, so neatly covered by Howard Colvin in the final three pages of "The Architectural Profession" at the start of his *Dictionary*.[12] Today's architect draws up designs and estimates the financial implications of those designs, but no longer oversees the workmen on the building site, merely attending occasional site meetings. It is in this respect that men such as Stone and Edward Jerman differed from the architect of today. They were responsible for both design and construction, not simply design, leading to the rather clumsy nomenclature of designer/surveyor, or architect/surveyor, for there is no single word which incorporates both aspects of their responsibilities.

How much of the design of Goldsmiths' Hall can be credited to Stone is open to debate, and the subject has been discussed by John Newman in a closely argued article.[13] As early as the beginning of February 1634/5, Stone presented the Court with plans for the Hall, and also with a set of exterior designs. However, one senses the spectre of Inigo Jones hovering nearby, for Stone "gave this Court to understand that in the doing thereof, Mr. Jones, his Majesty's Surveyor, took especial care and did advise and direct before the perfecting and finishing of each piece". The Company was aware, and clearly grateful that Jones had played some considerable part in the designs, for "Mr. Wardens were moved about some gratuity to be given to Mr. Jones . . . for his care and directions in the drawing the Company's plott for their buildings . . . a chain to be given to him . . . as a token of this Company's love".[14]

By the spring of 1635, work was underway, and in July of that year, articles of agreement were indented between Robert Hooke, on behalf of the Company, and Anthony and Hugh Jerman as carpenters for the rebuilding. I have transcribed this minutely detailed indenture in full from a slightly damaged document preserved at Goldsmiths' Hall.[15] The full transcript is set out in Appendix 3, but some parts are worthy of mention here as an example of a contract between a builder (the Goldsmiths' Company) and craftsmen (Anthony and Hugh Jerman) in the first half of the seventeenth century. The Jermans, for their part, were to supply all the "timber, boards, nails, carving, workmanship and materials whatsoever belonging to carpenters' work for the erecting, building and fitting up of a Hall and other buildings adjoining thereinto". The timbers were all to be of oak, and the floorboards of good, well-seasoned deal. Every joist, rafter, beam, purkin and raising plate was enumerated and its exact dimensions laid down for every part of the building. The Jermans agreed to follow all Stone's directions and to finish all the carpenters' work with "all convenient speed, making no neglect or delay but as speedily as the masons and bricklayers do make ready the same . . . so that they shall not be hindered by any such neglect of the carpenters". Presumably, similarly detailed indentures were drawn up with the masons and bricklayers, each being admonished not to keep the others waiting.

Under Hooke's direction, the Goldsmiths set down the payment for each of the minutely detailed items of carpentry. Each floor and ceiling of every individual room was valued at a different rate "by the measure", as would be advocated by Wren, Pratt and Gerbier. Certain items of carpentry were to be assessed for payment by two "indifferent" men, and the Jermans were to receive £150 on exchange of contracts, the "payments as shall be found fitting and needful to be paid as the work shall go forward". The final payment would be made when all

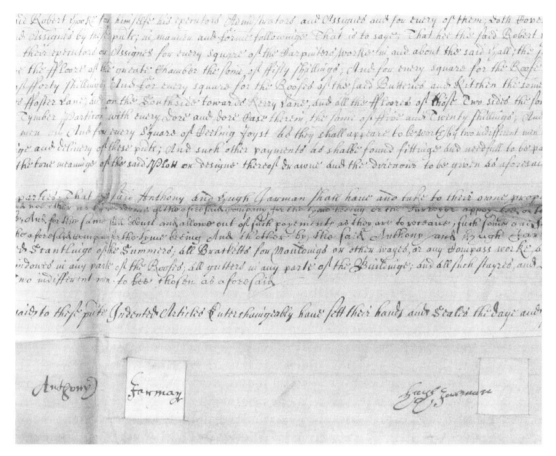

6.1 Signatures of Anthony and Hugh Jerman concluding an agreement with the Goldsmiths' Company (1635).

the carpenters' work was completed according to the design and it had been measured and approved. Although John Parker was responsible for the financial transactions between the Company and its workmen, it is not clear whether the final measuring of the work would have been the responsibility of Hooke, or of Stone himself. These indented articles were endorsed by Anthony and Hugh Jerman (Figure 6.1), and were presumably referred to whenever queries arose concerning materials or payments.

The indenture was signed on 18 July 1635, and work on the building proceeded, although it was constantly hampered by lack of funds. Much of the money required for rebuilding had to be borrowed at between 5 and 10% interest, and it is clear that the Company was walking an extremely taut tightrope. One entry in the Court Book reveals that, having borrowed several sums of money between £100 and £1,000, the Court considered it better to be indebted to a few persons in great sums (if they might be had) than to several persons for smaller sums.[16]

Although seventeenth-century working methods and payments, as set out in the previous chapter, appear relatively clear-cut, it seems that workmen and their employers did not always see eye to eye when it came to remuneration. Problems arose over discrepancies both in the measuring of completed work and over the amount of materials, notably timber, that were used. So it was that by April 1636, problems were arising between Anthony Jerman and John Parker about payment for work done. Jerman requested that measurements be made by an independent assessor, and because he claimed he was "a greater sum out of purse", he was given an interim payment of £100.[17] The situation rumbled on, and by April 1637, Jerman was clearly becoming very anxious that much of the carpentry work on which he had spent the previous year was about to be covered up by the plasterers, rendering measurement impossible. He therefore urgently desired that all his work might be immediately viewed and measured "otherwise he would be the loser by it".[18]

These measurements were not forthcoming until September 1637 when Jerman presented "a note of the report of the view and measuring of his work in the building of the Hall". However, the following January, the Court decided that the work should be re-measured, this time by two carpenters chosen by Jerman, and two by the Company, in the presence of a member of the Court. Two months went by and still no payment had been received. At a Court on 21 March 1637/8, Jerman, together with the bricklayers Burridge and Osborne, demanded all the money due to them, and this time, the Assistants and Wardens agreed to examine the account books in an attempt to settle the matter. A year later, no settlement had been made because the two parties had failed to agree on a mutually acceptable payment for the work, but the Court, seemingly exasperated, resolved that the Wardens should pay Jerman "what they shall think fit". Financial wrangles continued right up until 1639, with Jerman serving an affidavit on the Company for the recuperation of all the money due to him, at which time, the matter was finally settled.[19]

At this point, it is worth pausing briefly to consider financial arguments between company officials and workmen, for we find instances of such altercations with relation to Roger Jerman, Thomas Lock and Thomas Cartwright. Perhaps these master craftsmen, who were very often obliged to fulfil many different roles for the companies that engaged them, felt that they were insufficiently rewarded for the variety of work demanded of them. Certainly, in May 1670, there were "doubts, questions and differences" between the Fishmongers' Company and Thomas Lock over his carpenter's bills, resulting in his work being viewed and measured by an independent surveyor. As a result, a substantial sum was deducted from his final bill, and in 1674, the Court ordered that "Thomas Lock, carpenter, by reason of his very ill management of this Company's affairs in the building of their Hall shall henceforth never be any more employed to do any manner of carpenters' work for this Company".[20] Final indeed. Sir Roger Pratt, too, had cause to query Lock's charges in 1666 over the carpentry work at Horseheath Hall. "All his pretensions upon the rack came to about £1,500 as may be seen in particular accounts. Memo: that his quantities of lintelling were most easy to have been disproved by the circumference of the building. His agreement for slabs with my lord paid the sawing of his great timber and his price for the rail and baluster in all places most excessive".[21] One further example of Lock's decidedly less than honest approach where his timber dealings were concerned is found in a small book in the Fishmongers' archives. Entitled "Estates, Surveys and Reports", this little book contains plans of houses and land leased by the Fishmongers' Company, and we find, alongside one plan, "The premises marked F and G were leased to Thomas Lock, carpenter, who was head workman in building the Company's Hall, and it is said with the chips that he picked up at the Hall, erected these two messuages".[22]

Similarly, the Joint Committee of the Mercers and the City wrangled over payment with Roger Jerman about carpentry work at the Royal Exchange from April 1669 until January 1670/71,[23] and considered mason Cartwright's demand for money for his Exchange work excessive in 1667. Cartwright would fail to gain the mason's contract for work on the rebuilding of Goldsmiths' Hall in 1667 because his estimate was considered exorbitant, exceeding all the other submitted valuations. Perhaps, because of their acute shortage of money following the Fire, the companies were holding a very tight rein and questioning any charge they considered unreasonable, or simply did not feel obliged to pay their workmen more than they considered the job to be worth. On the other hand, human nature being what it is, certain specialised craftsmen might have had an inflated idea of their worth, or, with the City being one big building site, were greedy for as much money as they could attain.

The financial disagreements of 1636-39 did not spell the end of Anthony Jerman's association with the Goldsmiths, and once the new Hall was finally finished, the Company seems to have attempted to regularise payment to its craftsmen. In October 1646, the Court decided that the Company Bricklayer and Company Carpenter should have a yearly salary of four nobles (a gold coin worth one-third of a pound), to attend all views when required. Their intent was that when any tenant wished to renew his lease, the premises would be viewed by one or two Wardens together with the workmen (the Company Bricklayer and Carpenter), who would report in writing to the Court. A similar view would be taken of property requiring repair or even demolition. One such view was made in 1649 by Anthony Jerman and John Burridge concerning property leased to Sir John Wollaston, an Alderman, and former Lord Mayor.[24] The details of this view, signed by Burridge and Jerman, are interesting when compared with the cursory reports submitted by the Wardens when they were obliged to view company property. A report made in March 1655 will serve as an example, and both views, together with one made by Edward Jerman and John Burridge in 1652, are transcribed in Appendix 4. Comparing the assessments, it is no wonder that the Jermans were required to do the bulk of this work. It was clearly far too technical for the Wardens to discharge in any satisfactory fashion, and again serves to illustrate the wide-ranging capabilities of these master-craftsmen.

Following Anthony's death in 1650, it was Edward who succeeded him as Company Carpenter, not the young Roger who had been so eager to achieve the prestigious post (see Chapter 3). This was Edward's first company appointment, but by this time, he was already much involved in City work as City Carpenter, and would be appointed a City Viewer a few months later. Right from the start, Edward's work seems to have been that of a surveyor rather than a carpenter. During the great part of the 1650s and early 1660s, the Goldsmiths' Company was refurbishing property and developing land that they owned near the Hall. These northern and western holdings lay outside the City walls, the northern ones near the fashionable Aldersgate Street, around Redcross Street and Jewen Street. The western block was bounded by Fetter Lane and Shoe Lane, to the west of the Fleet River. Here, the Company was developing new streets and encouraging members of the Court to build in the area, as an example to others.

Edward Jerman not only planned these developments, but also supervised the work. Dozens of entries in the Court Books record his involvement with these projects. They were clearly a huge asset to the Company which would generate much-needed income in the form of fines and rents. The Goldsmiths might have been aware that in Edward Jerman they had found a gifted and reliable employee, for they paid him on a regular basis sums of money "with which he was well satisfied and thankful to the Company, affirming that it was more than he expected".[25]

Each of these projects will be considered separately, to avoid confusion, although they all ran concurrently. However, an early commission which may have sown the seeds of Jerman's interest in pageantry, an interest which would occupy a considerable amount of his time between 1656 and 1664 when he was not actively engaged on Goldsmiths' business, will be considered first.

In 1651, Edward was asked to work with Mr. Allen, the herald painter, on the construction and positioning of the arms of the benefactors of the Goldsmiths' Company around the Hall premises. Presumably, as no other carver is mentioned in the minutes, Jerman was responsible for the woodwork which would have involved the fashioning of mythical creatures, foliage, armour, and the personification of virtues. This must have been good preparation for a man who would be creating similar, but larger props for the Lord Mayors' Shows. From Mr. Allen, he would have learnt to appreciate the use of colour, not only as a heraldic device, but also to stress particular aspects of design. (A few years later, he would oversee the setting up of arms of the Fishmongers' Company in the Goldsmiths' Hall, no doubt a further expression of the amity existing between the two Companies). Finally, in 1662, he was required to draw "the form or figure for a representation of the Company to set forth their mystery by way of pageantry for the way of pageant entertainment of their Majesties". This was the Goldsmiths' contribution to the water pageant *Aqua Triumphalis* performed between Hampton Court and Whitehall, when Charles II presented his Queen to the people (Figure 6.2). A stage was to be set up at the head of the Company's barge, and Edward devised three scenes to represent the "mystery" of the Goldsmiths: Justice, with

6.2: *Aqua Triumphalis*. Water Pageant. Dirck Stoop etching, 1662.

a balance and touchstone; Jupiter, with her attendants holding golden cups and hammers; and a forge. Roger Jerman and Mr. Dacres, described as "the carpenter and the painter", fashioned these scenes from Edward's drawings. Edward's career could, in this respect, be likened to that of Inigo Jones, for both men spent several years on figurative work before extending their talents to architecture. Jones, apprenticed to a joiner in St. Paul's Churchyard, became a designer of court masques, creating costumes and ephemeral architecture while Jerman, although arguably less talented, less educated and certainly less travelled, pursued the same path, but in a City rather than a court environment. His vehicle was the pageant-wagon rather than the royal stage, but, had he enjoyed the patronage of the Court rather than that of the City fathers, wider horizons might have opened up to him.

The Goldsmiths' first venture into urban development under Jerman's supervision, albeit on a small scale, was that in the area to the west of the City walls. In 1650, Edward Jerman and John Burridge presented the Court with a draft of a new street on the south side of Shoe Lane, and of the houses that might be built there. The plans were accepted by the Court, and building went ahead. Meanwhile, some of the older property in the vicinity was in need of repair, and Jerman was required to take views here and to suggest possible improvements including the paving of streets and the maintenance of passageways together with their gateways.

The Goldsmiths' Shoe Lane development was, by 1661, stretching the sewer beyond its limits, and Jerman was ordered to meet with Peter Mills (who was still a City Surveyor) to view the same, "it being alleged by the City's artificers that by reason of the new building belonging to the Company, and of the drain there lately made, the sewer was overcharged with the water falling from the said buildings".[26] Jerman pointed out that the fault did not lie with the Company. The gate over the sewer had been removed from its original position, and to compound the problem, the street was full of soil, blocking the drain and causing the "annoyance". Jerman was also quick to point out that the Company had "done the City a far greater kindness in leaving a passage or cartway in order to an improvement in the City's interest in their land behind St. Giles Cripplegate".

The Committee, comprising Peter Mills and the City artificers, "did thereupon waive all further debate concerning the said charge". Edward Jerman was clearly becoming something of a diplomat, not only absolving the Company from blame, but also demonstrating the advantages to the City of the Goldsmiths' urban development programme.

The Goldsmiths' next project, starting around 1653, was the redevelopment of a street to the north of the Hall, called Jewen Garden. Seven new tenements were to be built there, under Edward Jerman's direction, but here again he seems to have been responsible for drawing up leases as well as for planning and building.[27] Jerman's knowledge of financial matters could not have been insignificant if the *Goldsmiths* were leaving this work to him, and were sufficiently pleased with the way he managed it to give him "as the Company's gift and goodwill" the sum of £20. The expense of the Jewin Garden development far exceeded Jerman's original estimate, but he was sufficiently confident to stand up before the Court and defend it.[28]

In the ten-year period between 1650 and 1660, there are no fewer than 90 entries in the Goldsmiths' Court Books detailing work done and payments made to Edward Jerman. These show that, once the rebuilding of their Hall was no longer a financial drain on them, the Goldsmiths developed a policy of systematic improvement and refurbishment of their extensive holdings around the north and west of their new Hall. Jerman viewed property and oversaw construction in Fetter Lane, Gutter Lane, Bachelors' Court, Aldersgate Street, Broad Street, Harding Street and Foster Lane itself. He was asked to arbitrate between tenants over ancient lights and water-courses, and to give his opinion on an estimate for carpenters' work submitted by the Skinners' Company Carpenter when the two Companies were planning a shared bargehouse. His work was therefore hugely varied and, one would imagine, very time consuming, although in some of it his son-in-law Isaac Dun gave him a helping hand.[29]

Edward continued to work more as a company surveyor than as the Company Carpenter which was his title, only on very rare occasions being paid specifically for carpenter's work. This is not really surprising because, from 1654 onwards, Roger Jerman was also employed by the Company as a carpenter (though not as the Company Carpenter). Roger's first work for the Company seems to have been on the Jewin Garden project, and thereafter he spent considerable time on the refurbishment of Bachelors' Court, next to the Hall. Edward had viewed this property in 1652 and found it "so extremely decayed" that the whole building was endangered (see Appendix 4). He suggested that, if the Company spent the requisite amount of money to put things right, according to specifications which he laid down, there should be "not more trouble in the space of 20 years".[30]

After he had completed the Bachelors' Court project, Roger was engaged on odd carpentry jobs for several properties around Aldersgate Street, and also worked on the kitchen and cellars of the Hall itself in 1659, and the bargehouse in 1660. While it fell to Edward to carry out whatever work was necessary in preparation for General Monk's dinner at Goldsmiths' Hall on 13 July 1660, Roger, as we have seen, was requested to execute the carpentry work for the Goldsmiths' barge in the Water Pageant of 1662. The records reveal that "the trimming and adorning of the pageant is wholly left unto the painter and carpenter who are requested to use the best of their care and skill for the well performing of the same".

From 1663 until he viewed the Hall after the Fire, there are very few records of Edward's work for the Goldsmiths' Company, apart from one view of Company property each year. He had resigned from the last of his City posts in 1662, and negotiations about timber, particularly for the Fishmongers' Company, seem to have comprised the bulk of his work. One cannot help wondering, therefore, whether he was unwell between 1663 and 1666, and two entries, in the Goldsmiths' and Haberdashers' minutes, point in this direction. In July 1666, Jerman asked the Court of the Goldsmiths for some remuneration for work done for them in 1664 and 1665, and the Court granted him £3. When one remembers not only the salary, but also the gifts of £20 which had been paid to him in the 1650s, one can only assume that he had undertaken very little work for the Company in those two years. Moreover, the entry continues "yet taking his present condition into consideration, being now under restraint . . . he should be given a free gift of the Company". Perhaps Jerman had already suffered the first exacerbation of the tuberculosis which, according to the burial register (see Chapter 2), claimed his life in 1668. The second piece of evidence is found in the Court Minutes of the Haberdashers' Company in May 1663: "This Court being now put in mind that no remembrance hath been hitherto given to Mr. Jerman, lately the City Surveyor and Carpenter to this Company for his pains in surveying and measuring the Company's houses in and near this City . . . and now he is fallen into decay in his estate, and doth need the same".[31] It seems likely that Edward Jerman was a sick man even before he started the gruelling task of viewing, designing and overseeing so many buildings in the post-Fire period. No wonder, therefore, that his health gave out after two such frantic years.

In September 1666, to return to Jerman's work for the Goldsmiths' Company, the Court of Assistants called him in almost at once "to take a view of the chimneys belonging to the common Hall", which were thought to be in danger of falling. The Court was keen that these chimneys should be retained if possible, but left the decision to Jerman. When the rubbish and damaged materials had been cleared, the Committee for Rebuilding was "entreated to consider and advise with Mr. Jerman touching the repair of the Hall". As a result of this meeting, Edward Jerman, speedily, "presented a draft in paper of the Company's common hall and of the rooms and officers' houses . . . and gave an estimate of the carpenters' work for the roof and flooring thereof . . . that timber might amount to £1,600, but the flooring part might be forborne at present, and only joists laid into the walls for the better strengthening thereof to support the roof".[32] This was going to be an extremely expensive undertaking in terms of timber alone, and Jerman was trying to keep costs as low as possible.

Damage to the Hall was evidently greater than Jerman had appreciated, for he was again asked to assess the damage and to estimate the cost of repairs. In July 1667, the Court gave him a reward of £20, "his employment in the Company's affairs for this year past having been much more than for some years past". This seems a further piece of evidence that Edward had been ill and unable to carry out much work for the Company in the previous two or three years. If he had contracted tuberculosis around 1663, which seems likely from the Goldsmiths' and Haberdashers' records, the disease was following the classic course of this untreated, and at this time, untreatable scourge. The primary tuberculosis infection produces no signs or symptoms, and in the vast majority of sufferers passes unnoticed, only a few patients experiencing febrile illness.[33] Edward Jerman was unlikely, therefore, to have known that he had contracted the disease until it progressed to the post-primary pulmonary phase, associated with tiredness, weight loss and respiratory symptoms such as cough and shortness of breath. As Susan Sontag explains, "Tuberculosis is understood as a disease of extreme contrasts, white pallor and red flush, hyperactivity alternating with languidness".[34] In the years immediately preceding the Fire, the disease must have been taking hold, extending through Jerman's lungs, leaving him weak and tired. In the post-Fire period, a phase of febrile activity took over which, combined with his personality, loyalty and penchant for hard work, enabled him to undertake so much work. Such fever, causing raised body temperature, can produce a feeling of euphoria, and, it has been suggested, can result in exceptional creativity. Keats, for example, is supposed to have written some of his best poetry at such phases of his illness. Perhaps this is why Jerman, emaciated by disease, could over-ride such physical symptoms and create so many designs in so short a time before his sudden death in November 1668; one remembers that he was recorded as being actively engaged on Fishmongers' Hall and the Royal Exchange until the end of October.

The last entry in the Goldsmiths' Court Books relating to Edward Jerman during his lifetime sums up the workload that their "ancient servant" (then aged 63) shouldered on their behalf. It reads, "At this Court, consideration was taken of Mr. Jerman's pains as well as his views and attendances on the Committee for Building at their weekly courts, as for the surveying of the Company's buildings at the Hall for the last year past, of whose care and fidelity therein, the Court being fully satisfied . . . Mr. Jerman shall have given to him £40".[35] The Court of Assistants of the Goldsmiths' Company was fully aware of the debt it owed Edward Jerman in his capacity as a town planner and as a surveyor as well as his official position as Company Carpenter, and in February 1668/9, Edward's widow was given £20 as a result of "information given of the present wants and necessities of the widow of Edward Jerman, the Company's late Surveyor and their ancient servant, in respect of his faithful service".

Thus a carpenter of Edward Jerman's proficiency was able to breach the boundaries of his craft, to rise above the role of an artificer and attain the status of a designer, and it was as a designer that the Joint Committee of the City and the Mercers' Company engaged him to work on the Royal Exchange.

CHAPTER 7

Edward Jerman's Royal Exchange

Until the 1997 publication of the London Topographical Society's book *The Royal Exchange*, edited by Ann Saunders, there had been little printed literature on this subject since the mid-nineteenth century, and such writing as there was concentrated on Sir Thomas Gresham's role in the genesis of the First Exchange. The essays contained in the LTS publication, especially those contributed by Ann Saunders, namely "The Building of the Exchange", "The Organisation of the Exchange" and "The Second Exchange", together with Jean Imray's "The Origins of the Royal Exchange", are invaluable to our understanding of the origins, form and organisation of the first two Exchanges, and the part they played in ensuring the supremacy of the City of London as a European financial centre. With these essays as a guide, I have transcribed and studied much of the Gresham Repertory for the years 1666-1669, in order to discover the details of Edward Jerman's role in the design and construction of the Second Exchange. The Repertory also sheds light on Peter Mills' participation during the consultative period, and on the work executed by, and the wages paid to the master-craftsmen, including Roger Jerman and Thomas Cartwright. The parts played by the Mercers' Company, the Corporation of the City, and indeed the King, in the development of the Exchange are also revealed. Alongside these written records, I have studied many images of Jerman's Exchange, and shall demonstrate that, although obliged to follow the plan and arrangement of its predecessor, Jerman succeeded in making the form of the building his own.

When fire consumed the City in September 1666, it destroyed two buildings which, above all others, had embodied its secular and religious nerve centres, the Royal Exchange and St Paul's Cathedral. The rebuilding of these two proud edifices was to be the cause of much debate between the City and the Crown, and all those who submitted plans for a new City laid stress on these two structures, recognising their great significance as symbols of a City reborn, financially and spiritually. The two chosen to design the new Exchange and the new Cathedral were very different men; one a carpenter-turned-designer, the other an astronomer-turned-architect; Jerman, trained in his father's craft, Wren, of Westminster School and Oxford University, and a Gresham professor. For the survival of the City, of London, and indeed of England, the speedy reconstruction of an imposing Exchange was more urgent than that of a great Cathedral. Building started on Jerman's Exchange in the autumn of 1667, and it was opened by the Lord Mayor on 28 September 1669, while work did not actually commence on Wren's Cathedral until 1675, a service of thanksgiving for its completion being held on 22 November 1709. The City and the Mercers, responsible for the rebuilding of the Exchange, had been well satisfied with the design of its predecessor, which had stood for a hundred years and received much praise throughout Europe. They suggested that a similar form should be adopted, and the new Exchange should be built on the old foundations.[1] The new St Paul's went through many gestations before everyone concerned was able to agree on a design acceptable to all of them. Jerman's Exchange strongly resembled its predecessor, Gresham's Exchange, and its prototype, the Antwerp Bourse, while Wren's cathedral displayed a form unknown in England, a domed Latin cross with a strongly centralising stress, which rivalled the great churches of Rome and Paris.[2]

Gresham's Exchange

From time immemorial, Lombard Street had been the meeting place for London merchants: "it does appear that the bourse of Lombard Street is of longer antiquity than any other bourse is known to be of that is within all Europe".[3] Merchants came to London from all over Europe to sell their commodities and to buy English cloth, and together with brokers and speculators, transformed the Lombard Street area into a hub of activity during trading hours. The discomfort they endured by conducting business in the open street was graphically chronicled by Stow:

> The merchants and tradesmen, as well English as strangers from many foreign nations now residing in London, for their general making of bargains, contracts and commerce . . . did usually meet twice every day in Lombard Street . . . but their meetings were unpleasant and troublesome by reasons of walking and talking in an open narrow street, being there constrained either to endure all extremities of weather, viz heat and cold, snow and rain, or else to shelter themselves in shops.[4]

Business was translated in any available premises, and shops, taverns, guild headquarters and coffee houses often served as alternatives to the open street.

As early as 1521, proposals were put forward to use Leadenhall as a bourse. This Hall had been bought by the City Corporation in 1411 but, as it was already used for a wide variety of activities, from storage of the City's ammunition and timber to the preparation of pageants, the plan was met with hostility. By 1527, the congestion and danger caused by a melee of carts, carriages and merchants when meetings were in progress prompted the Court of Aldermen to order a chain to be put across Lombard Street during trading hours. Finally in 1534, the Court of Common Council recommended the creation of "a bourse, and a place meet and convenient for merchants to treat of their feat of merchandise, as is accustomed and used in other noble cities in other outward parts beyond the sea".[5] These other "noble cities" included Bruges, Antwerp and Amsterdam, the bourse typically comprising a quadrangular courtyard surrounded by arcades, similar to monastic cloisters.[6]

Following the Common Council's recommendation, four Aldermen and twelve commoners drawn from the Great Twelve Companies were ordered to deliberate on the matter. It is interesting to note that the City companies were thus involved in negotiations from the start. At this time, houses in Lombard Street were considered the most satisfactory location, the merchants being accustomed to the site.

The impetus was lost, however, until Thomas Gresham, a Mercer, royal agent and European trader, realised both the necessity and the advantages of a properly housed bourse if the City were to maintain its importance as a financial and trading centre. Gresham's business took him to Antwerp, where he lived close by the new Bourse which had been built in 1531 by Dominicus van Waghemaker. This was an elaborate, flamboyant adaptation of its predecessor, and was a three-storey building with arcades set around an open courtyard, having shops on the upper levels and a tall tower at one corner. It was described by Francesco Guicciardini in *Descrizione di Tutti i Paesi Bassi* (1567) as "veramente bella".

What motivated Gresham to create a bourse is open to discussion. It could have been family tragedy linked with a desire to perpetuate his name; altruism, giving the City the advantage of his huge wealth; or self-interest, in the form of rich receipts from shop tariffs. For whatever reason, Gresham advised the City that he would build a bourse at his own expense, as long as the City, for its part, provided a suitable site. However, as Charles Knight comments, "This was not the munificence of a donor, but the calculation of a projector and capitalist. The whole work was done, not by a private citizen, but by many citizens and City companies and the Corporation of London. Moreover, compulsion was used from the first".[7] In January 1565/6, the City accepted Gresham's "gentle and friendly office" and on 9 February that year, Gresham promised that within a month after the bourse should be fully finished he would present it in equal moieties to the City and the Mercers' Company. This was the City's first intimation that it would not have the bourse to itself. Further frustrations ensued when Gresham's will was read following his untimely death in 1579. Not only was the Exchange left jointly to the City and the Mercers, but the profits from it were to be burdened in perpetuity by salaries to be paid to seven lecturers at Gresham College (a new institution of learning set up in Gresham's Bishopsgate house, which he had built in 1559-62), as well as by payments to almsfolk, prisons and hospitals. These outgoings amounted to half the annual income, causing the City and the Mercers to complain that they "take upon them the charge without profit".[8]

Building of the Exchange began in 1566 under the direction of a Flemish architect and contractor, Henryck van Paesschen, a pupil of the renowned Cornelius Floris who was the architect of the Antwerp Town Hall (1561-65), the "proudest town hall of the sixteenth century". The timber frame was set together at Gresham's Suffolk estate, and from there brought to London, while some of the stone was quarried in Wales, and some at Gresham's Norfolk estate. However, most of the stone was shipped from Flanders and a substantial amount of the wainscoting and glass was prepared in Amsterdam. Although Gresham had obtained permission from the Court of Aldermen to employ "such strangers on work and about the making of the same bourse as to him shall be thought requisite and useful", the City's bricklayers were most resentful and caused a near riot.[9] Gresham came to a settlement with the Bricklayers' Company and the workmen were pacified, although the ornamental stonework, so apparent on contemporary engravings, continued to be imported from Amsterdam. The proximity of Gresham's Suffolk estate to Antwerp and Amsterdam facilitated this passage of both men and materials, and his factors, who were resident in the Low Countries, organised their shipment. As John Burgon states, "it is quite surprising to conceive to what extent at this period an English edifice was indebted to continental artificers, not merely for its decorations, but for most of its material features". He adds, "men in all ages have been prone to follow precedent and imitate an approved model".[10] This, of course, was to be equally true of Jerman's Exchange in its resemblance to its predecessor, and so to the Antwerp bourse.

Stow provides a concise history of the construction of the Exchange, which was completed by the end of 1567. Such was the impact of this large, stone, Flemish-style structure in the centre of the City that there remain many images and eye-witness accounts of it, together with poetry and a short play dramatising the reasons for and the form of the building. The Elizabethan age was one of travellers, many of whom kept diaries and wrote tourists' descriptions of the places they visited. Two accounts of Gresham's Exchange have found their way into the Vatican Library. One, in the diary of Zdenek Waldstein, compared its form to the Antwerp bourse, while the other, by the Frenchman L. Grenade, in 1578 concluded, "in all Europe you will not find as fine an edifice for the purposes to which it is dedicated".[11] Other and very diverse Europeans impressed by the grandeur of the building and its statuary, as well as the number of merchants and transactions, were Frederick, Duke of Wirtemberg (1592), Paul Hentzner, a lawyer from Brandenburg (1598), Thomas Platter, a Swiss doctor (1600) and the Duke of Stettin-Pomerania (1602).[12] Evelyn, reiterating the praise of these earlier writers, compared the Amsterdam bourse unfavourably with its London counterpart, "I do not look upon the structure of the Exchange to be compared to that of Sir Thomas Gresham in the City of London". He considered the galleries of the Paris bourse as "nothing so stately as ours in London", and the Venice bourse as "nothing so magnificent".[13]

Webster, Dekker and Middleton all alluded to Gresham's Exchange in their dramatic works, usually employing "lawn" to rhyme with "pawn" in a rather derogatory way. They were implying a certain decadence prevalent amongst the female customers who frequented the "gaudy shops" selling such fine and expensive materials. Thomas Heywood, the dramatist and pageant-poet, devised an entire drama, "The building of the Royal Exchange", as part of his larger two-part play entitled "The Troubles of Queen Elizabeth". He described the building and the unsatisfactory conditions endured by merchants before its erection:

Gresham: . . . it angers me
             That such a famous City as this is
             Wherein so many gallant merchants are
             Has not a place to meet but in this
             Where every shower of rain must trouble them
             . . .
             I'll have a mansion built, and such a roof
             That merchants and their wives, friends and their
                 friends
             Shall walk underneath, as now in Pauls. . . .

Later, the Exchange having been built, Gresham and a colleague discuss its form,
and the reason behind its particular design, providing us with a description every
bit as graphic as the eye-witness accounts:

Dr. Newell: . . . in all my time
             I have not seen a work of this neat form
             What is this vaultage for. . . .

Gresham: Stowage for merchants ware and strangers goods
             As either by exchange or otherwise are vendable.

Dr. Newell: Here is a middle round a far space
             The round is greater, and the space
             Seems open, your conceit for that?

Gresham: The grates give light unto the cellarage
             Upon the which aisle have my friends to walk
             When heaven gives comfortable rain unto the earth
             For that I will have covered.

Dr. Newell: And what of this part is overhead?

Gresham: . . . in this
             There is more ware than in all the rest,
             Here, like a parish for good citizens
             And their fair wives to dwell in, I'll have shops
             Where every day they shall become themselves
             In neat attire. . . .

Dr. Newell: Kind Mr. Gresham, this same work of yours
             Will be a tomb for you after your death;
             A benefit to tradesman and a place
             Where merchants meet. . . .[14]

7.1 Detail of a map of London (1560s) attributed to Ralph Agas, showing Gresham's Exchange.

Gresham's intention of perpetuating his name in the City by willing the edifice to be known as Gresham's Exchange, stressed here by Newell's reference to it as "a tomb for you after your death", was frustrated when Queen Elizabeth made her much chronicled visit in 1571 and proclaimed it not "Gresham's", but the "Royal Exchange".

Several contemporary, and many later engravings depict the Exchange. The huge woodcut map of London ascribed to Ralph Agas was composed in the 1560s, when the Exchange was barely finished. It is probably the earliest representation of the building, and it certainly manages to portray the novelty of the form compared with neighbouring structures (Figure 7.1). Gresham's emblem, the grasshopper, dominates the towers. An exterior view from an engraving by Francis Hogenberg (1569) and Hollar's 1644 depiction of the interior together supplement the written accounts.

Figure 7.2, taken from a "scarce engraving", depicts the south front, an asymmetrical facade of four storeys including shuttered ground-floor shops, two storeys of regular fenestration and dormers. A grand, central, double-arched entrance leads to the courtyard. This entrance is set between two projecting blocks, that on the east being Tendring House, possibly the administration centre of the Exchange, with its double, corner entrance flanked by Ionic columns supporting an entablature repeated in the courtyard. A three-storey tower surmounts Tendring House, complete with balconies, clock and belfry.

Hollar's 1644 engraving (Figure 7.3) provides a good impression of the bustle in the courtyard during trading hours. A groin-vaulted arcade defines the perimeter, its slender Doric columns supporting semicircular arches. The decorated spandrels are surmounted by a frieze of foliage swags. Above in niches, separated by Ionic pilasters, stand statues of England's monarchs. A pronounced block cornice stresses the line of the steeply pitched roof with its dormers. There was thus more than a hint of classicism here, in the symmetry, the stress on the

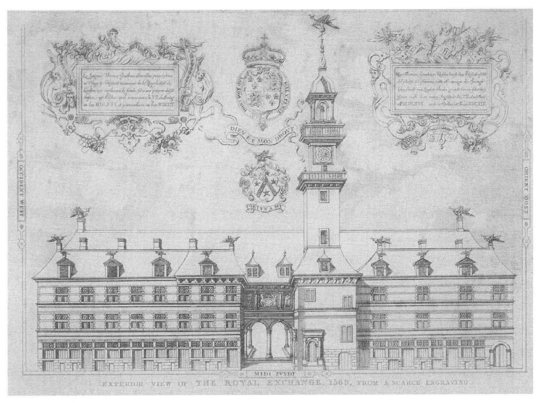

7.2 Exterior of Gresham's Exchange: engraving (1569).

horizontals, voids set upon voids and solids upon solids, and the correct use and form of the orders. As John Ward stated in 1740, "Gresham was unwilling that it should be inferior to any abroad, either for ornament or use, since London was then so eminent a City, both for extent and grandeur, as well as traffic".[15]

John Strype, writing in 1720, was fulsome in his praise of the Second Exchange, and in comparing its form with that of its predecessor, he indicates that Jerman's remit was the regeneration of a very convenient and much-admired building. Comparing Jerman's Exchange with Gresham's, Strype was emphatic that stone replaced wood and brick as the material of choice. He noted that "the stately building in a quadrilateral form, whose brick and wood was so covered with plaster that it imitated stonework" was now rebuilt in excellent Portland stone. Strype continued, "it is now rebuilt with such curious [ingenious] architecture that it far exceeds all other exchanges in Europe. The form of it now, as to the open court and the piazzas, is much the same as before, but without, it is much enlarged, having new piazzas on both the north and south sides, wherein are shops and walks. And whereas before there was but one single row of shops above stairs, there are now double rooms. (Possibly) it is the richest piece of ground in the world, for the ground on which it stands is but 203ft by 171ft and it does produce £4,000 yearly rent".[16]

7.3 Interior of Gresham's Exchange: Wenceslas Hollar engraving (1644).

Sir Thomas Gresham's Exchange stood for exactly a century before falling victim to the Fire on Monday, 3 September 1666. Accounts of the conflagration stress the speed of destruction once the flames had entered the galleries of the Exchange. Both Pepys and Evelyn noted the uncanny particular that all the royal effigies were shattered while that of Gresham, although fallen from its niche, remained intact.[17] For years, Londoners had listened to voices, ancestral and contemporary, amateur and professional, prophesying the doom of their iniquitous city. One of them, Thomas Vincent, although denouncing papists, foreigners, robbers and usurers as well as interpreting the Plague and the Fire as God's vengeance upon such wrong-doers, does actually seem to have been an eye-witness as the Fire consumed the Exchange. He considered that the speed with which the Fire spread was hastened:

> By the train of wood that lay in the streets untaken away, which had been pulled down from houses to prevent its spreading . . . the Royal Exchange itself, the glory of the merchants, is now invaded with violence, and when once the Fire was entered, how quickly did it run round the galleries, filling them with flames, then came downstairs, compasseth the walks, giving forth flaming volleys and filleth the court with sheets of fire, and by and

by down fall the kings upon their faces, and the greatest part of the stone
building after them.[18]
   The speed of the destruction also seems to have impressed Samuel Rolle, writing
in 1667, and poets of varying competence had a field day, many using the
destruction of the Exchange, as much as St Paul's, to exemplify the City's
degradation. Dryden, in 1667, wrote,

    One mighty squadron with a side wind spread
    Through narrow lanes his cumbered fire does haste
    By powerful charm of gold and sliver led
    The Lombard bankers and the change to waste.[19]

While Samuel Ford remarked on Gresham's "survival",

    Her next advance, the Royal change presents,
    Where Gresham thus she complements,
    Hail, flames survivor, though thy noble pile
    Be burnt (she said and wept the while).[20]

   The poem entitled "London's Lamentations" relates the destruction of the
company halls, commonly overlooked in these verses:

    Thus up and down th'incendaries range
    And lay in dust my Royal Old Exchange
    Of most my ancient and renowned halls
    My courts and offices the bared walls
    Those fouler skeletons of once so great
    And framed a beauty, stand in every street.[21]

As well as by the written word, the devastation of the fire was, of course, also
recorded by artists through the media of engraving, drawing and paint, and some
earlier engravings were quickly amended to be of immediate interest by the
addition of flames.

The financial business of the City was resumed as soon as the great intensity of
the Fire had abated, although sporadic outbursts continued for quite some time.
On 7 September, Pepys recounted discussions about reorganisation already
occurring: "this day our merchants first met at Gresham College which by
proclamation is to be their Exchange . . . much dispute where the custom house
would be . . . markets to be kept at Leadenhall".[22] Wren, Evelyn, Hooke, Mills,
Newcourt and Knight all devised plans for a new City which they submitted
with alacrity. Their tasks must have been made difficult by the fact that there had
been no comprehensive pre-Fire plan of the City, neither was the exact extent of
the burnt area known until Wenceslas Hollar, on 10 September 1666, was asked
by the King to "take an exact plan and survey of the city as it now stands after the
calamity of the late Fire".[23] The Exchange became an object of prime concern in
those days immediately following the Fire, and together with St Paul's it was
given pride of place in all the plans proffered to the City and the King.
   From *Parentalia*, we learn that Wren wished the Exchange "to stand free in the

middle of a piazza, and to be, as it were, the nave or centre of the town from whence the 60ft streets, as so many rays, should proceed to all principal parts of the City".[24] He also aimed to unite the halls of the Great Twelve Companies into one regular square, annexed to the Guildhall. In *London Redivivum*, Evelyn declared, "it will be necessary to amplify the old design which was much too narrow for the assemblies. If it should be erected near the Thames, let there be spacious piazzas about it".[25] Thus the sense of spaciousness and the cosmopolitan ambience of Inigo Jones' Covent Garden were clearly deemed worthy of emulation by both Wren and Evelyn. Both stressed the need for the Exchange to be situated in a really prominent position, with access either to great streets or to the river itself. It was indeed, to be at the very hub of the City, as befitted a building in which financial transactions which maintained the country's pre-eminence as one of the leaders in world trade were carried out.

Newcourt envisaged a City composed of squares, some larger, some smaller. In the centre of a great square, he set "a most stately Guildhall . . . and on the west side may be translated the Royal Exchange".[26] He allotted six smaller squares to the Great Twelve Companies, so that they might have terraces and gardens. Hooke, too, laid stress on open spaces. He set his churches and other public buildings in convenient locations, the Exchange as an island site with an open space on its southern aspect. Of course, all these grand plans were laid aside and came to nothing: the City could not afford to wait while the pros and cons of the various schemes were discussed. Time was the critical factor, and the renaissance of the Royal Exchange was crucial as the supreme symbol to present to the world that, for the City of London, it was "business as usual". The Exchange was rebuilt in two years, while other buildings, vital for the City's prosperity and safety, were not replaced with the same sense of urgency. Although severely damaged, much of the Guildhall survived the Fire, but repairs and renovations took ten years to complete. Newgate prison, totally destroyed and rebuilt with "great magnificence", was finished by 1672. The cost of these buildings was met by the coal tax. Wren's Custom House, built on its previous site at the King's expense, was back in business four years after the Fire.

Jerman's Exchange

Such was the determination of the Aldermen, that on 6 September, they convened a special court at Gresham House, beyond the ravages of the Fire, and ordered that "the Exchange shall be kept in the garden or walks of Gresham House which is to be speedily fitted and prepared for that occasion".[27] Gresham's Bishopsgate House, notable for its extent rather than any architectural beauty, was composed of one main storey and attics, its quadrangle with walks and trees imbuing it with an inward-looking, collegiate air. The spread of buildings round a central court, with brick arcades on the northern and southern sides (Figure 7.4) made it an obvious choice for the re-housing of the Exchange, especially since it was

7.4 Courtyard of Gresham College: engraving (1761).

already administered by the City Corporation and the Mercers. A delightful note creeps into the record, which reads, "the Governor of the East India Company is therefore desired to remove the pepper out of the said walks with all convenient speed",[28] presumably to prevent the merchants becoming further inconvenienced!

The first Joint Committee responsible for the Exchange, composed of the City and the Mercers' Company under the leadership of the Lord Mayor and Master, assembled at Gresham College on 18 September. Uppermost in their minds was the accommodation of the Exchange tenants. It was essential that the interruption to business should be kept to a minimum, but equally important was the income from rents. A subcommittee was appointed to allocate space at the College, every possible part being considered, including "the several lodgings of the lecturers and the public rooms thereunto belonging, as also the warehouses, cellars . . . sheds and other buildings in and about Gresham College, together with the almshouses". It was decided that the quadrangle could be divided "into about 100 shops which may accommodate the tenants of the upper pawn of the Royal Exchange, and some of the tenants below, appertaining to the City and the Company, upon a competent rent".[29]

On 19 October 1666, Edward Jerman and Peter Mills became involved with Exchange affairs: "to contrive a larger passage out of the yard on [the College's] Bishopsgate Street side into the place now used for the Exchange meetings". From Vertue's delightful engraving of the College (Figure 7.5), on which he indicated all the lodgings as well as the subsidiary buildings, we can appreciate that the

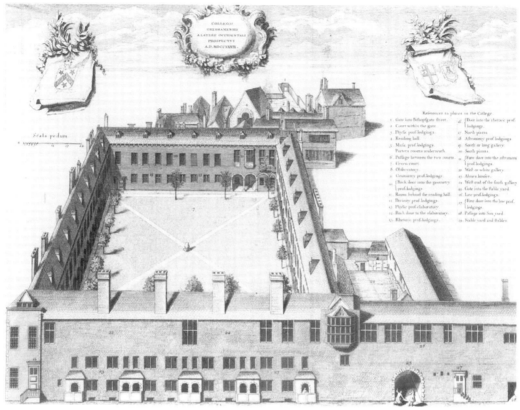

7.5 Gresham College: George Vertue engraving (1740).

original passage and gate through to Bishopsgate Street would have been totally inadequate for the numbers of people who were to start using it as a means of entry and exit. It was not only very small and narrow, but positioned at the easternmost point (top of image), at the furthest possible position from the centre of the complex.

At the same meeting, Mills and Jerman were also required to "view the Exchange ruins and to appoint labourers to separate the lead, iron, stone and rubbish, and to order some person to oversee the work and to look after the materials. Further, to view in what condition the arches over the vaults are, and whether they may be amended without taking down".[30] So, the same priorities applied here as with the Fishmongers, and indeed with any building of substance: to view the ruins, save whatever materials were redeemable, check on the viability of the remaining fabric, whether to amend or demolish, and appoint a supervisor. Over and above this, they were to "view the galleries in Gresham College, viz. whether they are sufficient without further support to bear the weight of the Exchange shops and concourse of people who frequent it".[31] The Committee was clearly fearful that the hundred-year-old house might collapse under the strain of so many people, and so much coming and going, it having been described, one remembers, as having a "quiet collegiate air".[32]

Jerman's and Mills' report came back very promptly on 23 October, providing detailed answers to all the questions which had been put to them: "We viewed the galleries of this house wherein are appointed shops for the Exchange tenants and do judge their strengths to be sufficient to bear the burden intended for them without any additional support". This must have been a relief for the Committee, for it meant that the tenants could be speedily re-housed and therefore obliged to pay much needed rents. Rebuilding could not be contemplated were there to be any long-term disruption to income. However, Mills and Jerman had less welcome news about the state of the Exchange: "We viewed the condition of the arches over the cellars which we found very bad viz: the north-west and south-east angles to be fallen in, and that on the north-east ready to fall which may cost £350 to make good, but do not advise the doing thereof before the City and the Company [i.e., the Joint Committee] do resolved to go in hand with the building, in regard it cannot be kept dry".[33] Thus Mills and Jerman were certainly not advocating piecemeal patching-up: they were both sufficiently experienced craftsmen to realise that was no long-term solution. They reported to the Committee that they had put in hand the separation of building materials and rubbish, with a view to re-using as much as possible, and that they had appointed two men to oversee this work and safeguard the materials.

Despite some grumblings, the Exchange tenants seem to have readjusted to their cramped conditions and to the general congestion, while the Exchange keepers acted as marshall at the Bishopsgate entrance. Stalls were set up in the quadrangle, making it an unusual cross-section of people who spent the next few years cheek-by-jowl in this Bishopsgate house. Their very clothing must have been so varied, from the aldermanic gowns of the City officials, to the new style petticoat breeches (a frivolity popularised by the euphoria of the Restoration) adopted by company dignitaries; from the flamboyant merchants, both English and foreign, to the stall keepers. Finally, there were the female customers, so criticised by the poets for their gaudy clothes of silk and lawn. Through this melee, Mills and Jerman passed regularly to discuss Exchange business. Did they dress as artisans or gentlemen? In Shakespeare's day, artisans had been identifiable by their clothes, viz: the start of *Julius Caesar*:

Flavius: . . . you ought not to walk
                 Upon a labouring day without the sign
                 Of your profession – speak, what trade art thou?
Carpenter: Why, sir, a carpenter.
Murellus: Where is thy leather apron and thy rule
                 What do'st thou with thy best apparel on?[34]

One cannot imagine that Jerman appeared at Gresham College complete with leather apron and rule. As a Surveyor, and a Company man of several years standing, he probably wore a less extravagant version of a City gentleman's outfit.

The City and the Mercers granted the Committee full powers to make decisions about the rebuilding, but before any such decisions could be made some estimate of cost was necessary. On November 2, Hooke, Mills and Jerman were requested to make an assessment of the state of the Exchange, to discover the condition of the foundations, what remaining materials might be useful in building, and then to estimate the cost of rebuilding upon the old foundations. Those grandiose City plans submitted to the King had been laid aside, and the Exchange was to be built on its old foundations, not as the centre of any cobweb street plan, nor with direct access to a quay. However, the best advice was being sought. It must be remembered that by this time, Hooke, Jerman and Mills had been appointed the City's representatives to survey the streets, along with Wren, May and Pratt, chosen by the King, and they were already starting their work. At the same time, Jerman, as surveyor to the Fishmongers' Company was travelling to and from Bray to check on timber supplies, as well as surveying the Company's houses and staking the bounds of their lands. For the Goldsmiths' Company, he was overseeing repairs to their Hall and property, and with Mills, he was reporting on damage and advising about repairs to Leadenhall. He was thus rapidly gaining experience in a diversity of fields vital for his work at the Exchange.

It is understandable that with such a workload Jerman was not present at the next meeting at Gresham College called one week later. Peter Mills attended, and "excused the not doing the work by reason of the shortness of time". Mills also explained to the Committee that the surveyors had not been instructed with what materials the new Exchange was to be built, so estimates of costs were not possible. The Committee assured Peter Mills that they intended to build "with such materials as were used in the former building", except for the columns, which they thought would be "better made of a certain marble found in the West country, rather than that of the Normandy stone of which they were made before".[35] Mills was asked to make an estimate "of the total charge". Meanwhile, Robert Hooke was asked to report and estimate, and from Hooke's report, we learn of what materials Gresham's Exchange was built. It had been composed, for the great part, of brick and stone, for Hooke informed the Committee that "there are more than half bricks enough to rebuild, and there is a great quantity of stone". The pedestals of the pillars were only slightly fire-damaged, and the arches and fronts of both entries "were little hurt". Hooke's estimate of the cost of rebuilding "in the same form as it was heretofore" must have gladdened the hearts of the Committee: "the whole charge will amount to £4,500 supposing all the materials are bought anew".[36] He was clearly considering patching up wherever possible, rather than a complete reconstruction. The Committee requested more details, but there is no evidence that Hooke ever made an exact survey of the site.

Over the next two months, the Committee played cat-and-mouse games, showing Hooke the Mills-Jerman estimate of work to be done, "the price only excepted" and requiring Hooke to "add prices thereto". Finally, in the new year, the Committee decided to commence the rebuilding, in ignorance of where it would lead them financially, so that "the season of the year may not be lost", and "for an encouragement for others". It was decided that the Lord Mayor should call a grand Committee to raise money, for money was "the only engine that can give vigorous motion to that great and needful work".[37] This meeting seems to have provided the impetus that had been lacking, and four days later Mills and Jerman were requested to review the ruins and to order "whatsoever may be preparatory to the building". The Committee decided that the creation of new streets on the east and west sides of the Exchange would be advantageous, and Mills and Jerman were asked how much ground would be necessary to realise such a plan, and to warn the tenants of such ground of the Committee's intention. At the same time, the masons Marshall and Young were required to investigate the cost of quarrying and carriage of Portland stone.

On 4 March 1666/7, the Committee finally decided that it was time to appoint "an able person or persons for surveyors and directors, and judging that none can be more serviceable than Mr Mills or Mr Jerman, they being now present were asked whether they could intend the business".[38] Peter Mills immediately accepted the post, but Jerman asked for some time to consider. A week later, Jerman was still unsure whether to accept the appointment, perhaps because he felt that the terms of his employment as "a surveyor and director" were less favourable than those of Peter Mills. The records are somewhat ambiguous, but it seems that there was some uncertainty, as we shall see, about his role vis-à-vis the street surveys, and he was awaiting the outcome of a Common Council meeting to clarify his position. By this time, the Mercers themselves had approached Jerman with a proposal to undertake the surveying not only the ground on which their Hall and Chapel stood, but all the contiguous ground, as well as that which they owned around Cheapside. On 20 March, his appointment as Company Surveyor for the rebuilding of Mercers' Hall and Chapel was formalised. Jerman already had long-standing commitments as Company Surveyor to the Fishmongers and Company Carpenter to the Goldsmiths, and one can sympathise with his hesitation in taking on an assignment such as the Exchange, with all its potential pitfalls.

The Committee met again a week later to discuss the question of masonry. Peter Mills was requested to compare his figures with those of Marshall and Young, only to find that the latter had come to no valuation of the turret, staircases and frontispieces "because of the present uncertainty how the same shall be built". The Committee was clearly looking for someone to help them out of this impasse, and lighted upon Thomas Cartwright, the mason, "to attend with the prices of stonework according to the valuation". It was Cartwright who would take over the responsibility for the Exchange after Jerman's death, and under whose direction the costs of the Exchange were to escalate. His estimates were on the table the following week.

By 15 April, the Committee was becoming extremely anxious that building time was being lost while they waited for a reply from Edward Jerman. He explained to them that "unless the City were pleased to put him into the same capacity of surveyor with Mr Mills, he could not attend the business, but was otherwise engaged to entertain such proffers as were made him by private persons". Jerman seems to have done little of the surveying of the devastated area, and it was left to Hooke, Mills and John Oliver to discharge the post-Fire surveys. Meanwhile, Jerman was accepting the "proffers from private persons", namely nine City companies (see Chapter 3). The Committee, well aware of his capabilities and experience was most determined to engage Jerman, "a known artist, rather than any other that may be commended to them, less known, and in whom they cannot have that satisfaction". The failure to achieve a formal agreement with Mills and Jerman had sprung "from the over much business [heavy workload] of Mr Mills and from some dissatisfaction in Mr Jerman", and the Committee hoped that "such small remorse may no longer stop the carrying on so great and so considerable a work as rebuilding the Royal Exchange".[39]

By 22 April 1667, in spite of the consensus on the urgency of the project, the Joint Committee had not yet appointed a designer, nor come to any decisions about how closely they wanted the new Exchange to resemble its predecessor, nor the type of stone they intended to use. Perhaps the machinery had become unwieldy: too many people had been consulted and were making conflicting suggestions. As well as the Committee, which comprised nineteen men, Mills, Jerman and Hooke were involved, as well as Cartwright, Marshall and Young. It would take a resolute man to take charge of such a project.

After some initial hesitation, Edward Jerman proved to be that resolute man. On 25 April, he was finally persuaded to accept the position of designer/surveyor of the Royal Exchange:

> Forasmuch as Mr Mills, the City Surveyor, hath declared that he cannot perform the work alone, and the Committee being very sensible of the great burden of business lying upon him for the City at this time, and considering that Mr Jerman is the most able known artist (beside him) that the City now hath, the Committee unanimously made choice of Mr Jerman to assist the Committee with agreeing for, ordering and directing that work. And having declared the same unto him, he after much reluctancy and unwillingness (objecting, it might be thought an entrenchment upon Mr Mills, his right) at length accepted. . . .[40]

What greater compliment and acknowledgement, not only of his artistry, but also his organisational skills could have been paid to Edward Jerman? He, a carpenter by training, had progressed to become a Company Surveyor and had now metamorphosed into the architect of the most prestigious building in the City at the time, entreated to accept the post by that formidable and powerful group of City businessmen.

Edward Jerman immediately presented the Committee with eight "particulars", and required answers from them concerning the form of the building, whether it should follow exactly the pattern of its predecessor, the appointment of master-craftsmen, and the provision of materials. After the committee had read and considered the proposals, they agreed:

> That the Exchange shall be built upon the old foundations. That number of pillars and arches and the manner of their roof be left to Mr Jerman to

model according to the rules of art, for the best advantage of the whole structure. That Cartwright be employed for the doing of the mason's work upon condition that he will agree upon as easy terms as other able men of that trade will do it for. That the Committee provide stone of several sorts, timber for the floors and roofs, deal baulke and other necessaries for the fencing in the ground, and making centres for the arches. Agreeing with the mason, carpenter and bricklayer be all left to the care of Mr Jerman provided that when he hath brought the agreement with the workmen to an head, he do impart it to the Committee for confirmation.[41]

Thus Edward Jerman was cast in the role of architect-surveyor, in overall charge of the building. Just how much autonomy the master-craftsmen such as Cartwright and Roger Jerman (who had been appointed carpenter on 23 April) had is not clear, nor is there any indication of the degree of detail laid down in the designs Edward made following the acceptance of his stipulations. An intriguing reference to those designs for the Exchange was made by W. Tite Esq., in 1846 when he stated, "Two large and beautiful drawings of Jerman's designs for the building, executed in Indian ink upon vellum. . . . These drawings belong to R.W. Jupp Esq., of Carpenters' Hall and are considered to be contemporary with Jerman's building".[42] Unfortunately, extensive investigations have failed to find any further trace of these drawings which would have been so valuable in understanding Jerman's intentions for the Exchange.

Work was finally under way, and an exultant memorandum reads, "The 6 day of May 1667, the workmen began the work of rebuilding the Royal Exchange". Very soon, Jerman realised that the covered walks would have to be widened, and by convincing the Committee that the work could be effected without any further cost, he secured their consent. At the same time, he recognised that none of the salvaged bricks was suitable for his new arches and vaults, and was given permission to bargain for them "at the reasonablest rate" he could. He must have decided that the choice of stone was too important to delegate to others, and set off on a quest, visiting quarries on the Isle of Portland, in Somerset and Gloucestershire, with the aid of a warrant from the Surveyor-General Sir John Denham. He found Portland stone to be to his liking, and contracted with Mr Switzer, the chief quarryman, to have 300 tons delivered to the Port of London.[43] While preliminary work continued on the Exchange during the summer, Edward Jerman was busy with several other projects. He had prepared plans for the Mercers in July; for the Halls of the Drapers, Weavers and Fishmongers in August; and for the Haberdashers by the beginning of September. The output of this man was phenomenal, and when one considers the constraints put upon him, his skill was truly remarkable. Like Wren, pondering designs for his City churches, Jerman was for the main part required to build on old foundations, so was obliged to modify his ideas to existing limits. He was dealing with committees who all the time were stressing speed and economy, yet aimed to improve on the constraints imposed on them by their previous rather inconvenient accommodation. On top of these considerations, he was working for powerful men, in a rich, commercial world – a daunting prospect even for a robust personality.

On 20 September 1667 the Committee approved Jerman's designs, but before proceeding further decided that they must be shown to the King for his approval. Accordingly, the Lord Mayor and Edward Jerman, together with two representatives from the City and two from the Mercers, presented Jerman's drafts to Charles II (these were, possibly, the two designs on vellum mentioned above). Edward Jerman was moving in ever-exalted circles, and by declaring an interest in the project, the King was aiming to ingratiate himself with the City and to link his name with its functional heart. From this time on, the Committee no longer had a free hand in the design of the Exchange. Although throughout much of the seventeenth century, the relationship between the City and the Crown had been an uneasy one, the ranks of English monarchs lining the walls of Gresham's Exchange had expressed to the world the interdependence between the two. Charles II, whose effigy had been added to their numbers in 1660, was now to show an interest in the reconstruction of this pantheon.

A week later, the King gave his blessing to the design, singling out for praise the south portico. He considered, as had the City planners, that the Exchange should be set free from any adjacent buildings, "in regard it is of so public and eminent a concern for the honour of the City", but stressed that "no private person may be wronged in the inheritance without having just satisfaction given him for the same".[44] If the Committee were to follow the King's wishes, the City and the Mercers would inevitably be involved in the huge expense of a general clearance scheme, not to mention the time that would be lost wrangling over compensation. Indeed, the "private persons" proved to be determined to make as great a financial gain as they could in response to the King's request for proper recompense.

In October, in a show of royal solidarity, the King fixed the first pillar, and was entertained lavishly "in a shed built and adorned for the purpose upon the Scottish walk", while similar rituals were performed by the Duke of York and Prince Rupert. Rumours reached the Committee that some landlords were about to start rebuilding on ground intended for the enlarged Exchange site. Jerman was ordered "to give them all the lawful hindrance he may", and an appeal was made to the Court of Aldermen to obstruct such building "by the Supplemental Act presented to Parliament about building in the City". At this point, it is difficult to determine whether delay or cost was the Committee's greater headache, but on 9 December work started on the two major sides, the north and the south, seemingly riding roughshod over the tenants and owners of the contiguous ground. The Committee finally voted Jerman some "gratification for his pains about drawing drafts and directing the building". He was paid £50 upon account, "until further consideration of his merits". Meanwhile, Cartwright was paid £200, "Mr. Jerman having first satisfied the Committee that the work done did require so much money". A careful check was being kept on Cartwright's expenditure, and one must assume that a large proportion of the £200 comprised money paid out on materials and contract labour. The Committee urged Jerman "if he find any unnecessary persons at the Exchange, to turn them out of employment". Cibber, the sculptor, hoped that his early application to make royal statues, under the patronage of the Earl of Manchester, would ensure the commission, but, a terse reply from the Committee assured him that "the business of making staues is yet very remote from their thoughts, having the whole Exchange to build first".

Perhaps with the spirit of Christmas upon it, the Committee entertained Denham and May at the Sun Tavern. Denham was thanked for his help with the Portland stone, and May was able to reassure the Committee of the King's approbation of the Exchange design. However, the Christmas spirit seems to have been lacking when Sir John "assured the Committee that if the landowners and tenants refused reasonable compensation, and presume to build in contradiction and hindrance of the works, then His Majesty and Council will interpose their authority to give a stop to their proceedings until an Act of Parliament can be obtained".[45] Perhaps this was a seventeenth-century compulsory purchase order.

By February, the rising cost of materials was worrying the Committee, and although it paid £200 each to Cartwright and Roger Jerman, and £100 to Mr. Switzer, it urged Edward Jerman with the assistance of John Oliver to "consider a way of how extraordinary charges upon Portland stone may be reduced". Due to the amount of work being carried out all over the City, materials were becoming ever more expensive and more difficult to obtain; even street scavengers had trebled their charges.[46] Although the records furnish us with no details, we assume, as Ann Saunders states, that "work went doggedly on", but in September, the design of the Exchange was still under debate. The main problem facing the Committee was the number of shops that should be provided. The former lessees prayed that "the Committee would not think of building a double pawn of shops because it would bring ruin upon them". They feared that the Exchange would be unable to sustain so many shops, that a single row set around the perimeter of the first floor would be sufficient. However, the subtenants presented a petition, "praying that a double pawn of shops be built . . . because it will be more magnificent and pleasing to His Majesty . . . and showing the advantage it will bring to the City and the Company". To these subtenants, a double row of shops simply meant double the revenue.[47] Edward Jerman was not party to this discussion; his disease was beginning to manifest itself. The Committee, seemingly unaware, or perhaps indifferent to his ill-health, sent word to enquire about his absence and required him "to order and compose all differences, that the building may go cheerfully on". It would seem that the Committee, unable to agree upon this vital decision, was abdicating its responsibility in favour of Edward Jerman.

Throughout September, Jerman's alternative plans were studied: "one with a single pawn throughout and warehouses behind every shop and the other with a single pawn south and north . . . and a double pawn east and west", and on 1 October, the Committee, "having considered thoroughly all the reasons pro

7.6 Jerman's Royal Exchange: Robert White engraving (1671).

and con, they resolved to go on with the building porticoes on all sides and a double pawn of shops above".[48] The Committee chided the workmen about their slow progress through the summer, but received the sharp reply that their tardiness sprang from uncertainty about the form the building was to take. They were nonetheless urged to proceed with all haste. Edward Jerman's last dealings with the Exchange took place on 22 October 1668, in connection with the extortionate compensation one of the tenants was demanding for his ground, and within a week, Jerman was dead.

A month later, Thomas Cartwright "declared himself master of the whole design intended for the building", and the Committee asked him to proceed "vigorously with the work" and to give them an estimate of "the outside building viz. of the cupola and porticoes etc". All the time, the costs were escalating, "the charge given by the workmen since Mr. Jerman's death far exceeding the estimate given by him",[49] and in the next two years, when the bulk of Roger Jerman's carpentry work would be effected, he was reprimanded three times concerning demands

7.7 South front of Jerman's Royal Exchange: English School (1702-14), pen and wash on vellum.

for money. Finally, in January 1670/71, Cartwright was given authority to employ an alternative carpenter, should Roger's demands prove unreasonable.

By March 1668/9, the stone shell of the Exchange's exterior was completed, but the thorny problem of the porticoes had still to be concluded. The Committee realised that the King's wish that the Exchange should stand in grand isolation with porticoes all the way round, would involve endless negotiations over land acquisition, and so it persuaded Wren to disabuse the king of his resolve. Wren was successful; the king agreed that the Exchange should have porticoes on the north and south aspects only.[50] Suddenly, the frustration and setbacks were a thing of the past, and a new surge of energy seems to have infused the operation. Roger Jerman was urged to "speedily make and finish one of the corner cupola windows and two of the lucerne lights [see Figure 7.9] so that the Committee may be able to judge of their fitness to distribute light to the prospective shops before they give order for doing the whole", and to complete "the whole timberwork of the inner quadrangle, employing such a number of men, and such care and industry about the same that no other trades shall stay for him".[51] Clearly, Roger's timberwork did not hold up any of the other workmen, for on 10 July

7.8 South front of Jerman's Royal Exchange. Thomas Malton, pen and ink (1781).

1669, an inscription was set up over the south entrance inside the quadrangle:

Ex Cambium Hoc anno 1666 in cineres reductum in plusquam antiquum
splendorem, Praetore Will'mo Turnero, Equite, anno 1669, restitutum fuit.[52]

The Exchange was declared open for trading on 28 September 1669 by the Lord
Mayor. Thomas Jordan's pageant, though written especially for the occasion and
incorporating a perspective scene of the Exchange in ruins, together with music
by Purcell, was done "with but small ceremony", because "His Majesty came not
down according to hope and expectation". This must have been a bitter
disappointment to all those who had expended so much time and energy on the
project, particularly after the King's interest and intervention.

Meanwhile, Roger Jerman's work went on. During the early phase of the
construction, this would have entailed the erection of scaffolding, and centring
for the arches. Now, with the masonry more or less completed, he was working
on the shops, galleries and stairs. In April 1670, he laid floors in the galleries (or
pawns). These were to be of good yellow deal, while the joists and ground plates, the
weight-bearing members were of stronger oak. By August 1670, he was building:

the shops and pawn under the south and north porticoes according to the
draft made by Mr. Cartwright, for which he is to have the following rates viz.:

7.9 Interior of Gresham's Exchange: George Vertue engraving (1739).

For the front storey running measure with all ornaments per foot	£1-8s-0d
For flooring with one another per square	£2-0s-0d
For partitioning per square	£1-0s-0d
For each stair step	2s-0d
For rail and ballister per foot	1s-8d

By itemising the component parts of Roger's work, the Committee was trying to keep a track on expenditure; the cost of the building had far exceeded any forecast. Roger Jerman finished his part of the woodwork of the interior when he laid the rest of the floors in April 1671.[53]

Finally, we come to the question of the tower, a three-tiered structure that surmounted the south entrance of the Exchange. Whether Edward or Roger Jerman or Cartwright designed the tower is not clear, but as Ann Saunders states, the tower "was not unlike the steeples that Wren was designing for the City churches; it is perhaps worth noting that Cartwright was the contractor of St Mary-le-Bow".[54] In January 1670/71, Cartwright and Jerman conferred about "rates for the timberwork of the cupilo" and Roger requested the "liberty to frame the

7.10 Interior Courtyard of Jerman's Royal Exchange: English School, pen and wash on vellum (1702-14).

7.11 Interior of Jerman's Royal Exchange: Thomas Malton, pen and ink (1781).

cupilo in the Green Yard". The Committee agreed that this would be "near and convenient, and resolved that the Lord Mayor desired to move the Committee for the City Lands that lease may be granted accordingly". This "cupilo" might have referred to the whole of the three-storey tower, or simply to the uppermost section or even its domical roof: it is not possible to discern from images of what material the tiers were made. Ingvid Roscoe states that above the frontispiece was "a wooden tower, soaring up 178 feet",[55] and certainly, by 1821, the woodwork of the tower was found to be rotten and the entire structure was replaced in stone. Whether this total replacement was for aesthetic or structural reasons is not known.

The whole operation had taken just over two years, and cost £58,122-17s-4d, instead of Hooke's original estimate of £4-5,000. Of this, £51,456-7s-4d was spent on construction work, materials and labour, and £6,666-10s for additional land, particularly that required for porticoes, so much the preference of the king. The Corporation of the City was able to recoup a fair amount of its share of this money from the coal tax, but the half share that the Mercers were obliged to pay, together with the rebuilding costs of their own Hall and properties, brought them to the

7.12 North front of Jerman's Royal Exchange: Thomas Malton, pen and ink (1781).

verge of bankruptcy.

In the Mercers' Company Renter Wardens' account books between April 1667 and 1672, there are fifty-nine entries of payment to Roger Jerman, totalling about £3,500. This represented the Mercers' moiety of payment to him "for work and stuff at the Royal Exchange".[56] This sum, together with the City's share, would have brought his total earnings at the Exchange to £7,000. In the two years of Edward Jerman's employment, the Mercers' moiety to him was £60, his total earnings therefore being £120. However, his widow did receive £50, "in recompense of her late husband's pains in contriving and surveying the building of the Royal Exchange until his death". When one considers that the entertainment of Denham and May at the Sun Tavern, together with a gift of wine and gloves for the Surveyor-General amounted to £44, Edward Jerman's remuneration seems paltry indeed.

The accounts also reveal that, between 1667 and 1673, the Mercers paid Thomas Cartwright £8,000 as their half of his work at the Exchange. Cartwright's situation was different from Roger Jerman's, for he was not obliged to buy the stone; its purchase was negotiated directly between the Company and the quarries. From his payment, which was over twice that of Roger Jerman, he had only to pay his craftsmen. This seems to imply that the masonry work at the Royal Exchange far

7.13 North front of Jerman's Royal Exchange.

exceeded the carpentry work, if the men were on the same pay scale. From the payments to various groups of craftsmen, it is possible to discern that much of the wainscoting was done in 1668-69 by the joiners Thomas Turner and Richard Clere, the brickwork in 1669-70 (apart from the brickwork of the shops which was completed in 1670-71), and the glazing and plastering in 1671-72. In the year 1667-68, the total cost of stone, including freight, wharfage, cartage and loading was £4,600. Of course there is no record of the purchase of wood because that was supplied by Roger Jerman.[57]

Although Edward Jerman's plans for the Exchange have been lost, its reputation and importance ensured its commemoration in words and images. Engravings, many derived from Robert White's birds-eye view of 1671 (Figure 7.6), as well as oil paintings and pen-and-wash drawings were produced. Colen Campbell included a plan and south elevation in volume II of *Vitruvius Britannicus* (1725) and Thomas Malton's four views in his *Picturesque Tour through the Cities of London and Westminster* (1792) include a rare view of the Exchange's north front to Threadneedle Street. It is from such images, as well as eye-witness accounts, that one can build up a fairly clear picture of the form of Jerman's Exchange.

The south front to Cheapside, depicted in Figure 7.7, was the Exchange's principal entrance, with its tower and royal statues. It consisted of thirteen bays, compared with the twelve of its predecessor, the nine bays of porticoes being set forward of the two at each end. The three central bays, surmounted by the three-storeyed tower, were in the form of a triumphal arch, with a large central and two tiny lateral arches. Above the latter, in aedicules surmounted by open pediments, statues of Charles I and Charles II greeted the arriving merchants: these flamboyant figures were sculpted by John Bushnell in 1671. Above the aedicules were round windows wreathed by laurel leaves. Giant Corinthian columns supported semicircular pediments over these lateral bays, with the royal arms above the central archway. The three bays on either side of this central section showed some resemblance to the New Gallery (1661-62) of Somerset House which, in Summerson's words, "bore an interpretation of the Bramantesque theme of an order raised on open rusticated arches".[58] In the case of the Exchange, the order was in the form of Composite half columns set in front of pilasters, above which the full entablature broke forward. These half columns separated tall, square-headed windows with lugged surrounds and aprons with recessed panels – recurring features in Jermans' designs. An emphasised string course separated the rusticated arcades from the smooth piano nobile, and this strong horizontal stress was echoed by a crowning balustrade. It was therefore a restrained façade, and although James Ralph condemned the tower as "being a weight to the whole building and broken into so many parts that it rather hurts than pleases", he allowed that the entrance was very grand and august.[59] The tower provoked considerable criticism, and it certainly seems to have dominated the south front, demonstrating an encyclopaedia of architectural forms. Its three tiers were square in cross-section, with tall, round-headed windows on each face. The angles were stressed by columns set in front of pilasters, and these are particularly evident in Malton's preparatory drawing of 1782 (Figure 7.8). In each storey, a full entablature broke forward over the Composite capitals, that of the second storey being surmounted by a balustrade. The pedimented top section was crowned by a small cupola carrying a weather vane in the form of Gresham's grasshopper. Was this cupola Roger Jerman's contribution, as has been suggested, or Cartwright's adaptation of Edward Jerman's tower? No records enlighten us.

Although the exterior of Jerman's Exchange was thus very different from its predecessor, the plan and interior arrangement were very similar to Gresham's building (Figure 7.9), to the Antwerp Bourse and indeed the Amsterdam Exchange. The central courtyard was defined by four arcades, seven bays on the north and south sides, five on the east and west. The elliptical arches were supported by Doric columns set on low pedestals, while on the inner walls, the wainscoting reached the level of the groin vaulting. The black and white Turkey stones, carefully preserved from Gresham's Exchange, are evident in many contemporary images. White's engraving of 1671 (Figure 7.6) depicts the niches of the piano nobile anticipating their royal occupants, while the pen and wash drawing (Figure 7.10), made sometime between 1702 and 1714, shows many of the statues in

7.14 Foster Lane façade of Goldsmiths' Hall: engraving (1750).

position. The central bay on each side was stressed by a pedimented triumphal arch motif, the other bays being separated by pilasters. There was again a strong emphasis on horizontals and above the niches, Jerman introduced small elliptical windows with a horizontal axis, a motif which he repeated on the north front. Roger Jerman's corner cupolas and lucerne lights are visible behind the encircling balustrades, and the sectional portions give some indication of the extent of his carpentry as described. Malton gives us an artist's impression of the interior of the Exchange in his preparatory drawing of 1782 (Figure 7.11), stressing the ornamental features that appealed to him. This drawing predates a similar engraving (Plate 67) in *A Picturesque Tour*, and from it, we can appreciate such details as the necking of the Doric columns, the coffering of the arches and the cartouches surmounted by feathers which are set in the springing of the arches.

There are very few images of the Exchange's north front to Threadneedle Street, but Malton's drawing (Figure 7.12), reproduced in his *Picturesque Tour* (Figure 7.13) shows its thirteen bays, with a nine bay central projection of porticoes.[60] Emphasis was again laid on the central section. Here, Jerman played with rhythms, creating an interesting ambiguity. Using the notation A-B-A-C-A-B-A, where A is a small rectangular window with an elliptical one above, B is a large rectangular window and C is a large triangular pedimented aperture, the inner A forms can be read as belonging to the middle triad with C at its centre, or to the outer triad with B at its centre, thereby setting up a tension. Jerman was, of course, restoring

Goldsmiths' Hall at this time, and there, the three end bays of the eleven bay façade were composed of just the same window forms, one large rectangular and (in that instance) one circular (Figure 7.14). Thus Jerman was able to pluck this motif from Nicholas Stone's façade and create a lively dynamism from it. The lower central section was again rusticated, the large central archway being flanked by two triumphal arch forms whose central arches were surmounted by strangely raised semicircular pediments. Angle quoins stressed the limits of the projecting bays, and the arches, with pronounced keystones, were supported by rusticated pillars. Above these, Jerman's windows with lugs and aprons were topped by a balustrade. In the recessed lateral bays, Jerman has playfully reversed the axes of the elliptical windows from vertical to horizontal, echoing those of the interior.

Although sketchy and untitled, a pen and wash drawing by Giovanni David (1786) in the Royal Collection at Windsor, accords with Colen Campbell's plan (*Vitruvius Britannicus* 2: pl.23) and Malton's illustrations.[61] David's drawing makes the north front look more classical than does Malton's, probably due to the detail David has invested in the projecting pedimented section. However, it was the south front that captured the attention of eighteenth-century critics, including Strype, Hatton, Ralph, Maitland and Malton, and the tower, not built until well after Edward's death, which came in for most of the criticism.

Edward Hatton, in 1708, claimed that "the beauties of this structure are too many to be particularised", but then went on to give a most thorough description of all parts of the building, including a detailed architectural account of the tower. He passed no aesthetic judgement on the tower, but Malton condemned it as being "in very bad taste", suggesting that it should have been designed "in a more simple style". Maitland (1756) merely remarked on the dimensions of the Exchange, employed adjectives such as "substantial" and "regular", and dwelt on the statuary and heraldic devices.

For late seventeenth-century poets, the re-opening of the Exchange was reason for celebration, not criticism, as expressed in a poem of 1672:

> View now this front, and there thou may'st espy
> Such curious work, fitting for majesty
> Itself to dwell in; And we do believe
> In all thy travels, thou did'st ne'er perceive
> A place like this. And herein thou may'st say
> To all the rest, that they must now give way
> We have the Phoenix in our English nation
> All those who new it stand in admiration.
> View but the stars here on the southern side
> And thou shalt see some reason for our pride
> And present boasting, when we say there's none
> Which can compare unto this place of stone.[62]

CHAPTER 8

Edward Jerman's work
for other City companies

Edward Jerman's work for most of the City companies that employed him is more scantily documented than that for the Fishmongers and Goldsmiths, whose clerks assiduously recorded the detail of every committee meeting, with minute books extending over many volumes. The clerks of most companies, on the other hand, appear to have recorded meetings in an abridged form, the day-to-day business of the company taking preference over hall rebuilding, especially in the hectic post-Fire period. Some record books have suffered damage by wear and tear, and especially by water, probably due to the use of hoses during the Second World War, rendering many entries illegible. Of these remaining companies, only the Mercers, in their Acts of Court, provide anything in the way of details of Jerman's work for them. Even they reveal little information concerning hall plans and the rebuilding process, lingering instead over surveys and arguments between tenants, presumably in anticipation of litigation. What must be remembered, however scanty the records, is that Edward Jerman, in the two years between the Fire and his death, was making designs, viewing and measuring sites, reporting to Courts of Assistants, arbitrating between tenants and overseeing building work on eleven separate, important City buildings, with committees of powerful City men all the time demanding speed and thrift.

The Mercers' Company

Because of the very character of the Mercers' Company, its age and its historical connections,[1] it was inevitable that it would have more to lose in the Fire than any other City company. Simply, the Mercers owned, or were more responsible for, more property than other companies. This property included its Hall and Chapel site, with the contiguous shops and houses in Cheapside, Old Jewry and Ironmonger Lane, St Paul's School and the Royal Exchange, all of which were reduced to rubble by the flames. The Mercers also controlled the Whittington Estate, the entirety of which lay within the City, and most of which, together with the almshouses, was destroyed. The financial problems caused by the juggling of rebuilding costs, low rentals, long leases and the suspension of fines were such that it was not until the nineteenth century that the Mercers were back on a firm financial footing. As we have seen, Edward Jerman played a vital role in the rebuilding of the Exchange, jointly controlled, as it was, by the City and the Mercers. He took a similarly important part at the Mercers' Hall and Chapel site, and at St Paul's School.

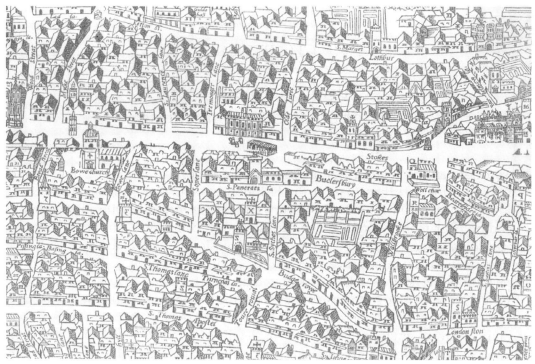

8.1 Detail of a map of London (1560s) attributed to Ralph Agas, showing Cheapside with Mercers' Hall.

It can be appreciated from sixteenth-century maps such as that attributed to Agas (Figure 8.1) that Cheapside was the widest east-west thoroughfare crossing the City. However, it had long served as the City's principal market place and was lined not only with permanent shops, but also with not-so-permanent stalls, no doubt made of and containing highly combustible materials. From Vincent's account of the Fire,[2] it is clear that the width of the street failed to serve as a fire-break, the collapsing houses on one side falling on to those across the way. The Mercers were lucky in as much as their Hall and Chapel had been constructed of stone, which was able, at least initially, to withstand the Fire sufficiently for them to rescue most of their plate and records. The sale of plate went some way towards the need for ready cash, and the salvage of the records has provided historians with insight into the circumstances and traditions of one of the oldest and most influential City companies.

The Mercers were more fortunate than other companies in having alternative accommodation in Gresham College, to which they repaired on 17 September 1666 for their first post-Fire meeting. They ordered the sifting of rubble and the saving of all re-usable materials, but the Mercers, like the Fishmongers, had to consider not only their own immediate affairs, but also those of their dependants, ranging from school children to tenants to almsfolk. The winter months were spent coming to terms with their situation, and it was not until March 1666/67, after the

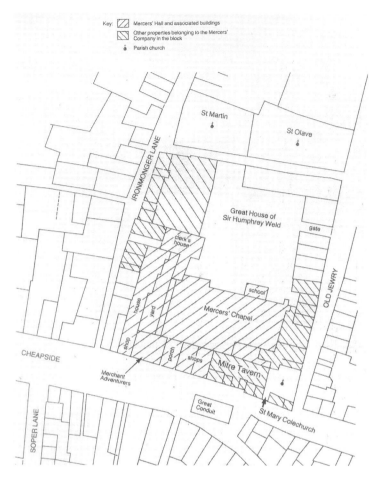

8.2 Diagrammatic representation of Mercers' Hall and
contiguous buildings (c.
1600).

passing of the First Rebuilding Act (February 1666/67) that the Mercers put their minds to the rebuilding of their Hall, Chapel and School. It was essential that the Cheapside site should be made to generate income as quickly as possible, and negotiations were started with the tenants. In order to create a uniform façade to Cheapside, the tenants' plot would have to be coordinated with any plans for the Hall and Chapel. The Foundations Committee therefore set about procuring "Mr. Jerman or some other able surveyor to view and measure the foundations and to make a draft of the same". Jerman was required to survey the whole of the Cheapside site, and to plan how best the land could be used to accommodate a Hall, Chapel and "Schoolhouse", as well as properties for the Company's use and some to be let to tenants.[3] This was a very sizeable site, and a complicated one (Figure 8.2), containing a network of intermingled buildings including a parish church and tavern. Even so, when Edward Jerman was formally requested to accept the post of Company Surveyor, he readily consented and was urged to "hasten the model of their grounds whereon to build their Hall, Chapel and Schoolhouse and the appertaining offices, that so they may resolve with to let".[4]

On 2 July 1667, Jerman's "draft or scheme" was scrutinised by the Committee who unanimously agreed that they should "fix upon it for a model".[5] Suffering the fate common to such plans, it has not survived, but it was probably a fairly rough sketch indicating the general measurements. What it did indicate to the Committee was that the separate entities could be built independently, thereby allowing work to proceed more rapidly on those shops and tenements that would generate income for the Company. In order to persuade tenants to build

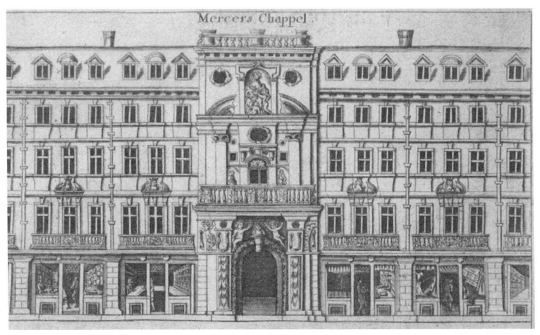

8.3 Edward Jerman: Mercers' post-Fire frontage to Cheapside, engraved 1700.

"substantially" and to achieve a homogeneous frontage in accordance with Jerman's plan, they were offered certain inducements, including longer leases, fixed rents and the waiving of entry fines. Although these inducements helped to solve the Mercers' immediate problem, in the long term, the price paid for such rapid rebuilding was a heavy one. Tenants had been offered leases of up to sixty-one years at a set rent, so no capital sums would be forthcoming until well into the eighteenth century.

Meanwhile, Edward Jerman was requested to oversee the workmen and labourers as they demolished walls and sifted materials which "for doing whereof, he is desired to agree with them by the great".[6] Presumably, the demolition work had been sub-contracted, and Jerman was acting here as an independent surveyor, albeit one with a vested interest. The Committee stressed that those tenants now in a position to start rebuilding must do so, "in conformity to the design of the Company, and in uniformity with the rest of the buildings which shall be erected before this Hall and Chapel".[7]

Figure 8.3 demonstrates how successful the Company was in attaining a balanced and harmonious frontage onto Cheapside, and a glance back at Figure 8.1 indicates the post-Fire changes. The tripartite form of the ground floor shops is stressed throughout by the grouping of the windows in the succeeding three storeys, and indeed the dormers. Each group of three is closely spaced and separated from its neighbour by vertical bands which look for all the world like drainpipes. The central window of each triad of the piano nobile has an unusual, open segmental pediment arising from three keystones, while all the other windows support single keystones. All have deep, projecting aprons contributing to the vertical emphasis of this façade, reaching a climax in the dormers. Here, each trio is crowned by a segmental pediment bounded by two triangular pediments. The overall verticality is, however, counteracted by a strong horizontal emphasis in the form of a pronounced architrave above the ground floor shops, balconies fronting the piano nobile windows, string courses above and below each tier of aprons and a marked modillion cornice.

The harmony achieved in this façade suggests that it was more than likely the work of Edward Jerman, but how much of the entrance porch can be attributed to him is more doubtful because the Company was unable to start work on it until well after Jerman's death. The contract signed with Cartwright (the same mason who took over from Jerman at the Exchange) and John Young in August 1669 stresses that Cartwright should build in accordance with John Oliver's design. Oliver had been appointed to replace Jerman in January 1668/9, when he had been shown Jerman's plans and promised "to make himself master of the intended designs". Whether Jerman had formulated detailed designs of the entrance is not known, and Jean Imray states that, although both Cartwright and Young were named in the contract, only Young received payment from the Company, implying that he did the work. To whose design did John Young build? Had he and Cartwright devised plans, or did he build to those of Oliver, or those of Jerman via Oliver? With such a variety of work being executed simultaneously, the accounts shed no light on this specific subject.[8]

Returning to 1667, Edward Jerman was spending a considerable amount of time viewing and measuring the maze of foundations which constituted the Hall and Chapel site, and advising the Committee whether to accede to the tenants' wishes about layout, some cases having to be referred to the Fire Court. The close proximity of the Mitre Tavern and the parish church inevitably gave rise to problems, and constant wrangling between two rich and influential tenants, Sir Theophilus Biddulph and Sir John Frederick,[9] must have tried Jerman's patience to the limit. However, acting as an arbitrator between such men, he learnt to become a first-class diplomat, a skill which he would have to employ not only on behalf of the Mercers, but also the Goldsmiths. All these negotiations took time.

In September 1667, the Committee decided that work must start as soon as possible on St Paul's School. Its construction had been delayed by the City authorities, who wished to widen the street between the Cathedral and the School, entailing the loss of a large block of school land. The Mercers had hoped to use the Fire to their advantage, to enlarge the School, and although Pepys heard tell that there were plans to relocate it outside the City, such plans came to nought.[10] Jerman was requested to make a draft, and was ordered to appoint a carpenter to drive stakes into the street in accordance with it, so that "at the coming of the King's Surveyor [Sir John Denham] it may the better appear what their desire is". Jerman's draft, taken over by Oliver in January 1668/9, was for a school very similar to its predecessor, being "built up again much after the manner and proportions as it was before".[11] The Committee, meeting in March 1669, approved "the upright designed by Mr. Jerman before his death", and was anxious that building should proceed a-pace.[12] It "considered the advantage etc that the building public schools will bring to the City by causing the inhabitants to settle the sooner where they can have the advantage for their children", and contracted with workmen to start.[13]

Hollar's 1670 engraving (Figure 8.4) shows a tripartite structure, two four-storey pavilions bounding a tall, single-storeyed central section, the schoolroom. This section comprises six bays, the two projecting central bays being topped by a pediment. Its tall, square-headed windows have plain architraves, whereas the round-headed windows of the side bays are bounded by Doric pilasters. All the windows have aprons with recessed centres, and the whole section is topped by a balustrade surmounted by urns and other devices. The pavilions are of three bays, and have a central attic bearing large volutes. The windows of the central bays are round-headed, all the others being square. They make a pleasing contrast with the central section, where the positions are reversed, resulting in a rhythm A-B-A-B-B-A-A-B-B-A-B-A, where A is a square head and B is a round head. Between the fourth floor and the balustraded attics of the pavilions are very large cornices. The whole structure was of brick with stone dressings, the uneven quoins, aprons, string courses, balustrades and semi-basement standing out in white stone against the red bricks. The central, hexagonal tower with a cupola appears to have been demolished by the time Nicholls made his pen, ink and wash drawing in 1697, a drawing now in the Pepys Library at Magdalene College, Cambridge.

Thus here again, Jerman created a harmonious, symmetrical building with many classically-inspired features, but somehow, maybe because of the conventions of the depiction, the total effect seems rather cluttered and fussy. The pavilions with their tall chimneys, the tower, and the fenestration give a markedly vertical feel to the façade, while Jerman's tall, segmentally topped windows, apparent here at the school and again at Barber-Surgeons' Hall, echo the smaller arches of the north front of the Exchange, enhancing this vertical emphasis.

James Ralph, writing in 1734, did not discuss the building, but as we saw in Chapter 7, he was no lover of Jerman's Royal Exchange. The posthumous 1783 edition of his *Critical Review* is quite damning of the School, concluding that "the architect has deviated exceedingly from the received rules, without offering anything in his performance which can induce us to excuse his presumption".[14] William Maitland, in 1756, offered no critical judgement on the architecture of the School, he merely discussed the number of pupils and the masters' salaries.[15] However, it did receive praise from some quarters. Edward Chamberlayne, in 1700, recorded that it had been rebuilt "in a far more magnificent, commodious and beautiful manner",[16] and Henry Chamberlain's "Society of Gentlemen" (1770) were fulsome in their praise, describing the School as a very singular and at the same time a very handsome edifice.[17] In his history of St Paul's School, William Coombe (1816) described the elevation as "uniform and, in a more advantageous

8.4 Edward Jerman: St Paul's School. Wenceslas Hollar etching (1670).

situation, would attract attention as an example of elegant architecture".[18]

The School was ready for use again in March 1671, John Oliver having been paid two sums of £50 as the Company Surveyor "for his pains about the directing and building of St Paul's School".[19] No record suggests that John Oliver had any part in the design of the School, and the report of the meeting in March 1669 seems to make it clear that Jerman was the sole designer.[20]

This was not the case where the rest of the rebuilding was concerned. Only the Clerk's House can be definitely ascribed to Jerman, and this was finished shortly after his death. The Cheapside entrance was not finished until 1671, the Chapel 1674, and the Livery hall itself until 1676. The delay was caused not only by lack of funds, but also by the intransigence of neighbouring tenants, and of course by Jerman's death in November 1668. The Mercers' Court turned to John Oliver and asked him to familiarize himself with Jerman's plans, so that he could advise them how best to proceed. In November 1669, he was requested to draw a design of the Hall and Chapel, and to prepare estimates of the cost. Oliver's design must have supplemented that made by Jerman in January 1667/8, namely "the draft of the new Hall and Chapel made by Mr. Jerman and now lying before the Court".[21] There is no written evidence linking their final design with either Jerman, Oliver, Cartwright or Young, although Colvin states that "His [Jerman's] plans for the Mercers' Hall were carried out after his death under the superintendence of John Oliver".[22]

The Foundations Committee continued to be "advised and assisted" by Jerman for the last six months of his life as he viewed, measured and made drafts of the several properties that lay interwoven within the Hall and Chapel site. He acted as arbitrator between tenants who claimed that their ancient rights had been violated, or that they had lost a few yards of ground because of the thickness of a neighbour's wall. Most of these tenants were rich, influential City men as we have seen, and there are twenty records of Jerman meeting with such men and having, as Company Surveyor, to persuade them, often against their wishes, to accede to the Company's overall plan.[23] It must have been an unusual situation for Edward Jerman to find himself in, and serves to illustrate yet again what confidence a Company such as the Mercers had in him, to allow him to conduct these delicate negotiations, as well as to design their showpiece buildings. For all Jerman's time, energy and ingenuity over the two-year period, the Mercers' Company rewarded him with two payments, one of £25 and one of £50.

Wax Chandlers' Hall

The extent of the destruction wrought by the Fire on Wax Chandlers' Hall is difficult to assess. The Hall lay in an area of the City where a number of the buildings were damaged, not destroyed, some of the local survivors being Goldsmiths' Hall (almost next door) and part of St John Zachary across the road. As the archivist at the Wax Chandlers suggests, the reason for thinking that a large part of the fabric survived is that the number of new bricks apparently

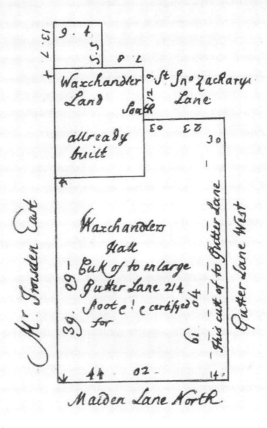

I sett out Wax Chandlers Hall 4th of March 1668 as designed below

8.5 John Oliver: plan of Wax Chandlers' Hall (1668).

bought would have been insufficient for a total rebuild. It is possible that a considerable amount of the old materials were re-used, and this could be the reason why, only one hundred years later, the Hall had to be rebuilt again as it was in a ruinous state. It seems unlikely that a building designed by Jerman should decay so rapidly, but we must remember that, having made the plans, Jerman was not alive to see those plans executed. Perhaps damaged bricks were incorporated in the structure, causing premature deterioration.

The accommodation provided by Jerman's design for the Hall was much the same as that of the pre-Fire building, although the western aspect was somewhat curtailed due to the widening of Gutter Lane as part of the City improvement scheme. There are two plans of the Hall drawn by John Oliver, in his capacity as a City Surveyor, one in 1668, which shows the street widening, and the other in 1696. The latter shows the completed Hall set round a small yard (Figures 8.5 and 8.6).

Unfortunately, no images remain of either the interior or exterior of Jerman's

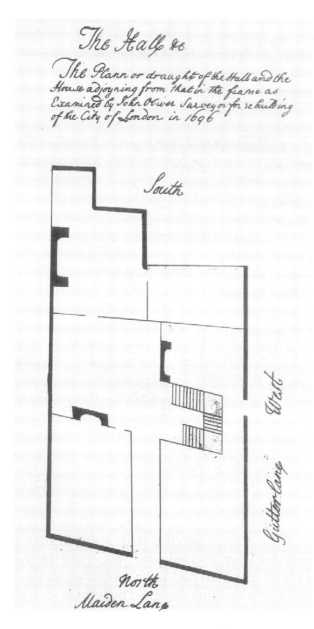

The Hall &c

The Plann or draught of the Hall and the House adjoyning from that in the frame as Examined by John Oliver Surveyor for rebuilding of the City of London in 1696

South

West

Gutter Lane

North
Maiden Lane

8.6 Wax Chandlers' Hall: ground plan of the Hall as completed (1696).

Hall, and descriptions of the building are scanty. Maitland simply referred to it as "handsome though not very spacious".[24] Jerman's plan was passed by the Committee in June 1667, and he was paid an initial fee of £50. He was later paid £38 "for work" and a further £100 "for work already done or to be done".[25] Meanwhile, Peter Mills received ten shillings (perhaps he was called in for advice), and "Jerman's man" was paid twelve pence for a job unspecified. Compared with other companies, the Wax Chandlers seem to have remunerated Jerman handsomely, although how much of this money was disbursed to workmen is not specified.

Rebuilding started in November 1668, just about the time of Jerman's death, and the first meeting was held in the completed hall on 29 September 1670. The Company records reveal no details about the building process.

Drapers' Hall

The Drapers' first Hall, built in the 1420s, was a typical timber-framed building with infill of plaster and stones.[26] It comprised a dining room, court room, financial chamber and ladies' chamber, as well as several service rooms. The great hall itself had a large chimney and a raised dais for the high table. In fact, it resembled, in most particulars, the houses of great nobles. From this hall, in 1541, the Drapers removed to the house of another great noble, Thomas Cromwell, who had been executed for treason in 1540. This property was a considerable one, with several smaller residences situated alongside, and extensive gardens. Stow told how

Cromwell enlarged his garden by requisitioning some of the Stow land: "My father had a garden there and a house standing close to his south pale; this house they loosened from the ground and bare upon rollers into my father's garden 22 foot ere my father heard thereof". Stow ruefully concluded that "the sudden rising of some men causeth them to forget themselves".[27] Nevertheless, for such a rich and distinguished Company, the property provided a most suitable headquarters.

The Hall was lost in the Fire, even though the house in the garden was partly demolished to act as a fire-break. Within a week, work had started to render any material remaining on the site safe and secure, since looting was very prevalent with such rich pickings lying around. In October 1666, a Committee was formed to "advise and consult with some surveyors of a fit form for a new Hall to be erected",[28] and in February 1666/7, the Committee resolved that "the Hall and its appurtenances shall be built as near as may be upon the old foundations, with such additions and alterations as shall be thought convenient. And that Mr. Mills the Surveyor do draw a model thereof accordingly". Three weeks later, Peter Mills attended the Court with a model for the Hall, "nine foot longer northward than before, and a parlour as large as the former but extending further westward".[29] There is no record of the Committee's approval of this model, and while the Court was deliberating the matter, Peter Mills became seriously ill from overwork and was replaced at the Drapers, as at the Royal Exchange, by Edward Jerman. Jerman was requested to make a model "for a new hall and two parlours and other necessary buildings in place of or near where the former stood, taking in Mr. Thynne's ground for the convenience and enlargement thereof".[30]

Jerman's model, "enlarged in length and breadth, with other convenient rooms", was approved by the Committee, and workmen were sought so that building might start as soon as possible. In January 1667/68, Peter Mills was paid £10 for the work he did before his "tedious fit of sickness", and £20 was paid to "Mr. Jerman our Surveyor, as an expression of this Company's sense of his great pains and long attendance in drawing models and overseeing and ordering the buildings of the intended hall".[31] It is clear, therefore, that Jerman was acting in the capacity of a designer/architect as well as a surveyor/contractor on the Drapers' Hall, as he had at the Royal Exchange and Fishmongers' Hall. Like many other companies, the Drapers made a gift of £20 to Mrs Jerman after Edward's death, when Cartwright assumed responsibility for the construction of the Hall.

Hatton, in 1708, seems to have been well pleased by Jerman's Drapers' Hall. He described it as "a very spacious, noble building containing the four sides of a quadrangle, each side elevated on columns and adorned with arches by which there are constituted piazzas".[32] Jerman had, therefore, reproduced the courtyard form of the previous hall (this time in brick and stone), and here again, he introduced an Italianate feel to the building, as he had at Fishmongers' Hall and the Royal Exchange, by the incorporation of arches. Jerman's plans have not survived, but when the Hall was again rebuilt following a fire in 1772, the architect was requested to draw up plans "in the same manner as before".[33]

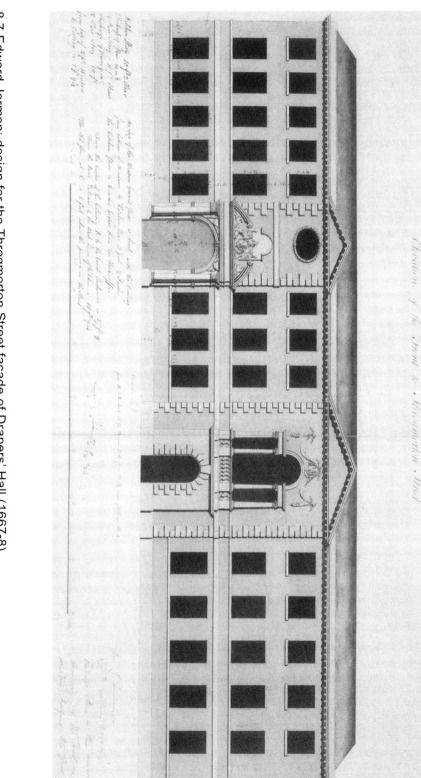

8.7 Edward Jerman: design for the Throgmorton Street façade of Drapers' Hall (1667-8).

A drawing showing the elevation fronting Throgmorton Street (Figure 8.7) is held at Drapers' Hall, and although it is unsigned, the Company has always accepted it as Jerman's work.[34] Certainly, it depicts many of the features one comes to associate with Jermanian facades: the projecting, pedimented sections accentuated by uneven quoins, the regular fenestration imbuing the building with a vertical feel, the conspicuous cornice and the stress on a rather elaborate pedimented entrance incorporating the orders. All these features were displayed on the Fishmongers' river front and all occur, individually or in combination, on Jerman's other façades.

The regular fenestration of this very long front, which extends round a slight bend in the street (as shown in a rough sketch below Jerman's drawing, and confirmed by Ogilby and Morgan's map of 1676), is broken by two projecting, pedimented sections. Only in these sections does Jerman depict any detail of the ornament he envisaged to enhance the façade. The smaller pedimented section is dominated by a very large, arched entrance supported by columns, similar to that which Roger Jerman was to execute at Vintners' Hall (perhaps Roger took this as his example), and better proportioned and less busy than that at Mercers' Hall. In the upper part of this section is a rather ill-proportioned oval window, quite unrelated to any of the rest of the fenestration (but possibly harking back to the north front of the Royal Exchange). The larger pedimented section, again stressed by uneven quoining, presents a tall, round-headed, rusticated entrance below, and above, an elegant Venetian window with a balcony. Four Ionic columns on pedestals emphasise the three parts of the window, and above, there is restrained festooning. This section seems to be the nearest Jerman got to pure classicism, and it is uncluttered, unlike so much of his work, by a surfeit of motifs.

Cartwright completed the Hall in 1671, and as Rev. A.H. Johnson so charmingly stated, "That we have no definite description of the Hall is unfortunate, inasmuch as a considerable part of Jerman's building was destroyed by another fire in 1772".[35]

Barber-Surgeons' Hall

The only part of the Barber-Surgeons' buildings to survive the Fire was Inigo Jones' anatomy theatre, lying isolated from the rest of the Hall buildings. The destruction of the Hall was reported by the Countess of Thanet, whose house in Aldersgate Street backed on to the Barbers' Hall, separated by the City Wall. She, having fled, wrote to a friend, "I hear it confirmed that Thanet House is safe, the nearest it [the Fire] came to my house was Surgeons' Hall, which is burnt to the ground".[36]

Immediately after the Fire, subscriptions were raised towards the rebuilding and on 3 March 1666/7 Edward Jerman was requested to make a plan for a new Hall. For this work, he was paid £5. There is no evidence from the records that Jerman oversaw the work, or made his usual reports to the Court, but his widow was paid £5 in 1669 for her husband's "pains".[37]

From plans of Jerman's buildings held by the Wellcome Trust, it can be seen that the mid line of his Livery Hall centred on the bastion of the City Wall, forming an

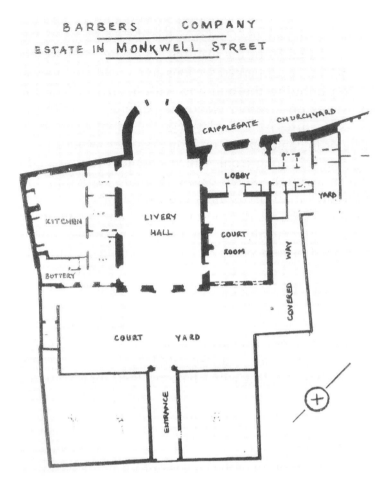

apsidal west end (Figure 8.8). The court room and parlours lay to the north, and the service wing to the south, creating a symmetrical composition described by Pepys as "very fine".

In a print held at the Guildhall Library, the courtyard façade gives every appearance of having been a simple, classical structure (Figure 8.9). A three-bay, two-storeyed, pedimented block separates two balustraded, three-bay, single-storey wings. The whole is of brick with stone dressings. The central door-case is rusticated and has a segmental pediment above a frieze with a stone block pressing down upon a figured keystone. Jerman has again brought rhythm to his fenestration viz. A-B-A-A-B-A-A-B-A, where A are round-headed and B are segmental-headed windows. There is considerable emphasis on stone enrichments here. The balustrade is balanced by a deep skirting, the arched windows of the wings are stressed by stone surrounds, and the central block displays very prominent quoins. The stone architraves of the square-headed windows of the lower storey and of the wings have lugs similar to those found in Palladio's Palazzo Chiericati in Vicenza and in Jones' first elevation of the Prince's Lodging (see Figure 5.8). Although the stone skirting, balustrade, string course and cornice create a strong horizontal emphasis, Jerman here again introduced verticality by means of projecting aprons beneath all the windows, together with the arch-like appearance of the tall segmental windows of the wings.

This façade of the Barber-Surgeons' Hall has a restrained elegance, and like the Drapers' Hall, seems to have avoided Jerman's tendency to over-elaboration. It was described by Hatton as "a spacious building of fine brick and stone", and by Maitland as "a magnificent building".[38]

8.9 Edward Jerman: courtyard façade of Barber-Surgeons' Hall. George Shepherd watercolour (1812).

8.10 Edward Jerman: the courtyard of Apothecaries' Hall, watercolour (1830).

Apothecaries' Hall

The first Hall purchased by the Apothecaries' Company in 1632 was a property which had been the guest-house of Black Friars Priory. It was known as Cobham Hall, and with it, the Apothecaries took possession of a garden and ground which extended down to the river, as well as a coach house and stables. Early in 1633, repairs were started on the fabric of the Hall, and Peter Mills seems to have been responsible for much of this work. He tiled three roofs and the gallery, re-pointed brickwork and repaired chimneys, and was paid £166-10s-9d for work "about the Hall and gable ends" (which implied that the Hall had a pitched roof). Further improvements were carried out to the Hall over the ensuing years, and in 1651, Mills was again called in, this time to inspect the workmanship. Mills' relationship with the Apothecaries was to be an on-going one, for he surveyed the Hall site after the Fire and was requested to keep a check on the Company's carpenter.[39]

Although their Hall was more or less gutted in the Fire, the Apothecaries decided to rebuild it on its old foundations. Like so many others in the same position, they salvaged and secured what they could until construction work could start anew in accordance with the Rebuilding Act's stipulations for safer, more substantial structures. The Apothecaries set up a Building Committee which, according to the Warden's Accounts, seems to have met in taverns and coffee houses. It also made visits to other company halls in its quest for ideas.

In July 1667 the Committee appointed, as Surveyors, Edward Jerman and Richard Ryder, Master Carpenter to the King. The two were requested to "survey the ground where the Hall stood",[40] and to have the survey ready for the following Court. There is, again, no evidence for Jerman's design, and only scant evidence of his dealings with the Company in the next year or so. He was accompanied to the site in August 1667 by the carpenter George Clisbie, and was present at a dinner in January 1667/8, provided by Mr. Corbett, the Company's Cook.[41] The last relevant entry appears on 4 August 1668, when the Committee, together with Jerman, viewed the Hall ground.

Thomas Lock, the Master Carpenter who took over from Jerman at the Fishmongers, did likewise at the Apothecaries, and seems to have adopted Jerman's design with few alterations. His main contribution was to give the Hall a flat roof, which Jerman's evidently had not.[42] Detailed supervision of the work is likely to have been carried out by Clisbie, appointed Company Carpenter in 1668. Lock accepted the sum of £40 for his work for the Apothecaries, while Clisbie was paid £1,318 between 1668 and 1671, for himself and his workmen. Both Hunting and Underwood agree that the smallness of Lock's remuneration suggests that Lock merely followed Jerman's plans in the construction of the Hall.[43] Although there is no mention of payment to Jerman, it is likely that he received a meagre sum here again in comparison with the master craftsmen. Roger Jerman's concentration on carpentry, rather than any incursion into surveying, begins to appear a wise decision financially.

The mason John Young designed the door-case, incorporating the Company's arms (1670). It was a more modest version of that at Mercers' Hall at which, as we have seen, he collaborated with Cartwright. Young's was also the stone staircase leading to the Hall, and the paved court. Both Hatton and Strype considered Jerman's Hall worthy of comment, describing it as "handsome and worthy of merit", and "a good building" respectively.[44]

A water-colour of 1830 depicts the courtyard (Figure 8.10). The façade containing the Livery hall is emphasised by a pediment. A rusticated ground floor supports a tall piano nobile of four bays, with tall, lugged windows whose verticality is further emphasised by what could be pulvinated friezes. Above these are the round windows favoured by Stone at Goldsmiths' Hall, but here, they are strangely positioned, seemingly squashed beneath the pediment. Again, Jerman stressed both horizontals and verticals, the verticality of the windows with their stone detailing being counteracted by the horizontality of the stone string courses and the very marked line of the cornices, so far above the windows themselves.

The overall impression given is that Jerman's design was executed by hands less able than his own – but perhaps it is the fault of the image and the water-colourist's eyes were insensitive to the subtleties of proportion.

8.11 Edward Jerman: the façade of Haberdashers' Hall. William Angus engraving (1811).

Haberdashers' Hall

The record books of the Haberdashers' Company have unfortunately become all but illegible due to fading ink and water damage. Mention is made of Jerman as Company Carpenter in 1663, the occurrence of the Fire is recorded, and there is some reference to the rebuilding of the Hall, but it is not until September 1667 that any details are available. Here, we find that "Mr. Jerman the Surveyor was desired to make a draft or scheme of the Hall and tenements with an estimate of the charges of the building thereof". One month later, Edward Jerman had already drawn plans for the new Hall, and the Haberdashers' Court had seen and approved them. By the end of November 1667, Jerman's "gate and gateway to the Hall" had been accepted,[45] and work seems to have gone ahead at speed, the Hall being in use by May 1668.

An engraving of 1811 (Figure 8.11) shows the Hall to have had a modest façade to the street, being a five bay structure of three storeys. The centre is stressed by a small pediment atop a strangely rudimentary entablature, and the windows of this projecting section are again embellished by lugs, supported in the upper storey by volutes, and in the piano nobile by pilasters. The entrance is extremely elaborate, with rusticated, banded columns carrying an ornamented broken pediment. This elaboration is clearly an attempt to impart some grandeur to an otherwise unimposing front, and the entrance bears some resemblance to Gerbier's York Water Gate of 1626-1627. No critical judgement of the Hall was made by either Hatton or Maitland.

Weavers' Hall

Their Hall having been laid waste in September 1666, the Weavers' first problem was to find a meeting place where they could discuss the problems of finding men, materials and money to build anew. Taverns proved both expensive and distracting, and finally, arrangements were made for them to rent a room at the unscathed Leathersellers' Hall. However, it was at The Angel in Moorfields on 1 July 1667 that Edward Jerman "was desired to view the Hall and garden and then present a draft thereof". The Building Committee clearly favoured the more congenial atmosphere of a tavern, for 26 August 1667 found the members meeting at the Sun Tavern in Bishopsgate with Thomas Cartwright, Jonah Lewis the master carpenter, and Edward Jerman. Here, they agreed that "the door-case to the Hall and gateway to the Hall shall be with stone as is demonstrated in the draft now presented by Mr. Jerman". The new Hall was to be of brick with stone dressings, and 10,000 bricks were ordered to be bought and rubbed for the front.[46]

Jerman was paid £5 for "his pains taken about the management of the Company building", while the Company spent twelve shillings and sixpence at the Sun Tavern, and eleven shillings and sixpence at The Angel during these negotiations. Mr. Seagood the bricklayer was asked to provide another 20,000 bricks for rubbing

8.12 Edward Jerman: entrance to Weavers' Hall. Thomas Shepherd pencil drawing (1840).

(these again must have been for the front, the greater cost of rubbed bricks limiting their use to façades). The bricklayer and carpenter were each paid £60 up to this point, while Cartwright was paid £50 for his work on the front, presumably for the masonry on Jerman's door-case and gateway.[47]

By the beginning of the next year, there seems to be a sign in the minutes that Jerman had taken on more work than his health would allow, and that Jonah Lewis had assumed the role of supervisor in his place: "Mr. Lewis do see Mr. Jerman's directions performed by all the workmen concerned".[48] Lewis was now acting as a middleman between Jerman and the workforce. Jerman was paid another £6 by the Company in April and June 1668 as the "Surveyor" rather than, as before, for "his pains about the management".

Although, like so many others, the Weavers had to borrow money to pay the workmen, building continued without interruption (no mention being made of Jerman's death) and the Hall was completed in the summer of 1669. It was a brick-faced structure with stone dressings and a wooden turret. Its façade encompassed two houses, between which was an entry from the street leading into a small courtyard (Figure 8.12). During discussions between Jerman and the Building Committee, it had been decided that there should be no balconies on the new Hall front, in accordance with the Rebuilding Act.

From the account books, it seems that the materials were supplied and the labourers engaged by the master craftsmen, who were therefore working by the great, but, at the same time, were remunerated on a salaried system, as discussed in Chapter 5.

There is no mention of a replacement for Jerman. Perhaps the Committee felt that the building was sufficiently advanced for each of the master craftsmen to take care of his own field of operation.

Vintners' Hall

Vintners' Hall in Upper Thames Street underwent a complete refurbishment in the 1580s, but all was destroyed in 1666, and it was not until 1671 that the company set about the task of rebuilding. Edward Jerman had died in November 1668, and it was to his brother Roger that the Vintners turned for help in the building of their new Hall. In the period immediately following the Fire, the energy of most Londoners had been channelled into the continuation of the City as the nerve centre of the country: its people had to be housed, its markets needed to trade, its prisoners restrained and its government to legislate as best it might. The Vintners, like the Weavers and many other companies, realised that for the time being, they could conduct their affairs in the rooms of nearby taverns (which, perhaps, they felt to be appropriate), and they preferred to postpone rebuilding until they had set their finances in order. For the next four years, they raised money by selling their plate, and indeed their rubble, and by increasing their apprenticeship fees and fines.

The old Hall of wood and plaster was to be replaced, by law, with brick and stone. The Vintners chose to leave the design of their new Hall in the hands of three master-craftsmen engaged for the building work: Roger Jerman the

8.13 Roger Jerman: courtyard doorcase of Vintners' Hall. George Shepherd watercolour (1810).

carpenter, Mr. Lem the bricklayer and Mr. Hammond the mason. Because there was no overall designer, plans were debated between the Committee and the craftsmen, and any adaptations considered appropriate were effected accordingly. One such debate took place in July 1672 when Roger Jerman, Lem and the Committee discussed the possibility of a kitchen and offices being sited under the great hall, and after a view, it was agreed that this could be effected "with much convenience and safety".

The craftsmen seem to have had a considerable amount of autonomy, but it is recorded that Roger Jerman proceeded with a door-case "without order". The old demarcation dispute between the Joiners and the Carpenters resurfaced and Jerman was reprimanded and advised not to "meddle with any Joiners' work belonging to the Hall".[49] The door-case in question (Figure 8.13), an open-pedimented structure supported on columns, giving access to the courtyard, was a simplified version of that designed by Edward Jerman for the Drapers' Hall (Figure 8.7). In December 1673, Roger was requested to make a handsome pair of gates for the front of the Hall, and by 1675, the rebuilding was complete.

Throughout his employment with the Vintners' Company, from 1668 until 1678, Roger Jerman was paid an annual salary of 13s and 4d – presumably as a retainer.

8.14 Payment received by Roger Jerman for work done in the City of London, April 1671.

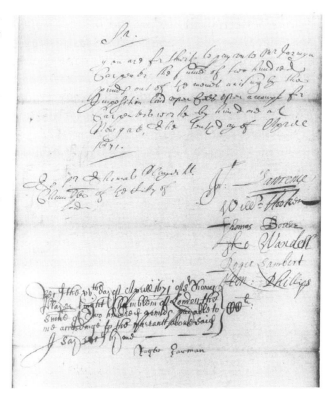

However, during that period, he was also paid a total of £575 "for work done at the hall". From this sum, he would have paid his workmen, but there is no mention of materials. The records state that he offered to "do the work well", and that, if the Company did not think he deserved the price he had put down, then "what they think it is worth, to pay him".[50] The Company must have been satisfied with his work, paying him regular sums on account.

Unlike his brother Edward, Roger Jerman spent the greater part of his working life as a master-carpenter rather than as a surveyor. As a result, compared with Edward, he made a large amount of money, which, according to his will, he invested in land and property. From 1662 until his death in 1678, Roger was the City Carpenter, and was therefore intimately involved with the rebuilding of many of the great City edifices that had been damaged or destroyed. These included the Guildhall and its adjoining properties, Newgate Prison, Moorgate and the markets, and Roger was paid a total of £2,200. This money was raised by coal dues,[51] and in the Newgate Prison accounts held at the Corporation of London Record Office is a warrant for one such payment, signed by Roger Jerman (Figure 8.14).

A separate ledger, held at the Guildhall, which itemises work done on City buildings between 1666 and 1675, reveals that Roger Jerman was paid a further total of £10,596-16-7d for "workmanship and materials".[52] When one recalls that he was also paid about £7,000 by the Mercers and the City for work at the Royal Exchange, the details of his will are somewhat less surprising than they might at first seem. He was paid a total of over £20,000 by the City, the Mercers and the Vintners alone. Financial advisors confirm that £20,000 in 1666 is worth about £1,500,000 today. Even assuming that Roger paid his own workmen and was responsible for the purchase of most, if not all of the timber he used, this is an enormous amount of money to have passed through the hands of a master-carpenter in sixteen years.

In 1670, Roger Jerman leased a piece of land he owned in Dorset Gardens to

Thomas Betterton, the actor, and others, for the construction of a new theatre.[53] This enterprise was supported by Charles II to the tune of £1,000, and was then patronised by the Duke of York, its name changing from Dorset Garden to Duke's Theatre.[54] Tradition has it that Wren designed the building, although there is no documentary evidence. Ned Ward enjoyed "the stately edifice whose front was supported by lofty columns",[55] while John Evelyn was impressed by the magnificence of the scenes and machines.[56] Roger Jerman was indeed a man of property.

Conclusion

The title of my thesis, on which this book is based was "From Artificer to Architect, the Metamorphosis of the Master-Craftsman Edward Jerman". This title evolved gradually, as my research brought to light more and more details of the work, not only of Edward Jerman, but also of the other six members of his family, all master-carpenters, who worked in the City of London between 1538 and 1678. Edward was alone amongst his family in his metamorphosis, the evolution starting in 1657, when he resigned from his post of City Carpenter. After that, there are no records of any carpentry work carried out by him, even for the Goldsmiths' Company where his official title was Company Carpenter. Although Anthony Jerman, Edward's father, made one major foray into the world of designing (for the Goldsmiths), his draft was rejected and it seems he never tried again. Edward was therefore unique, passing through the chrysalis stage of Viewer and Surveyor, to attain his wings as an architect in the post-Fire period. Indeed, Edward was unique not only amongst his family members, but also amongst his contemporary master-craftsmen – carpenters, masons and bricklayers – for both the output and the quality of work he accomplished in the City of London.

Edward Jerman's working life was intimately bound up with the Corporation of the City of London and the City companies. Their minute books furnish us with a comprehensive record of the variety of employment available to a seventeenth-century master-carpenter, and also demonstrate that Edward did, in fact, fulfil many of those options open to such master-craftsmen. Before the Fire, he worked for the Corporation of the City in the roles of City Carpenter, City Viewer and City Surveyor. At that time, too, he was personally involved in small-scale speculation as well as large-scale town planning for the Goldsmiths' Company. As Surveyor to the Fishmongers' Company, he was in charge of the fabric of their properties, together with the maintenance of their extensive woodlands. He also used his artistic flair, as well as his technical skills, to create pageants for the Lord Mayor's shows over a ten-year period.

By the time of the Fire he had achieved recognition as the City's best artist (beside Peter Mills), but we have little evidence of the artistry on which that recognition was based. No City buildings have been associated with his name. He had not been called upon to design any new company halls, or even extensions to existing ones. However, all that was to change with the Fire, when the City requested his services as a Surveyor for Rebuilding and the companies called on his expertise and imagination as a designer. He very soon found himself being courted by no less than eight City companies (including four of the Great Twelve), to design new halls for them, and it should be remembered that most of Jerman's halls were in occupation before any public buildings were complete, or a single City church was rebuilt. This speed of construction was due to two factors: the companies' need to rebuild quickly, in order that the City should maintain its supremacy as a centre of trade, and Jerman's capacity for work.

The halls were, on the whole, favourably received by eighteenth-century critics,[1] and most continued to fulfil the tasks for which they had been designed until fire or war destroyed them. None remain today, although images of them are plentiful and demonstrate certain features that recur in Jerman's buildings, so that we may refer to a "Jermanian style". Jerman imbued his façades with a vertical feel by linking his windows with aprons, and by emphasising the angles of projecting, pedimented sections with uneven stone quoins. He stressed the contrast of brick and stone, and enlivened his facades with string courses, balustrades, modillion cornices and skirtings. Where appropriate, Jerman ennobled his buildings by the incorporation of the orders, Venetian windows, pediments and other classical features. He enjoyed introducing rhythm into his fenestration, playfully reversing the positions of square and round-headed windows to inject dynamism into a façade.

Because of Jerman's sudden death in 1668, the authorship of some of these details must inevitably be open to debate. However, the facades of all his buildings demonstrate these Jermanian features to a greater or lesser degree, suggesting that his designs suffered little adaptation by those who saw them to completion. His style was one that seems to have satisfied his City patrons, by all accounts men of no great aesthetic taste compared with their contemporaries at Court, but nevertheless, men who were sufficiently well-versed in the "new architecture" to expect and appreciate Jerman's interpretation and utilisation of it.

By the time of his death, Edward Jerman must have been the best-known architect in the City of London, a figure familiar to members of the Corporation of the City and City companies alike. Although no portrait of any member of his family has, so far, come to light, record book entries are so abundant that it is fairly easy, in the mind's eye, to conjure up a picture of these men; their characters leap out from the pages.

I feel that a fitting postscript to Edward Jerman has been provided by Samuel Angell, writing in 1838:

> Mr Jerman has never enjoyed that degree of reputation to which he was
> fairly entitled. The Exchange was not the only design he made which has
> been attributed to Wren; the Fishmongers' Hall and the Drapers' Hall were
> both designed by Jerman. Mr Herbert in his *History of the Twelve Companies*
> has made this fact known, and has thus performed an act of justice to an
> architect of great talent.[2]

I hope I have further enhanced Edward Jerman's reputation.

Notes

Introduction

1. MC.GR (ii) fo. 293, 25 April 1667.
2. Metcalf, P., *The Hall of the Fishmongers' Company*, London, Phillimore, 1977; Imray, J., *The Mercers' Hall*, London, London Topographical Society, 1991; and Saunders, A., ed., *The Royal Exchange*, London, London Topographical Society, 1977.

Chapter 1 – Setting the Scene: Edward Jerman in Context

1. The Repertories are the minutes of the meetings of the Court of Aldermen of the City of London. For details of the hierarchy of Aldermen and Common Councilmen, see Chapter 3.
2. These include the City's cash ledgers, the City Lands Grant Books, Coal Duty Account Books and the Chamberlain's Acquittance Book.
3. MC.GR (ii) fo. 293, 25 April 1667.
4. Jerman's porch for Mercers' Hall was demolished in 1880 and re-erected at Swanage Town Hall. For an illustration of this see Imray, J., *The Mercers' Hall*, London Topographical Society, 1991, p.60.
5. Strype, J., *A Survey of the Cities of London and Westminster . . . by John Stow*, London, A. Churchill, 1720, vols. 1 and 2.
6. Hatton, E., *A New View of London*, London, Chiswell and Churchill, 1708, vol. 2, pp. 593-622.
7. Jupp, E.B., *A Historical Account of the Worshipful Company of Carpenters*, London, Pickering and Chatto, 1887, p. 625.
8. Alford, B., and Barker T., *A History of the Carpenters' Company*, London, Allen and Unwin, 1968.
9. Ridley, J., *A History of the Carpenters' Company*, London, Unicorn Press, 1995, p.60.
10. Newman, J., "Nicholas Stone's Goldsmiths' Hall. Design and Practice in the 1630s", *Architectural History*, vol. 14, 1971, pp. 30-39. Colvin, H., "Inigo Jones and the Church of St. Michael le Querne", *The London Journal*, vol. 12, no. 1, 1986, pp. 36-9.
11. Colvin, H., *A Biographical Dictionary of British Architects 1600-1840*, New Haven and London, Yale University Press, 1995, pp. 545-6.
12. Imray, J., *The Mercers' Hall*, London Topographical Society, 1991; Doolittle, I., *The Mercers' Company 1597-1959*, Leeds, W.S. Malley and Son, 1994.
13. Saunders, A., ed., *The Royal Exchange*, London, London Topographical Society, 1997.
14. Metcalf, P., *The Halls of the Fishmongers' Company*, London, Phillimore, 1977.
15. T.F. Reddaway acknowledged that he "knew so little about Edward Jerman that to set it down is to risk disparaging him". Reddaway, T.F., *The Rebuilding of London after the Great Fire*, London, Jonathan Cape, 1940, p.59.
16. Whinney, M., and Millar, O., *English Art 1625-1714*, Oxford, Clarendon Press, 1957, p. 152-3.

17. Downes, K., *English Baroque Architecture*, London, Zwemmer, 1966, p. 111.

18. Summerson, J., *Architecture in Britain, 1530-1830*, London, Penguin, 1991, p. 190.

19. Summerson, J., *Georgian Architecture*, London, Pimlico, 1988, pp. 39- 40.

20. Wall, C., *The Literary and Cultural Spaces of Restoration London*, Cambridge, Cambridge University Press, 1988, p. 152. Cynthia Wall mistakenly attributes to Jerman a plan for the new City. Wall, C., op.cit. p. 152.

21. Jeffery, P., *The City Churches of Sir Christopher Wren*, London, Hambledon Press, 1996.

22. Bell, W.G., *The Great Fire of London in 1666*, London, Jonathan Cape, 1940. Reddaway, T.F., op.cit.

23. Porter, S., *The Great Fire of London*, Stroud, Sutton, 1998.

24. Beier, A., "Engine of Manufacture: The Trades of London", A.L. Beier and R. Finlay, eds, *London 1500-1700. The Making of the Metropolis*, London, Longman, 1980, pp. 141-167.

25. Earle, P., *The Making of the English Middle Class: Business, Society and Family Life in London 1660-1730*, London, Methuen, 1989. Ibid, p. 329.

26. Woodward, D., *Men at Work, Labourers and Building Craftsmen in the Towns of Northern England 1450-1750*, Cambridge, Cambridge University Pres, 1995, pp. 35-91.

27. Wren's letter to the Bishop of Oxford, Letter III, 25 June 1681, in "Tom Tower, Christ Church, Oxford", ed. W.D. Caroe, Oxford, Clarendon Press, 1923, p. 27.

28. Rappaport, S., *Worlds within Worlds. Structures of Life in Sixteenth-Century London*, Cambridge, Cambridge University Press, 1989, p. 232 et seq.

29. Topsy, in *Uncle Tom's Cabin* by H. Beecher-Stowe, 1852, when asked "Do you know who made you?" replied, "I 'spect I grow'd, don't think nobody ever made me".

30. Shakespeare, W., *Hamlet*, Act IV, Scene 5, line 78, Geoffrey Cumberlege, Oxford University Press, Oxford, 1956.

31. The Weavers' Company paid £2-2-10d for a "full court dinner, being the first in the Company's new building", on 27 January 1668/9. GLMS 4648-1.

32. For an account of the Commissioners for Rebuilding, see Chapter 3.

33. For evidence of May's Royalist tendencies, see Porter, op. cit. p. 87-8; Colvin, *Dictionary*, p. 646. For Pratt, see Mowl, T., and Earnshaw, B., *Architecture without Kings. The Rise of Puritan Classicism*, Manchester, Manchester University Press, 1995, p. 55; Evelyn, J., *Memoirs*, ed. Wm Bray, London, printed for Henry Colburn, 1818, vol. 1, p. ix. For Wren, see Downes, K., *The Architecture of Wren*, p. 3.

34. See Reddaway, op. cit., p. 58.

35. This point is also made by Elizabeth McKellar. See McKellar, E., *The Birth of Modern London. The development and design of the City 1660-1720*, Manchester, Manchester University Press, 1999.

36. For Crosby Place, see Schofield, J., *Medieval London Houses*, London and New Haven, Yale University Press, 1994, p. 38; for Drapers' Hall, see Chapter 8 and Girtin, T., *The Triple Crowns*, London, Hutchinson, 1964, p. 120 et.seq; for details of Thanet House in Aldersgate, see Mowl and Earnshaw, op. cit., p. 137; for Bacon House, see Kingsford, C.L., "Historical Notes on Medieval London Houses", in *London Topographical Record*, vol. 12, 1920, pp. 28-31; for Browne's Place, see Kingsford, C.L., "A London Merchant's House and its Owners, 1360-1614", *Archaeologia*, vol. 74, 1924, pp. 137-158.

37. Hatton, op. cit., p. 127.

38. Hyde, R., *The A to Z of Restoration London*, London, Guildhall Library, 1992, pp. 25-8 and 35-8.

39. See Elizabeth McKellar pp. 127-8 for the use of drawn plans as a form of legal documentation.

40. Lock, master-carpenter, took over at Fishmongers' and Apothecaries' Halls; Cartwright, master-mason at the Royal Exchange and Drapers' Hall, and Oliver at Mercers' Hall.

Chapter 2 – The Jerman Family seen through the Records
of the Carpenters' Company

1. Carpenters' Company Warden's Accounts, GLMS 4326-2 fo. 250. Apprentices were usually presented by their masters at the age of seventeen or thereabouts, most of them serving an apprenticeship of between seven and nine years. Thus, if Roger followed the usual apprenticeship route to becoming a freeman, his birth can be set about 1520.

2. Michael Pinhorn gives dates of the births, marriages and deaths of some members of the Jerman family. See Pinhorn, M., "The Jerman Family", *Blackmansbury 1*, nos. 5-6, 1965. Roger enjoyed a close relationship with Christ's Hospital, and from the mid-1570s, he rented a house and carpenter's yard from them. Christ's Hospital Treasurer's Accounts, GLMS 12819-2, 1576.

3. This church, close by Mercers' Hall and the conduit in Cheapside, was situated on one of the most prominent sites in the City, and in the late 1630s its rebuilding was to be the subject of considerable acrimony between the church wardens, the Privy Council and Inigo Jones. Anthony Jerman, Roger's grandson, was requested to make a wooden model of the church early in 1637, as recorded in the Churchwardens' Accounts, GLMS 2895-2, 1637-38. For a full discussion of the circumstances surrounding the rebuilding of the church, see Colvin, H., "Inigo Jones and the Church of St. Michael le Querne", *The London Journal,* vol. 12 (1), summer 1986, pp. 36-39.

4. *Records of Carpenters' Company Court Book*, vol. 6, 1573-1594, fo. 79,1577.

5. "John Tarrant, apprentice of Edward Jerman, deceased". Ibid., fo. 234, 8 July 1587.

6. Ibid., fo. 86.

7. It is possible that, because Roger (Edward's father) and Elias (Anthony's father) were both freemen of the Carpenters' Company, their sons could have been made free by patrimony. This privilege allowed the by-passing of the formal apprenticeship system. The son of a freeman could be made free by patrimony at the age of twenty-one, enabling him to cut three or four years off his apprenticeship.

8. GLMS 4326-6 fo.102.

9. Goldsmiths' Company Court Minutes, Vol. T, fo. 191v., 19 June 1639.

10. Pinhorn, M., op. cit., p. 6.

11. GC Internal Activities, E 12(a), 18 July 1635.

12. Christ's Hospital View Book, GLMS 12834-2 fo. 146, 21 February 1666/7.

13. St. Giles Cripplegate Church Wardens' Accounts, GLMS 6419-8.

14. In the parish of St. Giles during 1665, 8,000 deaths were recorded, the great majority documented as due to the plague. Most were buried in the Pest House Burial Ground, while some were interred in the small graveyard surrounding the church. During 1665, 1,200 loads of earth were carted in to cover the corpses with two feet of soil. As a result, the churchyard was higher than the floor of the church and the neighbouring streets. The church escaped the Fire of 1666, and all interments were forbidden in the churchyard for seven years. Baddeley, J., *An Account of the Church and Parish of St. Giles without Cripplegate*, London, 1888, pp. 20-25. Edward Jerman must have been a much-respected parishioner to be granted a church burial at this critical time.

15. Whitebrook, J.C., ed., *London Citizens in 1651, being a transcript of Harleian MS 4778*, London, Hutchings and Romer, 1909, p.19.

16. GLMS 4326-9 fo. 152.

17. Van Lennep, W., ed., *The London Stage 1660-1800*, Carbondale, Southern Illinois University Press, 1963, pp. xxxix-xi; Hotson, L., *The Commonwealth and Restoration Stage*, Cambridge, Mass., Harvard University Press, 1928, p. 233.

18. For much of the information about the development, history and details of events concerning

the Carpenters' Company as described in this section, I am indebted to the works of E.B. Jupp; B. Alford and T. Barker; and Jasper Ridley. Their books published in 1887, 1968 and 1995 respectively, provide a thoroughly comprehensive account of the Company, the latter two utilising the extensive research carried out by E.B. Jupp in his capacity as Clerk of the Carpenters' Company.

19. The land lay at All Hallows by London Wall. Five old cottages on the land were demolished and replace by "a Great Hall and three New Houses".

20. Admission to the freedom by redemption required the payment of a fee or fine negotiable between the applicant and the company. See Chapter 3 for an explanation of routes to the attainment of the freedom of a City company.

21. This situation is well described in Vivienne Aldous' article "The Archives of the Freedom of the City of London 1681-1915", *Genealogists' Magazine*, vol. 23, no. 4, December 1989, p. 257.

22. GLMS 4329-1 fo. 192.

23. For a full account of these disputes, see Louw, H. J., "Demarcation Disputes between the English Carpenters and Joiners from the Sixteenth to the Eighteenth Century", *Construction History*, vol. 5, 1989, pp. 3-20.

24. Hebert, W., *The History of the Twelve Great Livery Companies of London*, New York, Augustus Kelly, 1968, vol. 1, p. 112.

25. *Carpenters' Company Warden's Accounts*, vol. 5, 1571-1591, fo. 91, ibid., fo. 121.

26. Ibid., fo. 179.

27. Ward, J.P., *Metropolitan Communities, Trade Guilds, Identity and Change in Early Modern London*, Stanford CA., Stanford University Press, 1997, p. 2.

28. *Carpenters' Company Court Book*, vol. 6, 1573-1594, fo. 109.

29. Ibid., fo. 102.

30. Ibid., fo. 251.

31. Ibid., fos. 167, 197.

32. Ibid., fo. 205.

33. *Carpenters' Company Court Book*, vol. 6, 1573-1594 fos. 77, 79.

34. Christ's Hospital Evidence Book, GLMS 12805 fo. 5.

35. Carpenters' Company Warden's Accounts, GLMS 4326-6 fo. 280, 2 September 1610.

36. Ibid., fo. 266.

37 Ironmongers' Company Court Minutes, GLMS 16967 - 1 fo. 182, 8 June 1586; 13 November 1587. The building which was supervised by a committee of twelve, was constructed in brick, lath and plaster, timber and tile. See Elizabeth Glover, *A History of the Ironmongers' Company*, London, Ironmongers, 1991, pp. 49- 50.

38. Moody, T., *The Londonderry Plantation 1609-1641*, Belfast, William Mullan and Son, 1939, p. 64.

39. Ibid., p. 280.

40. Moody, T., and Sims, J., eds., *The Bishopric of Derry and the Irish Society of London 1602-1670*, Dublin, Stationary Office, 1968, vol. 1, p. 89.

41. Carpenters' Company Warden's Accounts, GLMS 4326-7 fo. 213.

42. Ibid., GLMS 4326-7, September 1630.

43. Carpenters' Company Court Minutes, GLMS 4329-5 fo. 16v.

44. For details concerning City Viewers, see Chapter 3.

45. Carpenters' Company Court Minutes, GLMS 4329-5 fo. 2v.

46. Carpenters' Company Warden's Accounts, GLMS 4326-9, 12 August 1656.

47. Robinson, H., and Adams, W., eds. *The Diary of Robert Hooke 1672-1680*, London, 1935, p. 381.

Chapter 3 – Edward Jerman: City Worker

1. Riley, H.T., ed., *Liber Albus*, London, Longman and Roberts, 1859, p. xxix. The Liber Albus, Liber Custumarum and several similar volumes, including Liber Antiquis Legibus, compiled, translated and edited from the original Latin and Anglo-Norman, are chronicles of statues, transactions and customs relating to the City of London from 1178 until 1419.
2. An Assize, in this case, refers to a decree or edict.
3. Such precautions were still being recommended just before the Great Fire, but were largely ignored. Night-time baking was said to be the cause of the outbreak of fire in Pudding Lane.
4. Riley, H.T., ed., *Munimenta Gildhallae Londoniensis, Liber Custumarum*, London, Longman and Roberts, 1860, p. xxxiv. For details concerning the surviving texts of this and other building regulations, see Chew, H., and Kellaway, W., eds, *The Assize of Nuisance 1304-1431*, London, London Record Society, no. 10, 1973, p. ix et seq.
5. Sharpe, R., ed., *Calendar of the Letter Books of the City of London, C,* London 1899, p. 86. The Calendar of the Letter Books is a series of volumes lettered A to Z and AA to ZZ which record the proceedings of the Court of Common Council and the Court of Aldermen. The earlier volumes probably contain the only record of these proceedings prior to the fifteenth century, when they were first recorded in separate volumes known as Journals and Repertories respectively. The Letter Books, preserved at the Guildhall, are of vellum, while the Journals and Repertories are of paper.
6. *Assize of Nuisance*, Miscellaneous Roll DD no. 53. This has been transcribed by Chew and Kellaway, op.cit., p. 11. See also pp. xxxiii and xxxiv for a description of the membranes which constitute the Miscellaneous Rolls.
7. CLB. G, p. 279.
8. CLB. K, p. 276.
9. JOR 5 fo. 231.
10. CLB. M, p. 150.
11. CLB. D, p. 195.
12. Jupp, E.B., *An Historical Account of the Worshipful Company of Carpenters*, p. 193.
13. REP 72 fo. 80v., 14 March 1666/7.
14. REP 73 fo. 225.
15. Pearl, V., "Change and Stability in Seventeenth-Century London", in *The London Journal*, vol. 5, no. 1, May 1979, p.13.
16. REP 46 fo. 440v., 15 October 1632.
17. REP 57 (2) fo. 12, 19 March 1644/5.
18. Here, it is interesting to note that Edward Jerman had been appointed to an equivalent post, that of City Carpenter, when he was twenty-seven. It is difficult to know whether Anthony was an extremely ambitious father who, holding prestigious posts in both the City and the Carpenters' Company, was ensuring that his son should take on his mantle at his retirement, and was prepared to share the post of City Carpenter with Edward for seventeen years to guarantee this, or whether Edward was, in fact, an unusually talented young man. Perhaps both.
19. See Chapter 4 for reference to Peter Mills' country house designs, and also Colvin, H., "Thorpe Hall and its Architect" in *Essays in English Architectural History*, New Haven and London, Paul Mellon, 1999, pp. 158-178.
20. Christ's Hospital View Book 1622-1656, GLMS 12834-1 fo. 191.
21. REP 63 fo. 144 v., 13 July 1654.
22. Goldsmiths' Company Court Book Y 1648-1651 fo. 138v., 24 April 1650.
23. See Chapter 4 for details of these pamphlets, and Tatham's praise of Jerman.
24. Goldsmiths' Company Court Book 5 1665-1609, fo. 252, 5 February 1668/9. Edward Jerman's

work for the Goldsmiths Company is discussed in Chapter 5.

25. As stated in endnote 18, Anthony seems to have been ambitious for his sons. Not only did he introduce Edward to the Fishmongers' Company, but he had his oldest son Hugh working alongside him when he was engaged on the rebuilding of Goldsmiths' Hall from 1635 (see Chapter 5). He was eager to strengthen the family name within the world of the City master-craftsmen and City businessmen.

26. Colvin, H., "Thorpe Hall and its Architect", p. 169.

27. City Lands Grant Book 3 fo. 52, 4 December 1654.

28. City Lands Grant Book fo. 62v., marginal note, 21 April 1658.

29. For a discussion of development in the City, see McKellar, E., *The Birth of Modern London*, pp. 38-56. Although most of McKellar's discussion centres around the West End of London, she does mention City development, albeit post-Fire.

30. This Proclamation, which has been transcribed, can be found in Birch, W., ed., *Historical Charters and Constitutional Documents of the City of London*, London, Whiting, 1897, pp. 224-230.

31. *The Correspondence of Henry Oldenburg*, eds. A.R. Hall and M.B. Watson, Madison, University of Wisconsin Press, 1956-1986, vol. 3, p. 226. Pepys, too, mentioned in his Diary of 8 September 1666 that people were "speaking their thoughts about the rebuilding of the City".

32. *London Gazette*, no. 89, 20-24 September 1666.

33. JOR 46 fo. 123, 4 October 1666.

34. JOR 46 fo. 129.

35. Pepys, S., *The Diary of Samuel Pepys*, R. Latham and W. Matthews, eds., London, Bell and Hyman, 1970-1983, 28 February 1667.

36. JOR 46 fo. 148, 3 March 1666/7.

37. JOR 46 fo. 152.

38. John Oliver, after some persuasion, and after he had assisted Peter Mills in his work without taking any fee, agreed to accept a Surveyorship in January 1667/8. REP 63 fo. 72, 23 January 1667/8.

39. See Jones, P.E., ed., *The Fire Court*, London, Corporation of London, 1966, vol. 1, pp. 152-3 for details of Jerman's estimate of the case.

40. Ibid., pp. 99, 100. A "front" house was one which fronted a street or lane of note, while a "back" house was approached across a yard or through a narrow alley.

41. Mills' Survey, GLMS 84-1, 1667-68.

Chapter 4 – Edward Jerman as Pageant Maker

1. Bergeron, D, "Anthony Munday: Pageant Poet to the City of London", pp. 345-368 in *The Huntington Library Quarterly*, vol. 30, no. 4, 1967, p. 346.

2. Berlin, Michael, "Civic Ceremony in Early Modern London", pp. 15-27, in *Urban History Yearbook*, Avon, Leicester University Press, 1986, pp. 15-18.

3. *Liber de Antiquis Legibus. The chronicles of the Mayor and Sheriffs of London 1188-1274*, London, Trubner, 1863, p. 1.

4. Strype, J., *A Survey of the Cities of London and Westminster . . . by John Stow*, London, 1720, vol. 1, p. 265. ". . . on the vigil of St John the Baptist and on St Peter and St Paul there were standing watches in every ward and street of this City, there was also a marching watch that passed through the principal streets, with five hundred cressets being fired by the companies. There were also diverse pageants, Morris Dancers, constables, every one his henchman following him, his minstrels before him, the Mayor's officers for a guard before him all in a livery of worsted, the Mayor himself well mounted on horseback. The Mayor had besides his giant three pageants, the Sheriffs but two. This midsummer watch was accustomed yearly, time out of mind until the year 1539".

5. Bergeron, D., "Anthony Munday, Pageant-Poet to the City of London", p. 357; Bullen, A.H., ed., *The Works of Thomas Middleton*, London, John Nimmo, 1886, vol. 7, p. 389.

6. Hall, E., *Hall's Chronicle containing the History of England*, London, printed for Johnson and Rivington, 1809 edition, p. 798.

7. Berlin, M., op. cit., p. 19.

8. Machyn, H., *The Diary of Henry Machyn, Citizen and Merchant Taylor of London from 1550-1565*, London, printed for the Camden Society by J.B. Nichols and Son, 1848, p. 47.

9. Nichols, J.G., *London Pageants*, London, printed for J.B. Nichols, 1831, p. 99.

10. Robertson, J., and Gordon, G.J., eds., Collections III, *A Calendar of the Dramatic Records in the Books of the Livery Companies 1485-1640*, Malone Society, Oxford University Press, 1054, p. xxxii. As early as 1566, printed forms of speeches and songs had been distributed to the children who performed in the Shows. This was, presumably, an attempt by the organisers to help the children to learn their lines, or to remind them on the day should they forget, and these printed sheets were not circulated amongst the spectators.

11. For a full discussion of this argument, see D.J. Gordon "Poet and Architect, the Intellectual Setting of the Quarrel between Ben Johnson and Inigo Jones", pp. 152-178 in *Journal of the Warburg and Courtauld Institutes*, 12, 1949, p. 155. Gordon states that the "body" is the visual image and the "soul" is the *mot*, the verse, the words that must accompany it. David Bergeron draws a somewhat different distinction between the "soul" and the "body". For him, the thematic, symbolical, allegorical and emblematic nature of the entertainments is the concern of the "soul" while the stage properties, the expenses, the builders of the devices (the artificers) comprise the "body". Bergeron, D., *English Civic Pageantry 1558-1642*, London, Edward Arnold, 1971, pp. 3-4.

12. Bowers, F., ed., *The Dramatic Works of Thomas Dekker*, Cambridge, Cambridge University Press, 1955, part 2, p. 257.

13. As Gordon stated, "Jonson was aware of his dignity as poet and was hardly of a pacific disposition; and Inigo was certainly ambitious and proud of his Italian culture and techniques". Gordon, D.J., "Poet and Architect", p. 153.

14. Pepys, S., *Diary*, 23 April 1661.

15. Ward, N., *The London Spy*, ed. Paul Hyland, East Lansing, Colleagues Press, 1993, pp. 224-5. *The London Spy* originally appeared in monthly instalments beginning in November 1698, and was published in volume form in 1703. Another vivid description of crowd behaviour and the noise of the spectators at a Lord Mayor's Show is found in Malcolm Smuts' "Public Ceremony and Royal Charisma: The English Royal Entry in London 1485-1642", pp. 65-93 in *The First Modern Society: Essays in English History in Honour of Lawrence Stone*, eds. A.L. Beier, D. Cannadine and J. Rosenheim, Cambridge, Cambridge University Press, 1989, pp. 74-75.

16. Richards, K., "The Restoration Pageants of John Tatham", pp. 49-73 in *Western Popular Theatre*, eds. D. Mayer and K. Richards, London and New York, Methuen, 1977, p. 61.

17. Morrissey, L.J., "Theatrical Records of the London Guilds", pp. 99-113 in *Theatre Notebook*, 29, 1975, p. 104, quoting Haberdashers' Court Book 1651-1671, fo. 113.

18. Bergeron, D., *English Civic Pageantry 1558-1642*, London, Edward Arnold, 1971; this point is also made by Robertson and Gordon in *Collections III*, p. xxxviii, "What did the citizen audience make of it all when the familiar subject was translated into classical terms – when, for example, the forge of Lemnos appeared in the Ironmongers' pageant of 1618, or when Jason, Alexander, Hercules and Caesar appeared, identified by their appropriate emblems, as types of Honour achieved in the Drapers' pageant of 1621?"

19. Although Grinkin was the first artificer to receive such recognition, Bergeron states that the first time the identity of an artificer was known was in 1604, when Stephen Harrison designed triumphal arches for the royal passage of James I. Bergeron, D., *English Civic Pageantry*, pp. 71-2.

20. Bullen, A., op. cit., p. 395.

21. Ibid., p. 262.

22. Bergeron, D., "The Christmas Family: Artificers in English Civic Pageantry", pp. 354-364 in *English Literary History*, vol. 35, no. 3, 1968, pp. 360-61; Haberdashers' Yeomanry Wardens' Accounts 1601-1661, GLMS 15868, 1632, fo. 27v.

23. Withington, R., *English Pageantry*, Cambridge, Mass., Harvard University Press, 1920, vol. 2, p. 43. The legitimate theatre had also been forbidden in 1642, along with dancing and bear-baiting. Leslie Hotson gives a fascinating account of the running battles between actors and the authorities. The former regularly showed overt contempt for the law by staging plays that drew great crowds, only to find their theatres dismantled by the latter. Hotson, L., *The Commonwealth and Restoration Stage*, Cambridge, Mass., Harvard University Press, 1929, pp. 1-70.

24. Seaver, P., "The Artisanal World", pp. 87-100 in *The Theatrical City: Culture, Theatre and Politics in London 1576-1649*, eds., D. Smith, R. Strier and D. Bevington, Cambridge, Cambridge University Press, 1995, p. 92.

25. JOR 41 fo. 24v; fo. 248, 1 April 1661; ledger ex GL 289 lists the contribution of each of the City companies.

26. Gayton, E., *Charity Triumphant or the Virgin Shew*, London, Brooks, 1655.

27. Tatham, J., *London's Triumphs*, London, printed by Thomas Mabb, 1661.

28. Morrissey, L.J., "English Pageant Wagons", pp. 353-374, in *American Society for Eighteenth-Century Studies*, vol. 9, no. 3, Spring 1976, pp. 361-369.

29. Grocers' Company Calendar of the Minute Books, vol. 4, part 3, pp. 764, 768.

30. Grocers' Company Court Minutes, GLMS 7301-2 fo. 568, 2 October 1661.

31. Tatham, J., *London's Triumphs*, 1664.

32. REP 65 fo. 199, 13 October 1657, "It is ordered that Mr. Jerman have liberty to use the room in Leadenhall called the Pageant House for preparing of some pageants intended for the Lord Mayor's Day"; REP 66, fo. 320v., 11 October 1659, "it is ordered by this Court that such convenient place of Gresham College as Mr. Jerman shall appoint may be used for preparing the pageant against the Lord Mayor's Day".

33. Leathersellers' Company Court Minutes, 24 February 1633/4.

34. A description of the animal scenes, machines and props at this time can be found in *The London Stage 1600-1800*, William Van Lennep, ed., Carbondale, Southern Illinois University Press, 1965, part I, pp. lxxxiv-lxxxvi.

35. For a map depicting civic and royal processional routes, see Manley, L., *Literature and Culture in Early Modern London*, Cambridge, Cambridge University Press, 195, pp. 226-7.

36. Tatham, J., *London's Glory*, 1660.

37. CLRO ex GLMS 289

38. For a discussion of such precepts, see Edie, C., "For 'The Honour and Welfare of the City': London's Gift to King Charles II on his Coming into the Kingdom, May 1660", pp. 119-131 in *The Huntington Library Quarterly*, vol. 50, no. 2, Spring 1987, p. 123.

39. Ward, N., op. cit., p. 225.

Chapter 5 – Edward Jerman's Work for the Fishermongers' Company

1. Priscilla Metcalf's scholarly work, *The Halls of the Fishmongers' Company*, provides detailed account of the several Halls of the Company. Fishmongers' Company Accounts GLMS 5561-1, fo.77.

2. Munday, A., *The Fishmongers' Pageant 1616*, ed. G. Nichols, London 1859, p. 18. See also Chapter 4.

3. Herbert, W., *The Twelve Great Livery Companies*, p. 209.

4. Metcalf, P., *The Halls of the Fishmongers' Company*, p. 33.

5. There were no pageants between 1640 and 1655, due to the political situation. Jerman's clearest memories of pageant props must have therefore been those he scrutinised in 1639.

6. For a discussion of the building trades at this time, see also H. Colvin, *Dictionary*, pp. 21-28.

7. Wren Society, vol. IV, letter no. 3, 25 June 1681.

8. Ibid. See also McKellar, *The Birth of Modern London*, for a brief summary of contracting methods in the late seventeenth century, pp. 85-86.

9. Gunther, R., *The Architecture of Sir Roger Pratt*, Oxford, Oxford University Press, 1928, p. 87.

10. Ibid., p. 48

11. Gerbier, B., *Brief Discourse*, London, 1662, p. 26.

12. McKellar, E., op. cit., p. 86. For a description of seventeenth-century building contracts in general, and of those in operation during the building of St Paul's, see Lang, J., *Rebuilding St Paul's after the Great Fire*, Oxford, Geoffrey Cumberlege Oxford University Press, 1956, pp. 79-90.

13. Royal Exchange Renter Wardens' Account Books 1667-1672.

14. GLMS 5570-4 fo. 500, 15 May 1655. "Mr Jerman shall be allowed five shillings for every half day and ten shillings for every whole day whereon he shall view any house for this company".

15. Stow, J., *Survey of London*, Kingsford edition, vol. 1, p. 135.

16. Fishmongers' Company Court Minutes, GLMS 5570-4 fo. 430.

17. GLMS 5570-3 fo. 657, 1 May 1643.

18. GLMS 5570-4 fo. 448, 22 August 1654, "provided that he make a window there of the same height and breadth with the window directly over the same . . . with an arch roof of plaster, and that he consent to secure and damnify the building".

19. GLMS 5570-4, fo. 1066, 15 April 1663.

20. Albion, R., *Forests and Sea Power. The Timber Problem of the Royal Navy 1652-1862*. Cambridge, Mass., Harvard University Press, 1926, p. 100.

21. GLMS 5570-4 fo. 961, 20 August 1661.

22. GLMS 5570-4 fo. 1118, 8 February 1663/4. For a discussion of the demarcation disputes between various members of the timber trade, see H.J. Louw, "Demarcation Disputes between the English Carpenters and Joiners", *Construction History*, vol. 5, 1989, p. 14.

23. GLMS 5570-4 fo. 1066, 15 April 1663.

24. GLMS 5570-5 fo. 1, 13 September 1666.

25. Ibid.

26. MC.GR (ii) fo. 293, 25 April 1667.

27. GLMS 5570-5 fo. 49, 16 July 1667.

28. GLMS 5570-5 fo. 54, 27 August 1667.

29. GLMS 5570-5 fo. 73, 23 January 1667/8.

30. Scaffolding erected on the exterior of buildings was the master-carpenter's responsibility. P. Metcalf, op. cit., p. 69. GLMS 5570-5 fo. 90, 26 May 1668.

31. GLMS 5570-5 fo. 109, 29 October 1668.

32. Metcalf, P., op. cit., p. 70.

33. John Norden's 1600 view depicts this four-bay building.

34. The only other extant example of Jerman's draughtsmanship is a drawing of the front elevation of Drapers' Hall, described in Chapter 7.

35. Hatton, E., *A New View of London*, vol. 2, p.627.

36. This is referred to in GLMS 5570-5 fo. 298, 19 September 1672.

37. The extent of Lock's modifications of Jerman's plans is debateable. Although Priscilla Metcalf, in *The Halls of the Fishmongers' Company*, discusses Lock's activities during his period as surveyor, there is no evidence in the minute books of any further drafts following that of 1669.

38. See Chapter 6 for details of this Hall building.

39. Colvin, H., "Inigo Jones and the Church of St. Michael le Querne", pp. 36-39.

40. The degree of Jones' participation is still much debated. Mowl and Earnshaw seem to credit Jones with being the major designer, but Colvin is less convinced. He describes the evidence for Jones' involvement in the design of the house as "confused and perhaps apocryphal". Mowl and Earnshaw, *Architecture without Kings*, p. 53; Colvin, H., *Dictionary*, p. 560.

41. Newman, J., op. cit., p. 35.

42. Strype, J., op. cit., vol. 1, book 2, chapter 11, p. 182.

Chapter 6 – Father and Son at Goldsmiths' Hall

1. Stow, J., *A Survey of London*, Kingsford edition, Oxford, Clarendon Press, 1908, vol. 1, p. 345.

2. Hentzner, P., *A Journey into England, 1598*, ed. Horace Walpole, Strawberry Hill, 1757.

3. Prideaux, W.S., *Memorials of the Goldsmiths' Company*, London, Eyre and Spottiswoode, 1896, vol. 1, p. 134.

4. Calendar of State Papers Domestic 1634-1635, p. 28, Order of Council, 12 November 1634.

5. GC. CB R part 2 fo. 440, 20 March 1633/4.

6. Stow, J., op. cit. p. 305.

7. See Knowles, C., and Pitt, P., *The History of Building Regulation in London 1189-1972*, London, The Architectural Press, 1972.

8. GC. CB S part 1 fo. 23, 7 August 1634.

9. Ibid.

10. GC. CB S part 1 fo. 38, fo. 44, 6 November 1634.

11. GC. CB S part 1 fo. 77, fo. 81, 12 December 1634.

12. Colvin, H., *Dictionary*, pp. 43-45.

13. Newman, J., op. cit., pp. 33-37. "Nicholas Stone's Goldsmiths' Hall. Design and Practice in the 1630s", in *Architectural History*, vol. 14, 1971, pp. 33-37.

14. GC. CB S part 1, fo. 11, 4 February 1634/5, part 2 fo. 336, 8 January 1635/6.

15. Goldsmiths' Company Indented Articles E, The Hall, Internal Activities 2 (a), 1 July 1635.

16. Prideaux, W., op. cit., vol. 1, p. 170.

17. GC. CB S part 2 fo. 374, 5 April 1636.

18. GC. CB S part 2 fo. 508, 21 April 1637.

19. GC. CB T fo. 162, 15 February 1638/9, fo. 191v., 19 June 1639.

20. Metcalf, P., *The Halls of the Fishmongers' Company*, p. 78

21. Gunther, R., *The Architecture of Sir Roger Pratt*, p. 129.

22. GLMS 5860 fo. 4, 1669.

23. MC. GR (ii) fo. 377, 10 April 1669; MC. GR (iii) fo. 41, 7 January 1670/1.

24. GC. CB Y fo. 104v., 28 November 1649.

25. GC. CB Z fo. 31v., 25 November 1651.

26. GC. CB 3 fo. 60v., 23 January 1660/1.

27. "Taking into consideration Mr. Jerman's care and pains in ordering the affairs of the Company . . . relating to the letting of ground to build on in the new street in Jewin Garden . . . and also in taking the several dimensions of several leases granted by the Company for the long term of years mentioned in the said leases being a work not formerly upon leases for a short term, but conceived at present to be advantageous to the Company for the future". GC. CB Z fo. 273v., 16 June 1654.

28. "He [Jerman] hath made a far greater improvement of the business than either he or the Company did expect, for upon his proposal of building, the Company should have received but £7 a year and something by way of fine for the cellars and first storey for 40 years to come. And now they have received in fines £323 and shall receive £35 p.a. for 21 years . . . and Mr. Jerman did

further allege that though upon the first view it appeared to be a dear bargain to the Company, yet all things considered, the Company will receive £8.10s.% for the money disbursed in this building". GC. CB 1 fo. 150v., 3 April 1656.

29. Isaac, a relative of Mr. Dun of the City Works, was married to Edward's daughter, Judith, by whom he had three sons. The oldest of Edward's grandchildren, named Jerman, graduated from St. Catherine's College, Cambridge in 1673, and was admitted to the Inner Temple. See Chapter 2.

30. When the work on Bachelors' Court was nearing completion, the Court passed a directive that anyone wishing to be a tenant therein must be a bachelor, and a freeman of the Company. Every tenant was to have a key to the outer door and to keep the court "sweet and clean". Having spent so much money on both Hall and property in this renowned location close by Cheapside and Goldsmiths' Row, the Company clearly wished that it should remain an asset. Prideaux, W., op. cit., vol. 2, p. 102.

31 Haberdashers' Company Court Minutes fo. 100, May 1663. The date of Edward's appointment as Company Carpenter to the Haberdashers is not recorded in their minutes.

32. GC. CB. 5 fo. 95v., 22 March 1666/7.

33. Macloed, J., ed., *Davidson's Principles and Practice of Medicine*, Edinburgh, Churchill Livingstone, 1981, p. 253.

34. Sontag, S., *Illness as Metaphor*, New York, Random House, 1979, p. 11.

35. GC. CB 5 fo. 187v., 1 July 1668.

Chapter 7 – Edward Jerman's Royal Exchange

1. MC.GR (ii) fo. 257, 2 November 1666.

2. For an account of the discussions concerning the design of St Paul's, see Lang, J., *Rebuilding St Paul's after the Great Fire of London*, London, Geoffrey Cumberlege, Oxford University Press, 1956, pp. 35-63. In his review of Jerman's Exchange, Strype tells us, "The model was first shown to King Charles II who liked it well. But it was debated whether they should build after this model for fear of launching too deep in the expenses. Several were therefore against it, but the majority prevailed, having their eye upon the honour of the City". Strype, J., *A Survey of the Cities of London and Westminster*, Book 2, vol. 1, p. 137.

3. Hopkinson, H.L., *Ancient Records of the Merchant Taylors' Company*, London, 1915, p. 61.

4. Stow, J., *A General Chronicle of England*, London, Richard Meighen, 1631, p. 668.

5. JOR 13 fo. 417.

6. The very word "bourse" was derived from a square in Bruges, the Place de la Bourse, where bankers met, the square being named after the van der Beursse family who lived there, in a four-bay, ungabled house.

7. Knight, C., *The Life of Sir Thomas Gresham*, London, 1845, p. 185.

8. REP 15 fo. 406 v.; Imray, J., "The origins of the Exchange", pp. 20-35 in *The Royal Exchange*, ed. Ann Saunders, London, London Topographical Society, no. 152, 1997, pp. 34-35; also p. 425.

9. REP 15 fo. 406 v. A "stranger", at this time, was the term used for a foreigner, while a "forren" was a craftsman who was not affiliated to one of the City craft companies.

10. Burgon, J., *The Life and Times of Sir Thomas Gresham*, London, Effingham Wilson, 1839, vol. 2, pp. 117-20.

11. G. W. Groos, ed., *The Diary of Baron Waldstein*, London, Thames and Hudson, 1981, p. 289; Grenade, L., "Les Singularitez de Londres", quoted on pp. 48-9 in *The Royal Exchange*, 1997.

12. This information has been gleaned from the introduction to *The Diary of Baron Waldstein*, and subsequently from Rye, W.B., *England as seen by Foreigners in the Days of Elizabeth and James the First*, London, Smith, 1865, p. 8; Hentzner, P., *A Journey into England*, p. 40; Platter,

T., *Travels in England*, ed. Clare Williams, London, Cape, 1937, p. 157 and *Transactions of the Royal Historical Society* (1892), p. 61.

13. Evelyn, J., *Memoirs*, ed. Wm. Bray, vol. 1, p. 15, August 1641; p. 38, 3 February 1644 and p. 184, June 1645.

14. Heywood, T., *The Building of the Royal Exchange* (1606) Malone Society reprints no. 78, Oxford, Oxford University Press, 1934, line 540 et seq.

15. Ward, J., *Lives of the Professors of Gresham College*, London, Moore, 1740, pp. 11-13.

16. It is not possible to know how much stone was used in Gresham's Exchange. Indications that there was a considerable amount come from three sources. Firstly, Burgon states that stone was quarried from Gresham's Norfolk estate, and from Wales, and that many shiploads of stone were transported from Flanders. Secondly, eye-witness accounts of the Fire devastating the Exchange spoke of it as a stone building, and thirdly, as we shall see, Robert Hooke's report on the despoiled Exchange suggested that there remained a great quantity of stone with which to rebuild. The exterior piazzas were the porticoes that Charles II wished to see encircling the whole building. They replaced the closed shop fronts of Gresham's Exchange, evident in Figure 7.3. Strype, J., *A Survey of the Cities of London and Westminster*, vol. 2, ch. 8, p. 149.

17. Pepys, S., *Diary*, vol. 7, p. 276; Evelyn, J., *Memoirs*, vol. 1, p. 376.

18. Vincent, T., *God's Terrible Voice in the City*, London, 1667, pp. 61-62.

19. Dryden, J., *Annus Mirabilis*, London, printed for H. Heringham, 1667.

20. Ford, S., *London's Remains*, London, printed for Samuel Gillibrand, 1667.

21. London's Lamentations, York, printed for Francis Mawbarne, 1666.

22. Pepys, S., *Diary*, vol. 7, 7 September 1666.

23. Ibid., 10 September 1666.

24. Wren, C., *Parentalia*, London, printed for T. Osborn, 1750, p. 267.

25. Evelyn, J., *London Revived*, (1666), ed. E.S. de Beer, Oxford, Clarendon Press, 1938, p. 42. In her essay "The Second Exchange", Ann Saunders discusses the various City rebuilding plans, stressing the importance that was laid upon the positioning of the Exchange.

26. Hughson, D., *London, being an Accurate History and Description of the British Metropolis*, London, Robins, 1918, vol. 1, p. 254.

27. Mercers' Company R.E. box 4.10.

28. Mercers' Company R.E. box 4.10, 6 September 1666.

29. MC.GR (ii) fo. 228.

30. Ibid.

31. MC.GR (ii) fo. 250, 19 October 1666.

32. Knight, C., *The Life of Sir Thomas Gresham*, London, Knight, 1845, p. 200.

33. MC.GR (ii) fo. 251, 23 October 1666.

34. Shakespeare, W., *Julius Caesar*, Act I, Scene 1, line 3. Geoofrey Cumberlege, Oxford University Press, Oxford, 1956.

35. MC.GR (ii) fo. 258, 9 November 1666. See Endnote 16 for a discussion of the amount of stone used in Gresham's Exchange.

36. MC.GR (ii) fos. 261-263, 16 November 1666.

37. MC.GR (ii) fo. 269, 7 December 1666, fo. 277, 11 February 1666/7.

38. MC.GR (ii) fo. 283, 4 March 1666/7.

39. MC.GR (ii) fos. 291, 292, 15 and 22 April 1667.

40. MC.GR (ii) fo. 293, 25 April 1667.

41. MC.GR (ii) fo. 294, 3 May 1667.

42. W. Tite Esq., in *The Builder*, vol. 4, no. 152, 3 January 1846 (Figures 6.10 and 6.13 are not these drawings).

43. MC.GR (ii) fo. 298, 30 May 1667. Since Jones' use of Portland stone for the Banqueting House

(1619-22), it had been the preferred stone for important London buildings, being very durable. An ancient custom of the Manor of Portland gave the tenants the right to half the duty paid on stone from the common lands, the other half going to the Crown as Lord of the Manor. This duty paid for essential building and services on the island and meant that, while Charles II and his successors derived a huge income from the sale of stone, the islanders did reap some benefits from the quarrying. Bettey, J.H., *The Island and the Royal Manor of Portland. 1750 – 1851.* Weymouth, Shewen and Son, 1970, p. 58. Portland stone is quarried in massive blocks which can imbue an effect of monumentality to any building where it is used. This was ideal for an edifice such as Jerman's Exchange, although some contemporary critics might have agreed with Pugin's assertion (1841) that "large stones destroy proportion". Pugin, A., *The True Principles of Pointed or Christian Architecture*, 1841, p. 18.

44. MC.GR (ii) fo. 303, 27 September 1667.

45. MC.GR (ii) fo. 315, 316, December 1667.

46. Portland stone, because of its high quality, was an expensive stone per se, but transport charges by sea round to the City added considerably to its cost. It was not only materials that were giving Edward Jerman a headache. A Mr. Corden, who had lived in a house (appropriately called The Grasshopper) on the north side of the Exchange, had built himself a shed on his ground, and was living in it, together with a large amount of beer he had stored there. Jerman tried to reason with him that he must move, but to no avail. Finally, the Lord Mayor managed to persuade the wardens of St Bartholomew to build a shed on their land, to which Mr. Corden and his beer could repair! MC.GR. (ii) fo. 322, 4 February 1667/8. He was, no doubt, only one of many.

47. A double pawn implied a gallery with shops on each side.

48. MC.GR (ii) fo. 332, 1 October 1668.

49. MC.GR (ii) fo. 355, 24 February 1668/9.

50. MC.GR (ii) fo. 380, 27 April 1669. For a full transcript of the Committee's appeal to Wren to intercede on their behalf, see Ann Saunders' essay "The Second Exchange", p. 132.

51. MC.GR (ii) fo. 383, 30 April 1669.

52. MC.GR (ii) fo. 395, 10 July 1669. This may be translated: This Exchange, reduced to ashes in 1666, was restored to greater splendour than before by Mayor William Turner, Knight, in 1669.

53. MC.GR (iii) fo. 29, 20 August 1670; fo. 82, 2 April 1671.

54. Saunders, A., "The Second Exchange", in *The Royal Exchange*, p. 133. Paul Jeffery, referring to Cartwright's tower for St Mary-le-Bow, states that "it was the first classical steeple to be erected in the capital", adding, "strictly speaking, this claim could be made for Edward Jerman's tower of the rebuilt Royal Exchange, although this was neither ecclesiastical nor influential". See Paul Jeffery, *The City Churches of Sir Christopher Wren*, p. 49 and note 13.

55. Roscoe, I., "The Statues of the Sovereigns of England: Sculpture for the Second Building 1695-1831", pp. 174-187 in *The Royal Exchange*, p. 183.

56. The "stuff" implies that he supplied his own materials, and the "work" that he paid the craftsmen contracted him. The labourers were paid separately by George Widmerpool, the overseer.

57. In order to compare these amounts into present-day figures, they should be multiplied by a figure between 60 and 65, as set out in *How Much is that Worth*, by Lionel Munby, Chichester, Phillimore, 1996, pp. 38, 39.

58. Summerson, J., *Architecture in Britain*, p. 176.

59. Ralph, J., *A Critical Review of the Public Buildings, Statues and Ornaments in and about London and Westminster*, London, J. Wilford and J. Clarke, 1734.

60. Malton's three preliminary drawings have only recently come to light, and I am indebted to Ursula Carlyle, archivist to the Mercers' Company, for bringing them to my attention, and to the Company for allowing me to reproduce them.

61. See Howard Colvin's "The North Front of the Royal Exchange", in *The Royal Exchange*, pp. 1-7.

62. *Great Britain's Glory, a brief description of the present state, splendour and magnificence of the Royal Exchange by Theophilus Philalethes (pseud.)*, London, J. Edwin, 1672.

Chapter 8 – Edward Jerman's Work for Other City Companies

1. Keene, D., Introduction in Imray, J., *The Mercers' Hall*, London, London Topographical Society, 1991.
2. Vincent, T, *God's Terrible Voice in the City*, pp. 64 - 65.
3. MC. AC fo. 79, 5 March 1666/7.
4. Ibid., fo. 83, 23 April 1667.
5. Ibid., fo. 94 v., 2 July 1667.
6. Ibid. For discussion of working methods see Chapter 5.
7. Ibid., fo. 99, 30 July 1667. It is interesting to note that Mr. Strong, the gentleman to whom this passage refers, was to pay, for the first year, one peppercorn. According to the *OED*, this had been established as the quit rent or nominal rent since 1607.
8. Imray, J., *The Mercers' Company*, p. 51. The entrance porch was demolished in 1880, and re-erected at Swanage Town Hall, where it still remains.
9. Sir John Frederick was Lord Mayor in 1661, and a past-Master of the Barber-Surgeons' and the Drapers' Companies. Sir Theophilus Biddulph was a Member of Parliament and a past-Master of the Drapers' Company.
10. Pepys, S., *Diary*, vol. 8, p. 218, 16 May 1667.
11. Strype, J., *A Survey of London*, vol. 1, p. 186.
12. MC. AC fo. 181, 29 March 1669.
13. It is interesting to note that the habits of City dwellers have changed little in three hundred odd years. Not only were the Mercers assuming that parents would opt to live near a good school so that their children might benefit from a first-rate education, but we also learn that most of them went to the country at the weekends. In *Angliae Notitia* (1700) Chamberlain claimed that one of the reasons that the city was so devastated by the Fire was that it began at "the dead time of the week, being Saturday night, when traders were retired to their country houses". Plus ça change.
14. Ralph, J., *A Critical Review of Public Buildings*, ed. Wm. Nicholson, London, Wallis, 1783, p. 59.
15. Maitland, W., *History and Survey of London*, vol. 2, p. 1276.
16. Chamberlayne, E., *Angliae Notitia*, London, Hodgkin, 1700, p. 371.
17. Chamberlain, H., *A New and Complete History and Survey of the Cities of London and Westminster . . . from the earliest accounts to the beginning of the year 1770*, London, Cooke, 1770, p. 523.
18. Coombe, W., *The History of St Paul's School*, London, Ackerman, 1816, p. 27.
19. MC. Colet's Accounts, 1664-1680.
20. Sir Michael McDonnell, in *Annals of St Paul's School*, Cambridge, Cambridge University Press, 1959, p. 240, categorically states that "we may be quite certain that the architect was Edward Jerman".
21. MC. AC fo. 122, 21 January 1667/8.
22. Colvin, H., Dictionary, p. 545.
23. For examples of these negotiations, see the Mercers' Company Acts of Court fo. 114, 15 October 1667; fo. 117, 3 December 1667; fo. 123, 28 January 1667/8 and fo. 147, 11 August 1668.
24. Maitland, W., op. cit., vol. 2, p. 911.
25. Wax Chandlers' Company Warden's Accounts 1667-1669, GLMS 9481-2.
26. A detailed history of the Drapers' Company is provided by Johnson, A.H., *A History of the Worshipful Company of Drapers of London*, Oxford, Clarendon Press, 1914-1922, vols 1-4; while mention of the Hall is found in Girtin, T., *The Triple Crowns*, London, Hutchinson, 1964, pp. 36, 49 and 52, and in Penelope Hunting's book to which reference will be made in due course.

27. Stow, J., *Survey of London*, 1598, p. 181.
28. Drapers' Company Minutes and Records 1640 – 1667, fo. 317, 15 October 1666.
29. Special Committee on Rebuilding of Drapers' Hall, MB/TI fo. 1, 11 February 1666/7, 4 March 1666/7.
30. Drapers' Company Minutes and Records, MB 15, fo. 2 v., 18 September 1667.
31. Ibid., fo. 5 v., 11 January 1667/68.
32. Hatton, E., *A New View of London*, vol. 2, p. 602.
33. Jesse Gibson's survey (1819) reproduced in Penelope Hunting's *History of the Drapers' Company* illustrates the layout of the Hall, which is, presumably, that laid down by Jerman in 1667.
34. Hunting, P., *A History of the Drapers' Company*, London, Drapers' Company, 1989, p. 49.
35. Johnson, A.H., op. cit., vol. 3, p. 287.
36. Beck, R. T., "Halls of the Barbers, Barber-Surgeons, and Company of Surgeons of London", *Annals of the Royal College of Surgeons of England*, vol. 47, no. 1, July 1970, pp. 14-29.
37. Murray, I., and Hall, B., "The Hall and the Area in which we live", *The Company of Barbers and Surgeons*, ed. Ian Burn, London, Farrand Press, 2000, pp. 49, 50.
38. Hatton, E., op. cit., vol. 2, p. 596; Maitland, W., op. cit., vol. 2, p. 911.
39. Hunting, P., *A History of the Society of Apothecaries*, London, Society of Apothecaries, 1999, p. 82; Apothecaries' Company Warden's Accounts, GLMS 8202-2, fo. 464, 4 May 1668.
40. Apothecaries' Company Rough Court Book, GLMS 8201-1, 23 July 1667.
41. Apothecaries' Company Warden's Accounts, GLMS 8202-2 fo. 462, 9 January 1667/8.
42. "Upon the report of the Committee for Building, and for diverse reasons by them given, it is ordered that the Hall be built flat, contrary to the model". Apothecaries' Company Court Book, GLMS 8201-1, fo. 119 v., 20 October 1668.
43. Underwood, E.A., ed., *A History of the Worshipful Society of Apothecaries of London*, London, Oxford University Press, 1963, vol. 1, p. 320; Hunting, P., *A History of the Society of Apothecaries*, London, Society of Apothecaries, 1998, p. 84.
44. Hatton, E., op. cit., vol. 2, p. 594; Strype, J., op. cit., vol. 1, p. 194.
45. Haberdashers' Company Court Minutes, GLMS 15842-2 fo. 139 v., 3 September 1667, fo. 143, 27 November 1667.
46. Weavers' Company Court Minutes, GLMS 4655-4 fo. 63 v., 1 July 1667, fo. 77, 78 v., 26 August 1667.
47. Weavers' Company Accounts, GLMS 4648-1, August-September 1667, 12 November 1667.
48. Weavers' Company Court Minutes, GLMS 4655 – 4 fo. 102 v., 27 January 1667/8.
49. Vintners' Company Court Minutes, GLMS 15201-5 fo. 137, 31 July 1672, fo. 135, 19 July 1672.
50. GLMS 15202 – 5 fo. 24, 24 January 1671.
51. Coal Duty Account Book, vol. 4, CLRO 390D ex GLMS 273.
52. GLMS 184/4.
53. Betterton was described by Pepys as "the best actor in the world", *Diary*, 1 March 1660/61.
54. Van Lennep, W., ed., *The London Stage 1660-1800*, Carbondale, Southern Illinois University Press, part I, p. xxxix; Langhans, E., "The Dorset Garden Theatre in Pictures", in *Theatre Survey*, vol. 6, 1965, pp. 134-146.
55. Ward, E., *The London Spy*, ed. Paul Hyland, East Lansing MI, Colleagues Press, 1993, p. 119.
56. Evelyn, J., *Memoirs of John Evelyn*, vol. 1, p. 416, 26 June 1671.

Conclusion

1. Edward Hatton, in 1708, wrote of "the magnificent and beautiful halls of the companies". He specifically mentioned the merits of the Drapers', Fishmongers' and Mercers' Halls, as well as the Royal Exchange, which he considered "beyond compare". Hatton, E., op. cit., vol. 2, p. 627.
2. Angell, S., *An Historical Sketch of the Royal Exchange*, London, Jennings, 1838, p. 24.

Appendix 1

Election Day Dinner 1582

Thursdaye   Courte holden The Nyntenth daie of Julie Anno
Dni 1582 And in the xxiiijth yeare of the Raigne of our
Soveraigne Ladie Quene Elizabeth then beinge presente
Thomas Townson master, Roger Raynols Roger Shers and
Gilbert Thomplinson wardens, M^r butermore, m^r harper John
Lyffe Anthonie bear, Laurence puddle Thomas Wattes
William Silvester Robert Cawsie John bond and Gregorie
Newland.

A new Lyverie elected That is to saie John Golson, Roger bushe,
John peacoke, Stephen barton, Jefferie Abbott, Robert Fishar,
John Liff, peter Cobb, Roger Jarmayn, Richard Johnson,
John Ley and Anthonie bell withe proviso that ther shalbe
but eighte to serve and that if anie doe refuse of eight then
at the discrecyon of the m^r and wardens they shall appointe
others out of the nomber before named at wch tyme Roger
Jarmayne refused and for his fyne he paied xl^s Richard Johnson refused againe and in consideracon that he shalbe exempted
and called no more to be one of the liverie hereafter promiseth
to paie xx^s John Watson and Richard Smithe the yonger
excluded from the liverie for that their abilitie was not as
heartofore it was to mayntayne their liveries and to bear other
charges as they wer wont Besids it was agreed that the said
Eight persons according to thold auncient custome of this
companie shuld buye their gowne clothes at the hall and paied
for their hoodes xiij^s iiij^d a peice and xij^d a peice to the clarke
besides his liverie gowne clothe wch was fower yardes of pewk
and coste xvj^s the yard Som iij^{li} iiij^s besides his new hood
wch charge was borne emongest the said liverie and the laste
liverie before except x^s wch was allowed by the house And
further the said Eight persones did geve xx^s a peice viz xiij^s iiij^d
to the use of this companye and vj^s viij^d towardes their dynner
againste wch said dynner daie they made their newe gownes
and they and their wives according to the old custome dynned
at the hall and so did all the rest of the liverie and their wives
at wch dynner they had boyled capon Rosted beef geese vension
Rosted capon and custard as apereth by the accompt booke.

Charges expended uppon the elleccion daie wch was the generall meatinge of All the Liverie and their wives

Paied for bread xj^s Ale iiij^s ij^d bear vj^s	xxj^s ij^d
Paied for xvj gallons of claret wine xxvj^s viij^d ij gallondes of Sake v^s viij^d	xxxij^s iiij^d
Paied for iij dozen of Capons at xxij^d the peice iij^{ll} vj^s ij pullettes ij^s ij^d xviij geese xxxiij^s half a hundred of Egges xvj^d	v^{ll} ij^s vj^d
Paied for a firkin of sturgeon and the cariage	xx^s iiij^d
Paied for xij stoane and j^{ll} of beef at xiiij^d the stoane xiiij^s ij^d xvj maribons iiij^s and vij quarters of mutton xvj^s ij^d the cariag iij^d	xxxiiij^s vj^d
Paied for baking on buk and three quarters xxj^s baking vij pasties of mutton xiiij^s, xix custardes at ij^s vj^d the peice xlvij^s vj^d	iiij^{ll} xviij^d
Paied for v^{ll} of fine sugar vj^s x^d, iij^{ll} of corse sugar iij^s, proyns iiij^{ll} viij^d Curaunce iiij^{ll} xvj^d pep ij oz iiij^d, Nutmeges j oz v^d ginger ij oz x^d Safforne j^d Saunders j^d Large mace ij oz xxij^d Synamond j oz v^d, Cloves j oz viij^d barberies vj^d biskettes j^{ll} xvj^d iiij oz of musk comfeittes vj^d	xviij^s x^d
Paied to the Preacher for the Sermond	v^s
Paied to the Porters for keepinge the gate	xij^d
Paied for Trenchers iiij^s to the mynstrells v^s	ix^s
Paied to Nicholas Willyams the carver his fee	vj^s viij^d
Paied to his ij men in Reward	ij^s
Paied to the butler vj^s viij^d to his ij men in Reward xij^d	vij^s viij^d
Paied for a quarte of swet water xvj^d to the clarke of the churche xij^d to the cookes in reward xvj^d	iiij^s viij^d
Paied for water xij^d to the cookes Laborers	ij^s
Paied for half a peke of whit salte iij^d buter vj^{ll} xviij^d	xxj^d
Paied for varges iiij^d [a potle of] white [wine] vyneger xij^d psley iiij^d	xx^d
Paied for a quarte of sake and a quarte of whit wine	xj^d
Paied for pakthread ob stoane pottes iiij^d Straweng yerbbs ij^d	ij^s iiij^d ob
Paied for washing dishes	xij^d
Paied in reward for bringing a Buck from Roger Bushe	xij^d
Paied in reward for bringinge a Buck from Jefferie Abbott and Robert Fishar ij^s the hiring of ix garnishe of Pewter xj^s	xiij^s
Paied to the Clarke his Allowaunce for his messe of meat	vj^s viij^d

Soma xviij^{ll} xviij^s viij^d ob

Appendix 2

Anthony Jerman's property 1640

Christ's Hospital View Book 1622-1656 (GLMS. 12834/1), 22 January 1639/40. fo. 144.

The measure of the tenements and yard ground in the tenure of Anthony Jerman, carpenter, measured by John Clere, carpenter and Thomas Stevenson, clerk, taken the 22 January 1639 as followeth:

The yard is in length east and west 164ft and in breadth from north to south at the east end 68½ft and in breadth north and south at the west end 76ft little more or less, and breadth in the middle 72ft.

The entrance into the yard from Little Britain 45ft little more or less, in breadth 8½ft little more or less.

A messuage or tenement wherein the said Anthony Jerman lives, built part with brick and part with timber upon the length and breadth of the same ground, in length 48ft and in breadth from out to out 10ft.

One other tenement over the gate in length 14ft and in width towards the street 16½ ft little more or less.

Two tenements at the end of the yard next St. Botolph's churchyard on the south side, the one in length 30ft 9ins and in breadth 18½ft, and the other of the same length and breadth, the kitchen to it and rooms over the said kitchen built with brick at the east end thereof.

Appendix 3
Goldsmiths' Company Indented Articles E, The Hall, Internal Activities 2 (a)

Indented articles of agreement, 18 July 1635

Articles of agreement indented, made and concluded and agreed upon the 18 day of July anno domini 1635 between Robert Hooke, citizen and goldsmith of London for and on behalf of the right worshipful the Company of Goldsmiths, London, on their part and Anthony Jerman and Hugh Jerman his son, citizens and carpenters of London on the other part, as followeth:

Imprimus: The said Anthony Jerman and Hugh Jerman for themselves and their and both and either of their executors do jointly and severally covenant, promise and grant to and with the said Robert Hooke, his executors, administrators and assignees, by these put in manner and form following, that is to say that the said Anthony Jerman and Hugh Jerman, or one of them, their or one of their executors or assignees shall and will (for the consideration hereafter mentioned) at their or the sum of their own proper costs and charges ? supply ? timber, boards, nails, carving, workmanship and materials whatsoever belonging to carpenters work for the erecting, building or fitting up of a Hall and other buildings to be adjoining thereunto for the said Company of Goldsmiths, London, bounding upon Foster Lane, Gutter Lane and Maiden Lane, the scantlings and particulars to be as followeth viz:

All and every the timber to be of good, sound oak, and all the boards of the floors to be of good and well seasoned deal. And the scantlings for the roof of the Hall, the raising plates to be nine inches and seven inches and the beams to be eight inches thick and ten inches high. The joists thereof to be ten inches and three inches, to be well boarded. The principal rafters to be eight inches and nine inches, and the king pieces and the two assistants to the principal rafters to be eight inches and nine inches. The purlins on each side to be eight inches and nine inches, the single rafters to be five inches and four inches. Every bay of the foresaid floor and roof to be ten feet or near thereabouts. The first floor of the parlour, the summers to be sixteen inches broad and fourteen inches deep and not to lie above ten or eleven feet distance or thereabouts, to fit the piers between the windows. The joists to be sixteen inches deep and three inches thick and the floor be boarded with good spruce deal and well seasoned. The roof over the great chamber, over the parlour, the summers thereof to be fourteen inches broad and twelve inches thick, the joists to be twelve inches and three inches, the wall plates or raising pieces to be nine inches and seven inches, the principal rafters to be ten inches and nine inches, the purlins to be nine inches and eight inches, the single rafters to be five inches and three inches. For the ceiling of the roof, the collar beams framed into the principal rafters to be eight inches and five inches. The ceiling joists to be six inches and three inches. The scantlings for and over the two butteries and for and over the kitchen to be in like proportion in bigness so the Hall is appointed. The scantlings of the first floor towards Foster Lane, and also on the south side of the court towards Kerry Lane and consequently all the floors of those two sides to be as followeth viz:

The summers to be thirteen inches and eight inches, and not to lie above ten feet assunder, or thereabouts, as the piers fall out between the windows. The joists to be eight inches and three inches. The roof of those two sides, the wall plates or raising pieces thereof to be eight inches and six inches. The principal rafters to be eight inches and nine inches, the purlins to be seven inches and eight inches and the single rafters to be five inches and three inches. The collar beams to be seven inches and five inches, the ceiling-joists to be six inches and two inches. All partitions, the posts thereof to be six inches and eight inches, interstices to be six inches and seven inches, the quarters to be four inches and two inches. The doors and door cases for timber partitions to be laid about with an architrave. The doors to be glued and battened. The door cases in brick partitions, the frames thereof to be moulded with an architrave wrought out of the same timber. The doors likewise to be glued and battened. And shall substantially, neatly, artificially well and workmanly be performed the said carpenter's work belonging to the said building in all and every respect according to the draft or design thereof drawn. And such directions as shall be given them by Nicholas Stone surveyor appointed for the same building or such other surveyor for the same as shall be from time to time chosen or appointed by the Wardens and Assistants of the aforesaid company for the time being. And fully finish all and every the said carpenters work with all convenient speed, making no neglect or delay, but as speedily as the masons and bricklayers do make ready for the same. And so soon as the masons and bricklayers work shall be ready, the said Anthony and Hugh shall forthwith raise the same, whereby the masons and bricklayers shall not nor may not be hindered by any such neglect of the carpenters. And shall make the first floor over the two butteries to be as followeth viz: the summers to be twelve inches high and ten inches thick and the joist to be twenty inches and three inches. And to be neatly boarded with good and well seasoned deal.

In consideration whereof, the said Robert Hooke for himself, his executors, administrators and assignees and for every of them doth covenant, promise and grant to and with the said Anthony Jerman and Hugh Jerman, their executors, administrators and assignees here present in manner and form following, that is to say that he, Robert Hooke, his executors or assignees shall truly pay or cause to be paid unto the said Anthony Jerman and Hugh Jerman, their executors or assignees, for every square of the carpenters' work in and about the said Hall the sum of fifty shillings of lawful money of England. And for every square for the floorings over the said parlour, being the floor of the great chamber, the sum of fifty shillings. And for every square for the roof of the great chamber the sum of fifty shillings. And for every square for the floorings over the butteries, the sum of forty six shillings. And for ever square for the roofs of the said butteries and kitchen the sum of fifty shillings as of the Hall and parlour aforesaid. And for every square for the floorings of the first floor towards Foster Lane on the south side towards Kerry Lane and all the floors of those two sides, the sum of forty shillings. And for every square for the roofs thereof the sum of forty shilling. And for every square for every timber partition with every door and doorcase therein, the sum of five and twenty shillings. And for every door and every doorcase in every brick partition, so much as shall be thought reasonable by two indifferent men. And for every square of ceiling-joist, as they shall appear to be worth by two indifferent men. The several payments to be made as followeth, that is to say, one hundred and fifty pounds thereof at the ensealing and delivery of these present. And such other payments as shall be found fitting and needful to be paid as the work shall go forward. And the remainder when the said carpenters' work is set up and fully finished according to the true meaning of the said plott or design drawn. And the directions to be given as aforesaid and true admeasurement thereof made.

And it is agreed between the said parties that the said Anthony and Hugh Jerman shall have and take their own proper use and behalf all and every the timber of the old building now plucked down and to be pulled down, being such and not other as the Wardens of the aforesaid Company for the time being or the surveyor appointed or to be appointed aforesaid shall think fit to sell, as they the said Anthony and Hugh Jerman shall think fit to buy and not otherwise. And for the same shall endure and allow out of such payment as they are to receive one such sum or sums [hole in paper] ? as ? two indifferent men shall adjudge and award, the one to be chosen by the said Robert Hooke, or in his absence by the Wardens of the aforesaid Company for the time being, and the other by the said Anthony and Hugh Jerman. And it is lastly agreed that for all the furrings which shall prove to hang under any part of the propounded scantling of the summers all brackets for mouldings or other ways, or any compass work, all cartouches in all or under any part of the several roofs or floor etc, moulding of timber under them, all windows in any part of the roofs, all gutters in any part of the building, and all such stairs and staircases in and about the building to be performed. And they stand to such allowance as shall be thought meet by two indifferent men to be chosen as aforesaid.

In witness thereof, the parties aforesaid to these present indented articles interchangeably have set their hands and sealed this day and year above written.

Anthony Jerman   Hugh Jerman

Appendix 4
Views of Goldsmiths' Company Properties

Goldsmiths' Company, Court Book Z, 1 December 1652, fo. 113

". . .We, John Burridge, bricklayer, and Edward Jerman, carpenter, having viewed the several rooms situate lying and being in Bachelor's Court in Gutter Lane do find their decays following in and about the same. The ground plates next the yard are much decayed and for the greatest part thereof ought to have new plates in and foundations repaired. The most part of the ground floors want new boarding and joisting. The chimneys are much decayed in the foundations . . . the whole three piles are in danger of falling.

The roofs of all the buildings are so extremely decayed that there is necessity of taking them all off and new framing and tiling the same; also that through the insufficiency of the said roof, the outward storey is thrust out and the garret floor decayed which, if not repaired, may endanger the building.

The stairs leading up into four upper chambers are very inconvenient and dangerous and are necessary to be amended and that some of the upper stairs want mending.

Most of the glass windows are decayed, the glass broken, casements decayed and some doors, locks and hinges out of order.

Which said works being repaired in good and substantial manner for that in reason the Company may not in the space of 20 years be put to little or no trouble about further repair or support of the same, we, after due examination and consideration of each particular, are fearful they will cost less than the sum of £70 or £80, in testimony thereof, we have set our hands, the day and year above written.
John Burridge   Edward Jerman

Goldsmiths' Company, Court Book 1, March 1654/5, fo. 52

<u>View Westward</u>

Fleet Street.
  Mr. George Smith's . . . a back building of two rooms ready to fall down.

Shoe Lane.
  Mrs. Ladde's house wants plastering the third storey next the street.

<u>North and East View.</u>

Steyning Lane.
  Mrs. Jenisons house much out of repair.
  John Hancock's house the like.
  Flytte's house the like, very ruinous and all to pieces.

Little Wood Street.

Mr. Albrighton's house: a gutter of lead decays the house and a beam ready to drop down.

In Primrose Alley.

Mr. Howell's house much out of repair.

Mr. Jorden's houses are much out of repair, for they are ready to fall through the ceiling.

Goldsmiths' Company, Court Book Z, 1 December 1652, fo. 113

March 1656/7, fo.236

Steyning Lane.

Widow Jenison's house: . . . the jetty quite broken and the whole house is in much danger of falling.

Humphrey Flytte's house: the plastering and lathing on the second and third floors decayed.

Bibliography

Manuscript Sources

Guildhall Library Manuscript Department:
Company Records

Apothecaries' Company	Court Book	1661-72	GLMS 8201-1
	Warden's Accounts	1667-8	GLMS 8202-2
Carpenters' Company	Trade Records	1624-5	GLMS 4333
	Court Minutes	1533-1573	GLMS 4329-1
		1635-1656	GLMS 4329-5
	Warden's Accounts	1537-1546	GLMS 4326-2
		1574-1591	GLMS 4326-4
		1593-1613	GLMS 4326-5
		1592-1622	GLMS 4326-6
		1614-1647	GLMS 4326-7
		1647-1653	GLMS 4326-9
Fishmongers' Company	Court Minutes	1631-1646	GLMS 5570-3
		1646-1664	GLMS 5570-4
		1666-1699	GLMS 5570-5
	Warden's Accounts	1636-1658	GLMS 5561-1
		1658-1682	GLMS 5561-2
Grocers' Company	Court Minutes	1649-1661	GLMS 7301-2
	Warden's Accounts	1662-1671	GLMS 11571-15
Haberdashers' Company	Court Minutes	1652-1671	GLMS 15842-2
	Triumphs Accounts	1664	GLMS 15869
Ironmongers' Company	Court Minutes	1555-1602	GLMS 16967-1
Vintners' Company	Court Minutes	1669-1682	GLMS 15201-5
Wax Chandlers' Company	Warden's Accounts	1602-1671	GLMS 9481-2
Weavers' Company	Court Minutes	1666-1668	GLMS 4655-4
	Renter Bailiffs' Accounts	1666-1682	GLMS 4648-1

Guildhall Library Manuscript Department:
Other Records

Christ's Hospital	Register of Leases	1660-1683	GLMS 12879-1
	View Book	1622-1656	GLMS 12834-1
		1652-1722	GLMS 12834-2
	Evidence Book	1594-1612	GLMS 12805-5

	Committee Minutes	1666-1669	GLMS 12811-3	
	Renters Committees	1669-1676	GLMS 12811-4	
	Blackwell Hall Accounts	1666-1708	GLMS 12849	
	Court Minutes	1661-1677	GLMS 12806-6	
	Treasurer's Accounts	1608-1616	GLMS 12819-3	
		1614-1624	GLMS 12819-4	
		1624-1632	GLMS 12819-5	
		1652-1657	GLMS 12819-8	
		1657-1666	GLMS 12819-9	
		1667-1681	GLMS 12819-10	

St Giles Cripplegate   Warden's Accounts   1667-1672   GLMS 6419-8

St Michael le Querne   Churchwarden's Accounts   1605-1717   GLMS 2895-2

Corporation of London Record Office

Journals of Common Council	Journal 5	1454
	Journal 34	1627
	Journal 35	1632
	Journal 36	1633
	Journal 40	1644
	Journal 41	1650-1657
	Journal 45	1652
	Journal 46	1666-1668

Repertories of the Court of Common Council

Repertory 41	1627
Repertory 46	1632
Repertory 47	1633
Repertory 57	1644
Repertory 63	1654
Repertory 64	1655
Repertory 65	1657
Repertory 68	1662
Repertory 71	1666
Repertory 72	1667

City Lands Grant   Book 3   1652-1658

City's Cash   1/8   1653-1655

City's Cash   1/9   1655-1658

Coal Dues   1670-1673 misc. ms. 34.6

Coal Duty Account Book   1667-1676 CLRO 390 D

Coal Duty Account Book   1673-1674 misc. ms. 33.29

Newgate Prison Rebuilding 1670-1672 misc. ms. 136.1

Company Records retained at Halls

Clothworkers' Hall   Orders of Court   1649-1665

Drapers' Hall   Special Committee on Rebuilding
                               of Drapers' Hall   MB/T1

	Drapers' Company Minutes and Records	MB15
Goldsmiths' Hall	Court Book, R, part 2	1631-1634
	Court Book, S, part 1	1634-1635
	Court Book, S, part 2	1635-1637
	Court Book, T	1637-1639
	Court Book, V	1639-1642
	Court Book, W	1642-1645
	Court Book, X	1645-1648
	Court Book, Y	1648-1651
	Court Book, Z	1651-1654
	Court Book, 1	1654-1657
	Court Book, 2	1657-1660
	Court Book, 3	1660-1663
	Court Book, 4	1663-1665
	Court Book, 5	1665-1669
	The Hall: Internal Activities	2 (a)
Leathersellers' Hall	Court Minutes	1633-4
Mercers' Hall	Acts of Court	1663-1669
	Misc. Mss Box 2	MS 2.18
	Colet's Accounts	1664-1680
	Gresham Repertory (i)	1596-1625
	Gresham Repertory (ii)	1626-1669
	Gresham Repertory (iii)	1669-1676
	Renter Warden's Accounts	1662-1672
	Records of the City and Books of the Gresham Committee	R.E. Box 4.10
Skinners' Hall	Warden's Accounts	1656-1657

Printed Sources

Airs, M., *The Making of the English Country House 1500-1640*, London, Architectural Press, 1975

Airs, M., *The Tudor and Jacobean Country House: A Building History*, Stroud, Sutton, 1995

Albion, R., *Forests and Sea Power: The Timber Problem of the Royal Navy 1652-1862*, Cambridge, Mass., Harvard University Press, 1926

Aldous, V., "The Archives of the Freedom of the City of London 1681-1915", *Genealogy Magazine*, vol. 23, no. 4, December 1989, pp. 255-266

Alford, B., and Barker, T., *A History of the Carpenters' Company*, London, Allen and Unwin, 1968

Angell, S., *An Historical Sketch of the Royal Exchange*, London, Jennings, 1838

Anon., *A Short and Serious Narrative of London's Fatal Fire: a Poem . . .* , London, Dring, 1667

Archer, I., "The Nostalgia of John Stow", pp. 17-34 in *The Theatrical City. Culture, Theatre and Politics in London 1576-1649*, ed. D. Smith, R. Strier and D. Bevington, Cambridge, Cambridge University Press, 1995

Archer, I., *The Pursuit of Stability: Social Relations in Elizabethan London*, Cambridge, Cambridge University Press, 1991

Ashton, R., *The City and the Court 1603-1643*, Cambridge, Cambridge University Press, 1979

Aubin, R., *Topographical Poetry in XVIIIth Century England*, New York, The Modern Language Association of America, 1936

Aubin, R., ed., *London in Flames, London in Glory: Poems on the Fire and Rebuilding of London 1666-1709*,

New Brunswick, Rutgers University Press, 1943

Backscheider, P., *Spectacular Politics. Theatrical Power and Mass Culture in Early Modern England*, Baltimore, Johns Hopkins University Press, 1993

Baddeley, J., *An Account of the Church and Parish of St Giles, without Cripplegate, in the City of London*, London, Baddeley, 1888

Barker, F., and Jackson, P., *A History of London in Maps*, London, Barrie and Jenkins, 1990

Barton, L., *Historic Costume for the Stage*, London, Black, 1937

Beaven, A., *The Aldermen of the City of London, temp. Henry III-1908*, 2 vols, London, Fisher, 1908

Beck, R. T., "The Halls of the Barbers, Barber-Surgeons and Company of Surgeons of London", *Annals of the Royal College of Surgeons of England*, vol. 47, no. 1, July 1970, pp. 14-29

Beier, A. L., "Engine of Manufacture. The Trades of London", pp. 141-167 in *London 1500-1700. The Making of the Metropolis*, ed. A. L. Beier and R. Finlay, London, Longman, 1986

Bell, W. G., *The Great Fire of London in 1666*, London, John Lane, The Bodley Head, 1920

Bell, W. G., "The Rebuilding of London after the Great Fire of 1666", *R.I.B.A. Journal*, vol. 25, no. 7, May 1918, pp. 145-158

Bennett, J. A., "Architecture and Mathematical Practice in England, 1550-1650", pp. 23-29 in *English Architecture Public and Private. Essays for Kerry Downes*, ed. J. Bold and E. Chaney, London, Hambledon Press, 1993.

Bergeron, D., "Anthony Munday: Pageant Poet to the City of London", *The Huntington Library Quarterly*, vol. 30, no. 4, 1967, pp. 345-368

Bergeron, D., *English Civic Pageantry 1558-1642*, London, Edward Arnold, 1971

Bergeron, D., "The Christmas Family: Artificers in English Civic Pageantry", *A Journal of English Literary History*, vol. 35, no. 3, Sept. 1968, pp. 354-364

Bergeron, D., "Thomas Dekker's Lord Mayor's Shows", *English Studies*, 51, February 1970, pp. 1-14

Bergeron, D., *Thomas Heywood's Pageants*, New York, Garland, 1986

Berlin, M., "Civic Ceremony in Early Modern London", pp. 15-27 in *Urban History Yearbook 1986*, Avon, Leicester University Press, 1986

Bettey, J. H., *The Island and Royal Manor of Portland 1750-1851*, Weymouth, Sherrin and Son, 1970

Blackham, R., *The Soul of the City. London's Livery Companies: Their Storied Past, Their Living Present*, London, Sampson Low, 1931

Borer, M. C., *The City of London: a History*, London, Constable, 1977

Borsay, P., *The English Urban Renaissance, Culture and Society in the Provincial Town 1660-1770*, Oxford, Clarendon Press, 1989

Boulton, J., "Wage Labour in Seventeenth Century London", *Economic History Review*, vol. 49, no. 2, May 1996, pp. 268-290

Bradley, S., and Pevsner, N., *The City of London*, London, Penguin, 1997

Brett-James, N., *The Growth of Stuart London*, London, Allen and Unwin, 1935

Burgon, J., *The Life and Times of Sir Thomas Gresham*, London, Effingham Wilson, 1839

Campbell, R., *The London Tradesman*, London, T. Gardner, 1747

Chamberlain, H., *A New and Complete Survey of the Cities of London and Westminster . . . to the beginning of the year 1770*, London, Cooke, 1770

Chamberlayne, E., *Angliae Notitia*, London, Hodgkin, 1700

Charters, R., and Vermont, D., *A Brief History of Gresham College 1597-1997*, London, The College, 1998

Chew, H., and Kellaway, W., eds, *City of London Assize of Nuisance 1304-1431, a Calendar*, London, London Record Society, 1973

City of London Corporation, *Historical Charters and Constitutional Documents of the City of London*, London, Whiting, 1887

City of London Corporation, *Munimenta Guildhall Londoniensis: Liber albus, Liber custumarum, et Liber Horn*, 3 vols, ed. H. T. Riley, London, Longman, Brown, Green, Longmans, and Roberts, 1859-62

Clode, C., *The Early History of the Guild of Merchant Taylors*, London, Harrison and Sons, 1888

Colvin, H., *A Biographical Dictionary of British Architects 1600-1840*, New Haven and London, Yale University Press, 1995

Colvin, H., "Inigo Jones and the Church of St Michael le Querne", *The London Journal*, vol. 12 (1), Summer 1986, pp. 36-39

Colvin, H., "Thorpe Hall and its Architect" pp. 158-1173 in *Essays in English Architectural History*, New Haven and London, Paul Mellon, 1999

Colvin, H., and Newman, J., ed., *Of Building, Roger North's Writing on Architecture*, Oxford, Oxford University Press, 1981

Combe, W., *The History of St Paul's School*, London, Ackerman, 1816

Corporation of London, *The Corporation of London, its Origin, Constitution, Powers and Duties*, London, Oxford University Press, 1950

Cox, A., "Bricks to Build a Capital", pp. 3-17 in *Good and Proper Materials: The Fabric of London since the Great Fire*, ed. H. Hobhouse and A. Saunders, London, London Topographical Society, no. 140, 1989

Curl, J. S., *The Londonderry Plantation 1609-1914. The History, Architecture and Planning of the Estates of the City of London and its Livery Companies in Ulster*, Chichester, Phillimore, 1986

Dekker, T., *The Magnificent Entertainment given to King James . . . March 1603*, London, 1604

Doolittle, I., *The City of London and its Livery Companies*, Dorchester, Gavin, 1982

Doolittle, I., *The Mercers' Company 1579-1959*, London, Mercers' Company, 1994

Downes, K., *English Baroque Architecture*, London, Zwemmer, 1966

Downes, K., *The Architecture of Wren*, London, Granada, 1982

Dryden, J., *Annus Mirabilis. The Year of Wonders 1666*, London, printed for Henry Herringham, 1667

Eades, G., *Historic London: The Story of a City and its People*, London, Queen Anne Press and City of London Society, 1966

Earle, P., *The Making of the English Middle Class. Business, Society and Family Life in London 1660-1730*, London, Methuen, 1989

Edie, C., "For 'The Honour and Welfare of the City': London's Gift to King Charles II on his Coming into his Kingdom, May 1660", *The Huntington Library Quarterly*, vol. 50, no. 2, Spring 1987, pp. 119-131

Elmes, J., *Sir Christopher Wren and His Times*, London, Chapman and Hall, 1852

Eltringham, G., *Building Control and The Carpenters' Company 1588-1600*, London, The Author, 1954

Eltringham, G., *Notes on Apprenticeship in the Carpenters' Company in the Sixteenth and Seventeenth Centuries*, London, The Author, 1954

Evelyn, J., *London Revived: Consideration for its Rebuilding in 1666*, ed. E. S. de Beer, Oxford, Clarendon Press, 1938

Evelyn, J., *Memoirs*, ed. W. M. Bray, London, Colburn, 1818

Evelyn, J., *Panegyric to Charles II*, London, Crooke, 1661

Fairholt, F., *Lord Mayors' Pageants: being collections towards a history of these annual celebrations . . .*, Part 1. *History of the Lord Mayors' Pageants*, Part 2. *Reprints of Lord Mayors' Pageants*, London, Percy Society, 1843-44

Fisher, F., *London and the English Economy 1500-1700*, ed., P. J. Corfield and N. B. Harte, London, Hambledon Press, 1989

Forty, A., *Objects of Desire. Design and Society 1750-1980*, London, Thames and Hudson, 1986

Gayton, E., *Charity Triumphant, or the Virgin Shew, exhibited on 29 October 1655*, London, Brooks, 1655

Gerbier, B., *Brief Discourse Concerning the Three Chief Principles of Magnificent Building*, London, 1662

Gerbier, B., *Counsel and Advice to all Builders . . .*, London, 1663

Gilboy, E., *Wages in Eighteenth-century England*, Cambridge, Mass., Harvard University Press, 1934

Girouard, M., *Robert Smythson and the Elizabethan Country House*, New Haven and London, Yale University Press, 1983

Girtin, T., *The Triple Crowns. A Narrative History of the Drapers' Company 1364-1964*, London, Hutchinson, 1964

Girtin, T., *The Golden Ram. A Narrative History of the Clothworkers' Company 1528-1958*, London, Clothworkers, 1958

Glover, E., *A History of the Ironmongers' Company*, London, The Worshipful Company of Ironmongers, 1991

Godfrey, W. H., *A History of Architecture in and around London . . .*, London, Phoenix House, 1962

Godfrey, W. H., ed., "The Clothworkers' Company. Book of Plans of the Company's Properties made in 1612, with additions of various dates", pp. 51-97 in *London Topographical Record*, vol. 18, Cambridge, Cambridge University Press, 1942

Godfrey, W. H., ed., *The Survey of Building Sites in the City of London after the Great Fire of 1666*, 5 vols, London, London Topographical Society, 1946-65

Gordon, D. J., "Poet and Architect. The Intellectual Setting of the Quarrel between Ben Jonson and Inigo Jones", *Journal of the Warburg and Courtauld Institutes*, vol. 12, 1949, pp. 152-178

Gosling, W., *Seasonable Advice for Preventing the Mischief of Fire . . .* , London, 1643

Gotch, J. A., *Architecture of the Renaissance in England*, London, Batsford, 1894

Gotch, J. A., *The Growth of the English House*, London, Batsford, 1928

Gross, G. W., ed., *The Diary of Baron Waldstein, a Traveller in Elizabethan England*, London, Thames and Hudson, 1981

Gunther, R. T., *The Architecture of Sir Roger Pratt*, Oxford, Oxford University Press, 1928

Halfpenny, E., "'The Citie's Loyalty Display'd' (A Literary and Documentary Causerie of Charles II's Coronation Entertainment)", pp. 19-35 in *Guildhall Miscellany*, no. 10, London, Corporation of London, 1959

Hall, E., *Hall's Chronicle, Containing the History of England*, London, J. Johnson, 1809

Harding, V., "Citizen and Mercer: Sir Thomas Gresham and the social and political world of the City of London", pp. 24-37 in *Sir Thomas Gresham and Gresham College: Studies in the Intellectual History of London in the Sixteenth and Seventeenth Centuries*, Aldershot, Ashgate, 1999

Harris, E., *British Architectural Books and Writers 1556-1785*, Cambridge, Cambridge University Press, 1990

Harris, J., and Higgott, G., *Inigo Jones: Complete Architectural Drawings*, London, Zwemmer, 1989

Harris, T., *London Crowds in the Reign of Charles II: Propaganda and Politics from the Restoration until the Exclusion Crisis*, Cambridge, Cambridge University Press, 1987

Harris, T., *Politics under the Later Stuarts: Party Conflict in a Divided Society 1660-1715*, London and New York, Longman, 1993

Haslewood, J., *London Pageants: [cuttings from the "Gentleman's Magazine" . . .]*, London, 1824

Hatton, E., *A New View of London*, London, Chiswell and Churchill, 1708

Henderson, P., "The Loggia in Tudor and Early Stuart England, a Preliminary Survey", pp. 109-145 in *Albion's Classicism: The Visual Arts in England 1550-1660*, ed. L. Gent, New Haven, Yale University Press, 1995

Hentzner, P., *A Journey into England in the Year 1598*, ed. Horace Walpole, Strawberry Hill, 1757

Herbert, W., *The History of the Twelve Great Livery Companies of London*, New York, A. M. Kelly, 1968

Heywood, T., *If you Know not Me, you Know Nobody*, London, Malone Society, 1935

Hooke, R., *The Diary of Robert Hooke 1672-1680*, ed. H. Robinson and W. Adams, London, Taylor and Francis, 1935

Hope, V., *My Lord Mayor: Eight Hundred Years of London's Mayoralty*, London, Weidenfeld and Nicolson, 1989

Hopkinson, H., *Report on the Ancient Records in the Possession of the Guild of Merchant Taylors . . .* , London, Waterlow, 1915

Hotson, L., *The Commonwealth and Restoration Stage*, Cambridge, MA, Harvard University Press, 1928

Howgego, J., *Printed Maps of London 1553-1850*, Folkestone, Dawson, 1982

Hughson, D., *London: Being an Accurate History and Description of the British Metropolis*, London, J. Robins, 1918

Hunter, M., "The Making of Christopher Wren", *The London Journal*, vol. 16, no. 2, 1991, pp. 101-116

Hunting, P. *A History of the Society of Apothecaries*, London, Society of Apothecaries, 1998

Hunting, P., *A History of the Drapers' Company*, London, Drapers' Company, 1989

Hunting, P., *The Leathersellers' Company: A History*, London, The Leathersellers' Company, 1994

Hyde, R., "Ogilby and Morgan's City of London Map 1676", introduction to *The A to Z of Restoration London*, London Topographical Society, no. 145, 1992

Imray, J., *The Mercers' Hall*, London, London Topographical Society, no. 143, 1991

Imray, J., "The Origins of the Exchange", pp. 20-35 in *The Royal Exchange*, ed. A. Saunders, London, London Topographical Society, no. 152, 1997

Jeffery, P., *The City Churches of Sir Christopher Wren*, London, Hambledon Press, 1996

Jenkins, F., *Architect and Patron: A Survey of Professional Relations and Practice in England from the Sixteenth Century to the Present Day*, London, Oxford University Press, 1961

Jenner, M., "The Politics of London Air: John Evelyn's *Fumifugium* and the Restoration", *Historical Journal*, vol. 38, no. 3, 1995, pp. 535-551

Johnson, A. H., *The History of the Worshipful Company Drapers of London*, 5 vols, Oxford, Clarendon Press, 1914-1922

Johnson, P., "Jacobean Ephemera and the Immortal Word", *Renaissance Drama*, vol. 8, 1977, pp. 151-71

Jones, P. E., ed., *The Fire Court*, 2 vols, London, Corporation of London, 1966-70

Jose, N., *Ideas of the Restoration in English Literature 1660-1671*, London, Macmillan, 1984

Jupp, E. B., *An Historical Account of the Worshipful Company of Carpenters of the City of London*, London, Pickering and Chatto, 1887

Kaye, B., *The Development of the Architectural Profession in Britain: A Sociological Study*, London, Allen and Unwin, 1960

Kingdom, J., *Facsimile of the Grocers' Archives*, London, The Company, 1886

Kingsford, C. L., "A London Merchant's House and its Owners 1360-1614", *Archaeologia*, vol. 74, 1924, pp. 137-158

Kingsford, C. L., "Historical Notes on London Medieval Houses", pp. 1-66 in *London Topographical Record*, vol. 12, London, Chiswick Press, 1920

Knight, C., *The Life of Sir Thomas Gresham, Founder of the Royal Exchange*, London, Charles Knight, 1845

Knight, V., *Proposals of a New Model for Rebuilding the City of London*, London, 1666

Knoop, D., and Jones, G. P., *The London Mason in the Seventeenth Century*, Manchester, Manchester University Press, 1935

Knowles, C. C., and Pitt, P. H., *The History of Building Regulation in London 1189-1972*, London, The Architectural Press, 1972

Knowles, J., "The Spectacle of the Realm: Civic Consciousness, Rhetoric and Ritual in Early Modern London", pp. 157-189 in *Theatre and Government under the Early Stuarts*, ed., J. R. Mulryne and M. Shewring, Cambridge, Cambridge University Press, 1993

Lang, J., *Rebuilding St Paul's after the Great Fire of London*, Oxford, Geoffrey Cumberlege Oxford University Press, 1956

Langhans, E., "The Dorset Garden Theatre in Pictures", *Theatre Survey*, vol. 6, 1965

Lindley, K., *Popular Politics and Religion in Civil War London*, Aldershot, Scolar Press, 1997

Loengard, J., ed., *London Viewers and their Certificates 1508-1558*, London, London Record Society, 1989

London Intelligencer, vol. 85, Monday 31 October 1664

Louw, H., "Demarcation Disputes between the English Carpenters and Joiners from the Sixteenth to the Eighteenth Century", *Construction History*, vol. 5, 1989, pp. 3-20

Machyn, H., *The Diary of Henry Machyn, Citizen and Merchant Taylor of London, from 1550-1563*, ed. J. G. Nichols, London, Camden Society, 1848

Macleod, J., ed., *Davidson's Priciples and Practice of Medicine*, Edinburgh, Churchill Livingstone, 1981

Maidmont, J., and Logan, W., ed., *Dramatic Works of John Tatham*, Edinburgh, W. Paterson, 1879

Maitland, W., *The History and Survey of London from its Foundation . . . to the Present Time*, 2 vols, London, Osborne and Shipton, 1756

Malton, T., *Picturesque Tour through the Cities of London and Westminster*, London, T. Malton, 1792

Manley, L., *Literature and Culture in Early Modern London*, Cambridge, Cambridge University Press, 1995

Mawbarne, *England's Lamentations*, York, 1666

McDonnell, M., *Annals of St Paul's School*, London, Gavin Press, 1959

McDonnell, M., *The History of St Paul's School*, London, Chapman and Hall, 1909

McKellar, E., *The Birth of Modern London. The development and design of the City 1660-1720*, Manchester, Manchester University Press, 1999

Melton, F., "Sir Robert Clayton's Building Projects in London 1666-1672", pp. 37-41 in *Guildhall Studies in London History*, vol. 3, no. 1, October 1977

Mercer, E., *English Art 1553 – 1625*, Oxford, Clarendon Press, 1962

Metcalf, P., *The Halls of the Fishmongers' Company*, London, Phillimore, 1977

Middleton, T., *The Works of Thomas Middleton*, 7 vols, ed. A. H. Bullen, London, John C. Nimmo, 1885

Montaño, J. P., "The Quest for Consensus: the Lord Mayor's Day Shows in the 1670s" pp. 31-51 in *Culture and Society in the Stuart Restoration: Literature, Drama, History*, ed. G. MacLean, Cambridge, Cambridge University Press, 1995

Moody, T. W., *The Londonderry Plantation 1609-1641*, Belfast, Wm. Mullan and Son, 1939

Moody, T. W., and Sims, J., eds., *The Bishopric of Derry and the Irish Society of London 1602-1705*, 2 vols, Irish Manuscript Commission, 1968

Morrissey, L. J., "English Pageant Wagons", *American Society for Eighteenth-Century Studies*, vol. 9, no. 3, Spring 1976, pp. 353-374

Morrissey, L. J., "Theatrical Records of the London Guilds 1655-1708", *Theatre Notebook* vol. 29, 1975, pp. 99-113

Mowl, T., and Earnshaw, B., *Architecture without Kings. The Rise of Puritan Classicism*, Manchester, Manchester University Press, 1995

Munday, A., *Fishmongers' Pageant 1616*, London, The Worshipful Company of Fishmongers, 1844

Murray, I., and Hall, B., "The Hall and the Area in which we live", pp. 45-60 in *The Company of Barbers and Surgeons*, ed. I. Burn, London, Farrand Press, 2000

Neve, R., *The City and Country Purchaser and Building Dictionary*, London, Sprint, 1703

Newman, J., "Nicholas Stone's Goldsmiths' Hall. Design and Practice in the 1630s", *Architectural History*, vol. 14, 1971, pp. 30-39

Nichols, J. G., *London Pageants*, London, J. B. Nichols, 1831

Nisbet, J., *Fair and Reasonable: Building Contracts from 1550*, London, Stoke, 1993

Ogilby, J., *The Entertainment of His Most Excellent Majesty Charles II in His Passage through the City of London to His Coronation . . .* , London, Rycroft, 1662

Ogilby, J., *The Relation of His Majesty's Entertainment passing through the City of London to His Coronation*, London, R. Marriott, 1661

Pearce, D., *London's Mansions: The Palatial Houses of the Nobility*, London, Batsford, 1986

Pearl, V., "Change and Stability in Seventeenth-Century London", *The London Journal*, vol. 5, no. 1, May 1979, pp. 3-27

Pearl, V., *London and the Outbreak of the Puritan Revolution*, Oxford, Oxford University Press, 1961

Peck, F., *Desiderata Curiosa . . . a collection of divers scarce and curious pieces . . . relating chiefly to matters of English history . . .* , London, T. Evans, 1779

Peele, G., *The Dramatic Works of George Peele*, New Haven and London, Yale University Press, 1961

Pepys, S., *The Diary of Samuel Pepys*, 11 vols, ed. R. C. Latham and W. Matthews, London, Bell and Hyman, 1970-1983

Perks, S., "London Town Planning Schemes in 1666", *R.I.B.A. Journal*, 3rd series, (27), 1920, pp. 69-78

Pevsner, N., *A History of Building Types*, London, Thames and Hudson, 1979

Pevsner, N., "The Term 'Architect' in the Middle Ages", *Speculum*, Cambridge, Mass., Medieval Academy of America, vol. 17, 1942, pp. 549-562

Pinhorn, M., "The Jerman Family", *Blackmansbury*, vol. 1, nos. 5-6, 1965

Platt, C., *The Great Rebuildings of Tudor and Stuart England: Revolutions in Architectural Taste*, London, U.C.L. Press, 1994

Platter, T., *Travels in England*, translated by Clare Williams, London, Cape, 1937

Poole, A.L., *Medieval England*, 2 vols, Oxford, Clarendon Press, 1958

Porter, S., *The Great Fire of London*, Stroud, Sutton, 1998

Porter, S., ed., *London and the Civil War*, Basingstoke, Macmillan, 1996

Power, M.J., "Social Topography of Restoration London", pp. 199-223 in *London 1500-1700. The Making of the Metropolis*, ed. Beier, A. L., and Finlay, R., London, Longman, 1986

Prideaux, W., *Memorials of the Goldsmiths' Company*, 2 vols, London, Eyre and Spottiswode, 1896

Puttenham, G., *The Art of English Poesie*, ed. G. D. Wilcox and A. Walker, Cambridge, Cambridge University Press, 1936

Ralph, J., *A Critical Review of the Public Buildings, Statues and Ornaments in and about London and Westminster*, London, J. Wilford and J. Clarke, 1734

Rappaport, S., *Worlds within Worlds: Structures of Life in Sixteenth-Century London*, Cambridge, Cambridge University Press, 1989

Records of the Worshipful Company of Carpenters
    Volume 1, *Apprentices Entry Books 1654-1694*, ed. B. Marsh, Oxford, Oxford University Press, 1913
    Volume 2, *Warden's Accounts 1438-1516*, ed. B. Marsh, Oxford, Oxford University Press, 1914
    Volume 3, *Court Book 1533-1573*, ed. B. Marsh, Oxford, Oxford University Press, 1915
    Volume 4, *Warden's Accounts 1546-1571*, ed. B. Marsh, Oxford, Oxford University Press, 1916
    Volume 5, *Warden's Accounts 1571-1591*, ed. J. Ainsworth, London, Phillimore, 1937
    Volume 6, *Court Book 1573-1594*, ed. J. Ainsworth, London, Phillimore, 1939
    Volume 7, *Warden's Accounts 1592-1614*, ed. A.M. Millard, London, Phillimore, 1968

Reddaway, T.F., "Elizabethan London. Goldsmiths' Row in Cheapside 1558-1645", pp. 181-206 in *Guildhall Miscellany*, vol. 2, no. 5, October 1963

Reddaway, T.F., *The Early History of the Goldsmiths' Company*, London, Edward Arnold, 1975

Reddaway, T.F., *The Early History of the Goldsmiths' Company*, London, Edward Arnold, 1975

Reddaway, T.F., *The Rebuilding of London after the Great Fire*, London, Jonathan Cape, 1940

Reddaway, T.F., "The Rebuilding of London after the Great Fire, a Rediscovered Plan", *Town Planning Review*, vol. 18, July 1939, pp. 155-161

Reedy, G., "Mystical Politics: The Imagery of Charles II's Coronation", pp. 19-42 in *Studies in Change and Revolution: Aspects of English Intellectual History 1640-1800*, ed. P. J. Korshin, Menston, Yorks, Scolar Press, 1972

Richards, K., "The Restoration Pageants of John Tatham", pp. 49-73 in *Western Popular Theatre*, ed. D. Mayer and K. Richards, London and New York, Methuen, 1977

Ridley, J., *A History of the Carpenters' Company*, London, Unicorn Press, 1995

Riley, H. T., ed., *Chronicles of the Mayors and Sheriffs of London 1188-1274*, London, Trubner, 1863

Robertson, J., and Gordon, D. J., eds, *A Calendar of Dramatic Records in the books of the Livery Companies of London 1485-1640*, Oxford, Malone Society, 1954

Robinson, J. M., *The Wyatts. An Architectural Dynasty*, Oxford, Oxford University Press, 1979

Roscoe, I., "The Statues of the Sovereigns of England: Sculpture for the Second Building 1695-1831", pp. 174-187 in *The Royal Exchange*, ed. A Saunders, London, London Topographical Society, no. 152, 1997

Rye, W. B., *England as seen by Foreigners in the Days of Elizabeth and James the First . . .* , London, Smith, 1865

Salzman, L., *Building in England down to 1540: A Documentary History*, Oxford, Clarendon Press, 1952

Saunders, A., "Reconstructing London: Sir Thomas Gresham and Bishopsgate", pp. 1-12 in *Sir Thomas Gresham and Gresham College: Studies in the Intellectual History of London in the Sixteenth and Seventeenth Centuries*, ed. F. Ames-Lewis, Aldershot, Ashgate, 1999

Saunders, A., "The Building of the Exchange", pp. 36-47 in *The Royal Exchange*, ed. A. Saunders, London, London Topographical Society, no. 152, 1997

Saunders, A., "The Second Exchange", pp. 121-135 in *The Royal Exchange*, ed. A. Saunders, London, London Topographical Society, no. 152, 1997

Schofield, J., *Medieval London Houses*, London and New Haven, Yale University Press, 1995

Schofield, J., *The Building of London from the Conquest to the Great Fire*, London, British Museum Publications, 1984

Schwarz, L. D., *London in the Age of Industrialisation: Entrepreneurs, Labour Force and Living Conditions 1700-1850*, Cambridge, Cambridge University Press, 1992

Seaver, P., "The Artisanal World", pp. 87-100 in *The Theatrical City: Culture, Theatre and Politics in London 1576-1649*, ed. D. Smith, R. Streier and D. Bevington, Cambridge, Cambridge University Press, 1995

Shapin, S., "Who was Robert Hooke?", pp. 253-274 in *Robert Hooke: New Studies*, ed. M. Hunter and S. Schaffer, Woodbridge, Boydell Press, 1989

Sheppard, F., *London, A History*, Oxford, Oxford University Press, 1998

Smuts, M., "Public Ceremony and Royal Charisma: The English Royal Entry in London 1485-1642", pp. 69-93 in *The First Modern Society: Essays in English History in Honour of Lawrence Stone*, ed. A. L. Beier, D. Cannadine and J. Rosenheim, Cambridge, Cambridge University Press, 1989

Sontag, S., *Illness as Metaphor*, New York, Random House, 1979

Soo, L., ed., *Wren's Tracts on Architecture and other Writings*, Cambridge, Cambridge University Press, 1998

Stow, J., *A General Chronicle of England*, London, printed by Richard Meighen, 1631

Stow, J., *Survey of London*, London, 1633

Stow, J., *The Survey of London*, ed. C. L. Kingsford, Oxford, Clarendon Press, 1908

Strype, J., *A Survey of the Cities of London and Westminster . . . by John Stow*, London, A. Churchill, 1720

Summerson, J., *Architecture in Britain 1530-1830*, London, Pelican History of Art, 1991

Summerson, J., *Georgian London*, London, Barrie and Jenkins, 1978

Summerson, J., "Three Elizabethan Architects", *Bulletin of the John Rylands Library*, Manchester, 1957, vol. 40, pp. 208-228

Tatham, J., *Aqua Triumphalis*, London, 1662

Tatham, J., *London's Glory, represented by Time, Truth and Fame*, London, Godbid, 1660

Tatham, J., *London's Triumph, presented by Industry and Honour*, London, Mabb, 1658

Tatham, J., *London's Triumph, celebrated in honour of Thomas Allen*, London, Mabb, 1659

Tatham, J., *London's Triumph, presented by several delightful scenes*, London, Mabb, 1661

Tatham, J., *London's Triumph, in honour of Sir Anthony Bateman*, London, Brome, 1663

Tatham, J., *London's Triumph, celebrated in honour of Sir John Lawrence*, London, Brome, 1664

Tatham, J., *The Royal Oake, with other various and delightful scenes*, London, 1660

Thomas, V., *God's Terrible Voice in the City*, London, 1667

Thorold, P., *The London Rich. The Creation of a Great City from 1666 to the Present*, London, Viking, 1999

Treswell, R., *The London Surveys of Ralph Treswell*, ed. J. Schofield, London, London Topographical Society, no. 135, 1987

Unwin, G., *The Guilds and Companies of London*, London, Frank Cass and Co., 1963

Van Lennep, W., ed., *The London Stage 1660-1800*, part 1, *1660-1700*, Carbondale, Southern Illinois University Press, 1965

Wadmore, J., *Some Account of the Worshipful Company of Skinners*, London, Blades, 1902

Wall, C., *The Literary and Cultural Spaces of Restoration London*, Cambridge, Cambridge University Press, 1998

Ward, J., *Metropolitan Communities, Trade Guilds, Identity and Change in Early Modern London*, Stanford CA, Stanford University Press, 1997

Ward, J., *The Lives of the Professors of Gresham College*, London, J. Moore, 1740

Ward, N., *The London Spy*, ed. Paul Hyland, East Lansing MI, Colleagues Press, 1993

Webb, G., "The Architectural Antecedents of Sir Christopher Wren", *R.I.B.A. Journal*, 27 May 1933, pp. 573-583

Whinney, M., and Millar, D., *English Art 1625-1714*, Oxford, Clarendon Press, 1957

White, J.G., *History of the Three Royal Exchanges, the Gresham Lectures and the Gresham Almshouses*, London, Effingham Wilson, 1896

Whitebrook, J., *London Citizens in 1651: being a transcript of Harleian Ms. 4778*, London, Hutchings and Romer, 1910

Wickham, G., *Early English Stages 1300-1660*, 3 vols, London, Routledge and Kegan Paul, 1963

Williams, S., "The Lord Mayor's Show in Tudor and Stuart Times", pp. 3-18 in *Guildhall Miscellany*, no. 10, September 1959

Wilton Ely, J., "The Rise of the Professional Architect in England", pp. 180-208 in *The Architect: Chapters in the History of the Profession*, ed. S. Kostof, New York and Oxford, Oxford University Press, 1977

Withington, R., *English Pageantry: An Historical Outline*, 2 vols, Cambridge, Mass., Harvard University Press, 1920

Woodhead, J.R., *The Rulers of London 1660-1689: A Biographical Record of the Aldermen and Common Councilmen of the City of London*, London, London and Middlesex Archaeological Society, 1965

Woodward, D., *Men at Work: Labourers and Building Craftsmen in the Towns of Northern England 1450-1750*, Cambridge, Cambridge University Press, 1995

Wren, C., *Parentalia: or Memoirs of the Family of the Wrens*, London, T. Osborn, 1750

The Wren Society, 20 vols, Oxford, Oxford University Press, 1924-43

Yeomans, D., "Structural Carpentry in London Building", pp. 38-47 in *Good and Proper Materials: The Fabric of London since the Great Fire*, ed. H. Hobhouse and A. Saunders, London, London Topographical Society, no. 140, 1989

Index

Page numbers in *italic* refer to illustrations